The Green Wood Companion

Barry Mays

eco-logic books

Old beech tree

Dedication

Thanks to Peter Andrews at eco-logic books for publishing what is after all, a very unconventional book, and Helen Johnstone, who never failed to handle the text (and the enthusiastic author) with respect, empathy and just the right mix of camaraderie and gentle editorial authority.

I am grateful to my talented friend Alex Machin, who created the illustrations which undoubtedly brought alive the chapter on tree folklore and myth.

Salutations and thanks to Howard Brown, in France, for his unique craftsperson illustrations, and to Sue Bryant for her tree illustration.

Special thanks to Mike Trafford for generously allowing me to set up my first Cornish workshop at Turlea Farm, where I produced some of my best early creative work; and drank a lot of tea... and other liquids. Happy days.

My respects to the following talented, far-sighted and special human beings, who have directly or inadvertently inspired and assisted me in my personal journey down the green wood path with either their books, creations, work ethic, or personal communications – Daniel Mack, Jennie Alexander, Drew Langsner, Owen Rein, Sam Maloof; and on this side of the pond – Mike Abbott, Gudrun Leitz, John Brown, Jack Hill, Tim Stead, David Nash, Andy Goldsworthy.

This book is dedicated to my two precious sons, Matt and Louis, who enabled me to re-discover what love is.

What a journey!

First Published in 2016

by eco-logic books

www.eco-logicbooks.com

Text © Barry Mays 2016

Unless otherwise attributed, illustrations © Barry Mays 2016

Illustrations for Chapter 26 © Alex Machin

ISBN 978 1899233236

Illustrations:	Barry Mays, Alex Machin, Howard Brown and Sue Bryant
Editing:	Helen Johnstone
Design & Typesetting:	The Design Co-operative
Printed on 100% recycled paper by	Cambrian Printers

Further copies of this book can be purchased from eco-logic books: **info@eco-logicbooks.com**

eco-logic books publish and sell, mail order, a large range of books that promote practical solutions to environmental problems, organic gardening, sustainable living, permaculture and related topics. To view their list visit their website at www.eco-logicbooks.com.

The Small Print
Whilst every effort has been taken to ensure the accuracy of the information in this book the publisher and author accept no responsibility for errors and omission or as to any actions that may be taken as a result of reading this work.

Cover photograph: Alder trees in the Beaulieu River, New Forest © Jim Champion

CONTENTS

Bluebells in sweet chestnut coppice, Flexham Park, West Sussex

INTRODUCTION

Trees are sanctuaries. Whoever knows how to listen to them, can learn the truth.

Herman Hesse

The Green Wood Companion was born out of a need to gather information on a personal journey to becoming a green wood chair maker. Somewhere along the line I got carried away a bit. This book is the result.

When I first embraced the notion of leaving my city life and moving to the country to make chairs from trees, I had no idea where to start. I knew nothing about the countryside, trees, green woodworking and woodland terminology, tool names and types and where to get them, which wood to use, or even the right books to read. If only this publication had been available then!

I was determined to seek out this knowledge, and so

Part of Author's bookcase

began a fascinating journey of enlightenment into the green world. It soon became apparent to me that in the past, a craftsperson's skills were learned either through formal apprenticeships or handed down by close familiarity from father and mother to son and daughter. Almost nothing was written down. Materials, methodologies, designs and terminology had considerable regional variances and as industrialisation took hold, and then the two world wars depleted the population of skilled woods people and woodland craft workers, their knowledge and skills became in danger of disappearing altogether.

In recent decades, a handful of dedicated individuals have published some excellent and informative books on woodland management and country crafts (most of which appear in the *Recommended Reading* section of this book). Collectively, these books supply us with a comprehensive overview of the traditional sylvan practices and crafts.

Unfortunately, what I couldn't find was one single publication serving as a quick and easy-to-use reference book, containing specific answers to the questions that arise when working with wood, and covering the whole process, from the tree to the tools for working the wood.

Finally, after years of personal study and practice of woodland crafts, it dawned on me that I had inadvertently amassed a huge amount of information in my eclectic collection of books, notebooks, sketchbooks and on scraps of paper, old floppy discs and CDs, which was not only very useful to me almost on a daily basis, but could also be very useful to others. I had almost written a book, fuelled by an obsessive interest in my new career and lifestyle.

So what I'm attempting to achieve in this book is to bring together all these useful nuggets of information in a single publication, in what is, essentially, a quick reference book 'with knobs on', for everyone. Its purpose is to preserve and share this valuable specialist knowledge, and in its own small way, encourage the continuation of woodland crafts in Britain on a commercial, recreational and spiritual level, for the good of our countryside and our personal wellbeing.

Now, 15 years down the green wood path, I'm just starting to be in danger of knowing what I'm talking about – and I am still learning. I spend my days crafting chairs, stools and wood wares from green wood, and occasionally teach and mentor others. I have also met, corresponded with and read the work of many other dedicated and skilled practitioners of green wood skills, both in the UK and on the other side of the Atlantic, who have been extremely generous in sharing their individual specialist knowledge and skills.

Wood cultivation and crafts have been practiced for many hundreds of years. This knowledge should not be lost. It should be nurtured and shared with others. It is the sum of our endeavours; it is about us and the people who practised it before us, and we should be rightly proud of it.

So, for anybody with thoughts of trying their hand at green woodworking either as a hobby or a small business, for people already involved in this wonderful woodland crafts industry, for historians, or for those curious about

The author using a shaving horse in his woodland workshop

trees and the myth and folklore surrounding them – and for all those moments when you need a question about wood answered – I do hope that you will find my humble offering an informative, absorbing and helpful companion.

Barry Mays

Craftsmen and women

While there are plenty of women involved in woodland management and wood crafts now, it is difficult to ignore the fact that in many of our rural activities in the past, men were dominant.

Historically, 'sawyers' were men. This physically demanding profession necessitated teams of two, referred to as top man and pit man. Foresters, wheelwrights and coopers were almost always men. That does not mean to say that women were excluded from woodland and workshop activities; but they were generally occupied full-time in running the household.

During World War II, the Women's Land Army, generally known as the Land Girls, were very evident in the British woodlands, tending the land, growing the crops and managing the woodlands. In the US, women known as Lumber Jills worked in forestry professions. Many woodland crafts have always been practiced by women as well as men. Today, a refreshingly large percentage of women work full-time in this industry, especially in more recent years, and play a prominent part in local woodland shows across the country.

All this aside, I have decided to deal with this matter in a way that I hope is acceptable to everybody, as is it not my intention to show anything but great respect and encouragement for all woodland workers and crafts people, irrespective of their gender. In the chapters that follow, I have made studious efforts not to refer to one gender in my own writings, but have thought it necessary to faithfully reproduced short extracts from passages in some excellent books previously published, (some of which are now quite old) which will include words like 'craftsman' or 'he', as I am of the opinion that I do not have the right to re-phrase another author's work.

So, please enjoy this book for what it is, and what it is trying to share with everyone.

CHAPTER 1

The remarkable tree

The oaks and the pines, and their brethren of the wood, have seen so many suns rise and set, so many seasons come and go, and so many generations pass into silence, that we may well wonder what 'the story of the trees' would be to us if they had tongues to tell it, or we ears fine enough to understand.

From *Quotations for Special Occasions,* **Maud van Buren**

Bills' Oak, Tutwell

Trees are amazing! They are the longest living organisms on the earth. It would be impossible to over-estimate the importance of them.

Trees came into existence well over 300 million years ago, before dinosaurs trod the earth. Conifers were the first to appear, followed relatively recently by broadleaf trees, around 100 million years ago. They re-colonised Britain after the last ice age some ten to twelve thousand years

ago (depending who you talk to). This original growth has been referred to as wildwood. Old English words weald, wald and wold describe a 'wild', or 'wooded place.' The word 'tree' is derived from the Anglo Saxon word treow (while the Latin for forest is silva).

The British Isles host 33 true native species, but it is not clear just how many species there are worldwide. The difficulty seems partly down to the fact that zoologists and botanists don't always agree; different institutions have varying definitions of what a tree is. It is also complicated by the fact there can be many different species within each tree genus. For instance, there are currently thought to be 65 species of ash, 350 species of oak, willow species exceed 300, and the acacia can boast up to 1000 species. The list goes on, and will do, as new species are discovered and the experts continue to know best. So, for argument's sake, we could say that there are between 30,000 and 100,000 species of tree worldwide.

Tree canopy in the Tamar Valley

Edward Milner's book *Trees of Britain and Ireland* estimates 700 conifer species and 30-40,000 broadleaf worldwide. This sounds reasonable. Colin Tudge's book *The Secret Life of Trees* puts the number of known species currently at approximately 60,000, of which 600 are conifer; and these two broad estimates seem to be acceptable to most people.

Incidentally, of all the expert physical and technical definitions of how a tree should be described, my favourite comes from Colin Tudge's book previously mentioned above, which describes a tree as 'a big plant with a stick up the middle.'

As for how may trees there are, it is impossible to say, but a UN Food and Agriculture Organisation (FAO) Forest Resources Assessment in 2010 estimated that trees covered approximately 4 billion hectares (9.9 billion acres), or about 31 % of the Earth's landmass.

Why do trees have Latin names? Why not? Medieval scholars, who documented just about everything, spoke Latin, making it easy to standardise on a common tongue to avoid confusion – a bit like English being the international maritime language. So, for labelling flora and fauna, it seems that Latin, with a bit of Greek thrown in, has become the solution which has successfully stood the test of time.

The importance of trees

So, what's so good about trees then? What have they ever done for us? Well, for a start, trees not only sustain us with essential and useful things; they also sustain life on this planet. They provide the habitat for three-quarters of the planet's bio-diversity. Without trees, and of course, all other plants, we would have no suitable air to breath, because they absorb and lock in carbon dioxide from the atmosphere, and produce and release oxygen, which keeps us alive. They are the cornerstone of the delicate balance of life, on which we all depend.

Every single part of a tree has been useful to us ever since time began. Wood, bark, leaves, sap, roots, nuts, fruit and berries have provided us with all of our immediate basic needs; shelter, warmth, food, medicine, tool and weapon shafts and handles.

Coiled lime bast in basket harvested and woven by Carol Horsington of Cornish Willow

Even today, many byproducts from trees – pulp, chemicals, cellulose, food and medicine – are an essential part of everyday living and are impossible to directly simulate or replace.

For as long as humankind has walked the earth, trees have been revered throughout the world. They are part of history and culture. Myth, folklore and religion surround them. Trees are a natural wonder and the vital infrastructure of planet earth, and yet they are constantly under threat from the modern world.

They must battle with non-indigenous evasive plants, disease (Dutch Elm disease was responsible for 25-30 million lost elms in Britain), certain wild animals, insects, and spontaneous forest fires. These natural enemies are a perpetual danger; but not surprisingly, by far the greatest threat to our trees lies with the activities of an animal of the two-legged variety. Agriculture, expansion of roads, airports, motorways and housing, mining for other natural resources, tourism and recreation, pollution, logging and the general over-exploitation of our forests for medicine, foods and commercially related products, all contribute to the threat. As a species, humans have a lot to answer for.

The consequences of this intervention into the natural way of things is inevitably being revealed in global warming, endangered species, soil erosion, shade reduction, susceptibility to disease, the reduction in animal and plant life, the quality of our air and the loss of certain foods, medicines and related commercial products, and, of course, the demise of aesthetic landscape and human wellbeing. Humanity seems determined to shoot itself in the foot.

Despite this, trees continue to impress us with their sheer tenacity and natural sense of survival. You can even cut one down and many will re-generate from the stump! So how do they work? Prepare to be impressed.

How they work

Basically, a tree flourishes by embracing the four essential elements; earth, air, water and fire (the sun). Moisture, minerals and salts are absorbed through its root system and drawn up through the sapwood (also known as xylem) in the trunk and branches, along tubes, known as vessels.

Carbon dioxide (emitted by all animals, including us) is extracted from the air through microscopic holes in the leaves which also absorb sunlight, and through photosynthesis, form carbohydrates (or sugars). These

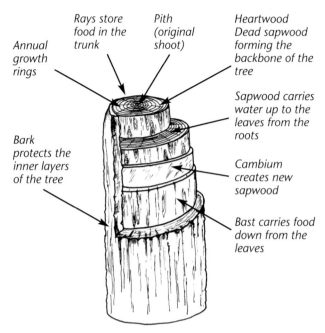

The layers of a tree

sugars are transported down the trunk though the bast, (also known as phloem or inner bark), a layer of cells just beneath the protective bark. Just inside the bast is another thin layer called the cambium. Within this layer, the carbohydrates convert into wood cells or fibres; forming the solid, but flexible structure and shape of the tree, in which vessels transport the water, and rays store food.

Once absorbed, carbon dioxide, which is harmful to air-breathing mammals, and to the Earth's atmosphere, is literally 'locked in' to the tree, only to be released if the tree dies, or is felled and burnt. Felling and making things out of the timber will retain the carbon dioxide locked within the wood, and so continue to serve humankind in a very positive way.

The roots of a tree play a dual role, in so much as they not only hold the tree up, but they collect water and nutrients from the soil and send it up for processing. When a seed germinates, it sends down a single tap root burrowing downwards into the soil to plug into the natural resources. Once the tap root is deeply established in the soil, many more sub-roots are formed which spread out in all directions to forage supplies for the tree.

The delicate root system expels certain chemicals which dissolve elements in the soil so that they can be transported with the collected water, up the trunk. Minute, specialist fungi – mycorrhiza – attach to the tree roots like microscopic root hair extensions, assist the tree roots in a

Exposed sycamore tree roots

symbiotic partnership. This mycorrhiza produces nitrogen, phosphorus and other nutrients, vital to the tree, which in turn allows the tree to produce more water, sugars and carbohydrates, benefitting the fungi in return.

In all woodlands, immense, complex subterranean networks of fungal root systems (mycelia) collectively weighing many tons, lie below the surface, interacting with all tree and plant species in a co-operative feeding partnership.

This essential co-operation between root and fungi can sometimes produce stunning effects within the tree timber. Brown oak is a valuable and coveted wood which owes its distinct russet colouration to the work of the beef steak fungi *fistulina hepatica*. The dark, irregular linear pattern occurring commonly on beech, and popular with bowl turners, is known as spalting. Again, this is a result of specialised fungi.

Tree roots stabilise soil and prevent soil erosion, ensuring that rain water is allowed to seep gradually into the earth. Depending on the species of tree, its roots can extend underground up to three times its height, with 90% of tree roots in the top 46cm (18 inches) of soil.

Tree profile

As the tree grows

Each year of tree growth produces a growth ring within the cambium layer. Over time, as the girth of the tree increases (approximately 2.5 cm a year on average) the inner cells become lignified; that is, filled with lignin – the semi-liquid 'glue' that binds wood fibres together. In this way, they become dormant, forming the 'skeleton' of the tree. These cells are known as the heartwood. The outer, living part of the tree below the bark where the sap still flows, is known as the sapwood.

A cross-section of a felled tree will clearly show each of these parts, as well as revealing an extremely accurate history of that particular tree. Dendrochronology is the practice of examining the cross-section of a tree to determine, amongst other things, its exact age, how fast it grew in any particular year, if it was crowded by other trees and had to fight for space, its position (on a slope, or on flat ground), weather and climate on each particular year, pest interference, and any evidence of forest fires, earth tremors or quakes.

Trees compete for light with each other quite ruthlessly in a deadly serious race to reach above other trees and spread a canopy of leaves. Fig trees have a parasitic tendency to engulf an unwilling host tree to provide it with a natural scaffold on which to entwine and reach towards the light, eventually killing the host. Walnut trees can, and do, secrete a poison from their roots called *juglone*, which is capable of killing nearby trees competing for light and moisture. Eucalyptus shed their toxic leaves, rendering the ground below uninhabitable to any other plant growth.

However, aside from the obvious traits necessary for basic survival, trees not only co-operate with fungi, bacteria, insects, birds and mammals for their very existence, they

Strangler fig on a host tree

also sometimes unwittingly help out their own neighbouring species, by communication.

When willows are attacked by webworms and caterpillars, they emit a volatile pheromone called *methyl salicylate;* a modified form of salicylic acid which acts as an airborne chemical alert signal to its other leaves, which respond by producing more tannin in their leaves, rendering them difficult to digest by the attacking insects. Any willow trees in the immediate vicinity will also 'pick-up' this airborne chemical alert and automatically produce their own boost of tannin in their leaves to protect themselves. Alder and Scots Pine react in the same way too.

African Acacias emit similar windborne chemical vapours when their leaves are under attack from giraffes. Mopane trees do the same to help combat hungry elephants. However, it is speculated that a mature and therefore wiser elephant, having dined on a tree downwind, will approach a second tree upwind to combat the airborne alert.

So, do trees communicate with anything else? Unlikely, but curiously enough, the common crow, an intelligent bird, will forsake a tree, even if it has been used as a nest site over many years, if they sense that the tree is going to

Cross section of a tree showing the growth rings

Elephant eating leaves

die. This may occur long before the tree shows any visible signs that humans would recognise.

How do trees reproduce? Being literally rooted to the spot cramps their style somewhat, but the resourceful tree manages to find a way in partnership with nature, insects and mammals. Put simply, moving pollen and seeds around happens with the aid of natural elements like water, wind, and insects – particularly flies, bees, and wasps (yes, wasps sometimes actually do useful things; particularly useful if you happen to be one of the 750 species of fig tree, entirely dependent upon their very own specialised species of wasp to pollinate for you). Birds eat seeds within the fruit of trees and then pass them through their gut, coated with some natural fertilizer, to get the new tree growing. Mammals like the bats, monkeys and squirrels also help the process – the latter, forgetting where it buried a few of its winter food store of acorns, enabling some to grow into mighty oaks. From little acorns to mighty oaks – sounds like a good line? Nah… it'll never catch on.

However, having justifiably given some credit to the

Red squirrel

squirrel for assisting in the propagation of oak, it is in fact the jay (garrulous glandarius), to whom we must bestow the award 'oak planter supremo'. A most resourceful and intelligent bird, being a colourful member of the crow family, will devote up to 10 hours a day collecting autumnal acorns in its gullet (usually two or three at a time, although they can hold up to 9), and burying them in natural holes under leaf litter and crevices in tree bark.

This remarkable and naturally shy bird can store up to 5,000 acorns in just one season. A German study revealed that 250 jays removed 3,000 kg of acorns in just 20 days.

Jay collecting acorns

A part of the environment

Trees induce rainfall by cooling the land and transpiring water into the sky from their leaves. One mature oak tree can draw many litres of water in a day from its roots and put up to 500 litres into the atmosphere. A hectare of woodland can give off up to 50,000 litres of water each day. This will return to the land in due course in the form of rain, either directly back onto the terrain from which it came, or, more than likely, tens or hundreds of miles away, depending upon the prevailing winds.

The leaves on a tree act as thousands of solar panels, constantly tilting themselves towards the sun, presenting the maximum surface area to collect the heat and produce chlorophyll derived from the blue and red light of the sun, giving the leaves their green colour. Leaves sense the changing of the seasons by the gradual change of daylight and darkness hours. In autumn, it is not the reduced length of the day (light) hours, but the extended length of the dark hours (longer periods of darkness), that the tree responds to.

The many colours of autumn leaves

Once the tree senses autumn, it will literally start to 'shut down' for the winter. Shorter days, and more significantly, longer nights, will automatically trigger off a chemical reaction, sending a substance down the stem to the joint in the twig holding the leaves, cutting off the vital supply of sap. Deprived of its life-giving substance, the chlorophyll, responsible for providing the colour green in the leaf, declines, revealing the familiar autumnal reds, yellows and browns of the other chemicals contained within it. The leaf will slowly dry, and eventually the once flexible stem will fracture, causing the leaf to separate from the tree and float down to the forest floor. There it assumes a new function protecting the tree roots and small wildlife for the winter. Eventually it rots down into a nitrogen rich fertilizer, aided by millions of industrious worms which pull the leaves down into the soil.

Now, sap ceases to flow and the tree's nutritional reserves are stored in the roots and branches, ready for use next spring.

Shedding such huge quantities of water-soaked summer leaves relieves the enormous weight on the branches by several tons on a larger specimen, leaving it more able to cope with severe winter gales and heavy snow until the following spring, when the tree will bud and grow its next generation of leaves anew, and continue to grow and serve the planet.

So, in summary, a tree is a completely self-sufficient, self-perpetuating moisture recycling and rain machine, a carbon dioxide prison, and a wood and oxygen factory. Prefect of our planet, regulator of our environment, provider of food, medicine, shelter and spiritual well-being. A giver of life.

How the forests are faring

Despite the importance of trees to life, our forests are still being cut down. In the pre-industrial era, forests spread over 5.9 billion hectares of the world's surface. That is now down to 4 billion hectares, or 31% of Earth's land.

In Britain, around 12% of total land area is forest, making it one of the most lightly forested countries in Europe. Scotland can claim around 17% of its land as forest, although less than one fifth is ancient woodland (400 years old), while 37% of the EU as a whole is forested.

According to the UN Food and Agriculture Organisation, the highest rate of deforestation worldwide was in the 1990s, but despite the growth of woodlands (both through natural growth and planting) in some areas, there was still a net loss of forests from 2000 - 2010 of approximately 5.2 million hectares a year. In the first decade of this new century UN data shows that we were still destroying 13 million hectares of forest each year.

Trees are inexplicably linked with our past, the present, and the future survival of our planet, and therefore, us. They are so much a part of the circle of life that they tend to be overlooked. This is a dangerous mistake.

Pine trees

One new tree every year

We need more trees – in the right places. For those people inclined to empathise with the philosophy of Buddhism, or, for that matter, anyone in tune with the environment, should take note from the teachings of Buddha, which suggested that every good Buddhist should plant, nurture, and see the establishment of at least one tree every year.

Dr E.F.Scumacher, in his classic book *Small is Beautiful* (a study of economics written in 1973, but amazingly as true today as it ever was), concluded that:

"If you could just establish an ideology which would make it obligatory for every able-bodied person in India to do that little thing – to plant and see the establishment of one tree a year, five years running, after just five years, you would have 2,000 million additional established trees.

"It could be achieved without a penny of foreign aid, savings or investments, and would produce foodstuffs, fibres, building materials, shade and water across India, whilst considerably reducing dust."

It is, in fact, starting to happen in India, and in other parts of the world too; the most notable being the Green Belt Movement in Kenya, founded by Wangara Maathai, a Nobel peace prize winner in 2004. Since she established the Green Belt Movement in 1977, a staggering 51 million trees have been planted and tended in Kenya, mostly by women. The purpose is to provide a renewable source of food, fuel, shelter and shade. Do the maths. Imagine if all countries of the world adopted this philosophy. Imagine!

The best time to plant a tree was 20 years ago. The next best time is now.

Chinese proverb

Now... let's all go for a walk in the woods.

Tree planting

CHAPTER 2

The fall and rise of woodland crafts

The best friend on earth of man is the tree. When we use the tree respectfully and economically, we have one of the greatest resources of the earth.

Frank Lloyd Wright

It is well documented that woodland knowledge, management and crafts declined dramatically during and after the industrial revolution in the late 18th century. Prior to this there had been an essential woodland industry throughout Britain for centuries, sustaining successive generations, stabilising the local economy and preserving a way of life that was the backbone of the country.

In his excellent book *Woodland Crafts in Britain*, first published in 1949, H.L.Edlin sets the scene:

"Until the woodman had done his task, there was scarcely another craftsman who could begin work. The toolmaker, called by some the master of all trades, had first to go to the woodman for hafts or handles cleft from pliant ash. The mighty smith could not light his forge until his charcoal had been charred, and his iron won from its ores, with wood from the forest. The woodman provided the potter with his wood fuel and his potter's wheel, the glassmaker with his charcoal and potash. The spinner came to him for spindle or spinning wheel, and the weaver for loom and shuttle. The tanner, and therefore every leather worker, was dependent on tan bark stripped from the woodland trees. Miners, quarrymen , and stone workers needed timber props, trams, and mallets to ply their trade. The woodman supplied the thatcher's pegs, the lace maker's bobbins and the net maker's needles. The brewer needed his casks and the

Thatcher at work in Escheburg, Germany

dairymaid her pails, whilst every kind of furniture and domestic gear – cheese presses, cider presses and the like – were framed by the woodworker's hands."

Almost every splinter of wood felled found a use locally in one way or another. One trade complemented and sustained the other, in parity with the ways of the natural world.

Making use of woodlands

This most essential produce was created by coppicing; a practice originating thousands of years ago. Woven hazel screens carbon date back 5,000 years B.C.

A sweet track discovered in Somerset is an excellent example of a perfectly preserved man-made trackway over marsh. It carbon dates to between 4,000 - 3,000 BC and is made from uniform, straight lengths of ash, elder and oak, strongly suggesting that its components were a product of coppicing.

Coppicing is the practice of managing and working a renewable and sustainable natural woodland resource by cutting some trees at a certain age (or when they reach a certain diameter) and allowing them to re-grow, while other parts of the woodland are cut and then left. This is covered in greater detail in Chapter 7.

In the past, Britain in particular made extensive use of woodlands, and records suggest that the range of hand tools and ingenious applications for them exceeded those of the rest of Europe.

Whilst coppicing was the backbone of the country, mature wood produced from standards (trees grown from seed and allowed to grow on for 100 years or so), together with the larger diameter coppiced wood, provided not only an essential raw material for housing, but also for transport, including carts, wagons, ships, boats, train carriages and

Baskets and hat made by Carol Horsington, Cornish Willow

track sleepers. Wood provided so many useful things: buckets, barrels, boxes, woven baskets, spinning wheels, looms, kitchenware, brooms, furniture, tool handles, blocks for the pattern making and printing industry, clothes and tent pegs, longbows, musical instruments, sports equipment, picture frames, and so on.

The end products were often beautiful as well as useful. Can you think of a single item produced from a tree that is not aesthetically pleasing and tactile? Most products made from wood perform better than the mass-produced plastic

Ash hurdle and willow screen made by Moreton Wood Coppice Products

offerings from the polluting petrochemical industry. Even trees themselves are beautiful to behold.

The return of wood

Wooden things seemed to 'go out of fashion' during the 60s, 70s and 80s. There was a sharp decline in woodland management and sustainable practices, half of England's ancient woodlands and hedgerows were systematically cleared in the six decades between 1930 and 1990, mass plantations of conifer replaced our native broadleaf trees, and there has been an uncontrolled importation of cheap timber. But there is good news! Although it never went away, wood is slowly making a welcome return to our lives.

Have you noticed a resurgence in the construction of timber-framed buildings? Many architects now appreciate that wood actually out-performs other building materials in many ways and include the use of it in many new builds. Wood is an ecologically and economically sound building material – far less expensive and polluting to produce than metal and concrete, longer lasting and more stable, requiring much less transportation if sourced locally, and of course, it looks good too.

Growing numbers of discerning people are becoming tired of mass produced, machine-made products with built-in obsolescence, that will end up in a landfill site within a decade or less. A beautiful piece of local handmade furniture on the other hand, will last you a lifetime. It is a future heirloom. It is unique; you know the maker's name and so the extra cost involved in the initial purchase is more than justified by quality and exclusivity, and the chances are that the wood used will have come from a sustainable source. When the item is in need of some renovation in a hundred years or so, this is easily done by the hands of a good furniture restorer; the tiny carbon footprint made in the manufacture having already been trodden a century beforehand.

Has anybody found a more efficient way to sweep a stone, concrete, tiled or brick floor or steps, or the leaves off a lawn, with anything else other than a beautiful, hand-made besom broom, consisting simply of a wooden handle and either a birch, heather or willow head? Isn't it sad that for hundreds of years we were happily using wooden chopping boards and eating from sycamore platters with wooden spoons before wood was suddenly condemned as a harbourer of bacteria and widely replaced by impersonal and irritatingly coloured plastic alternatives. Ironically,

Traditionally made besom broom by Mark Cottrell

research has proven that plastic is actually less hygienic that wood.

As we all know, heating oil gas has become very expensive. These materials pollute the earth more than wood. Burning wood for heat either in log fuel or biofuel is more efficient and less polluting, if you burn well-seasoned, sustainable, local wood. Although when you burn the wood, the CO_2 taken in by the tree is released again, if the tree came from a sustainable source, your tree will already have been replaced by another which is absorbing and 'locking in' CO_2 again.

The new era of woodland management

Woodland management (and permaculture) is undeniably common sense, but never forget that woodlands are pretty good at managing themselves. Farsighted people understand that in the long term, sustainable co-operation with woodlands and harmonisation with our environment is the solution to many of our future generation's local needs.

Steady interest in recreational training activities like hedge laying, coppicing, green woodworking, basket making and the like is extremely encouraging. Television now occasionally devotes prime time to programmes featuring traditional skills, like thatching, wheel making and chair making. Dedicated but struggling artisans now find that they can continue the craft they love by supplementing their modest income by running training courses on their specialist skill. This in turn passes on and spreads the appreciation and practice of these valuable

Discovering the woodlands with Little Oaks Forest School at Cotehele

skills and creates a local demand for sustainable timber, as people learn old skills to makes things for themselves (again).

Across our country, community woodland projects maintain and regenerate local woodlands, while providing social, environmental and community benefits. There is a new interest in alternative outdoor recreational activities, and woodland owners are increasingly inclined to start up their own businesses, or lease to other groups interested in setting up such activities. As well as education and training in traditional woodland management activities, there are now initiatives like tree surfing and climbing, bushcraft skills, mountain bike trails, and weddings taking place in our woodlands.

Local villages can and do own community woodlands, where all manner of activities entice people out into woodlands to rediscover a connection with nature and each other, while providing light physical activities like coppicing, firewood gathering and general maintenance. In many areas, local schools and nurseries are making ever-greater use of their local woodlands for educational and recreational purposes. There is growing demand for forest schools, which provide young children with a countryside learning and discovery environment, stimulating the senses and providing enormous, cheap and healthy fun.

Many under-woodspeople, managing the younger trees in a diverse woodland, have adapted to modern day trends and some now produce hurdles and gates, arbours and gazebos to grace the most prestigious of homes.

What more could woodlands provide?

Few recent figures exist about barbecue charcoal produced in the UK. Although there has been a resurgence in the availability of the British product over the last few years, a *Guardian* article in 2008 estimated that in U.K. we buy approximately 60,000 tons of the stuff, of which about 90% is imported from rainforests and mangrove habitats in South America, West Africa and South East Asia. The UK easily has enough overstood coppice (once, well managed coppice plantations now neglected for years) to provide our entire needs, so let's get to it.

The tree has provided us with free medicine in the past, and could probably supply the solution to many of our modern day illnesses, in areas where overpriced, synthetic drugs, controlled by profit driven cartels, are still failing to cure.

The Global Tree Campaign (a partnership between Fauna and Flora International and Botanic Gardens International) estimate that 50,000 plant species are used medicinally with

Ring kiln charcoal burning at Moreton Wood

In his book *Tree Medicine*, Peter Conway highlights the incredible properties of the Neem tree *azadirachta indica*, a native of India and Burma. It is an extraordinary insecticide effective 'against 200 different insect species, as well as fungal, bacterial, mite and nematode plant infections'.

Native hardwoods are gradually being reinstated into our woodlands. Coppicing re-emerges as a viable option for small businesses, or for personal sustainability as fuel. Value added wood products are finding a new market. Apprenticeships and training in our traditional wood-related skills are becoming available again, albeit on a small scale. Environmental awareness is now taught in most schools to our children, who will expect their own offspring to benefit from current efforts, and for subsequent generations to perpetuate the gradual return to common sense.

Yes, wood is gradually returning to our lives, but like everything in nature, it just takes time.

Traditional 'pimp' – 25 individual bundles of fire kindling – Moreton Wood Coppice Products

The future for woodland crafts

It is all too easy to paint a romanticised picture of days gone by, where jolly, red-cheeked woodland workers and rural craftspeople were to be found dotted around the countryside, cheerfully beavering away in a local community bubble, making a modest living from country crafts products.

The reality is that everybody involved in woodland management and crafts had to work extremely hard to earn even a basic living. Many end products like spoons and baskets were made at home in the evenings after a long day working outside in all weather conditions.

Most skilled craftspeople's prices were tied in to the local economy, and if their parents had charged a certain price for a product, the local customers expected the offspring to

global trade exceeding $60 billion per annum. In 2009, the Arthritis Research Campaign found Britons were spending around £450 million a year on all complementary medicines.

One notably fine example of the medical usefulness of trees is that of the English Yew, Taxus baccata, itself widely known as having poisonous leaves. These same leave are now being used successfully to treat breast cancer.

The point is, there must be so many more plant species yet to be discovered for the benefit of human kind, so doesn't it make sense to protect and explore our mysterious forests across the world, instead of chopping them down?

We are dangerously over-using modern chemicals to spray crops, resulting in very harmful short and medium-term damage to the local eco system, and potentially our own health, and that of our children.

The disappearance of bees in such alarmingly large numbers has been linked to indiscriminate usage of certain crop sprays. Without bees and other insects to pollinate trees, other plants and crops, the whole circle of nature will suffer catastrophic damage, resulting in a world food shortage on an unprecedented scale on an already over-populated planet.

Trees produce their own natural insect repellents to either discourage small insects from damaging them, or to attract larger, predatory insects to feed on the less desirable ones.

Traditional spoon carving

We work for ourselves. We engage in work that is stimulating, creative and enjoyable. We are outside in the fresh air every day, exercising our bodies and minds – acutely aware of the seasons and the environment. We are doing something with our hands. We have many skills. We look forward to going to work each day!

Our profession ensures a job with dignity and integrity; it can bring an inner calm and contentment, devoid of the common relentless triviality associated with so many jobs in the modern day world. Now, how many people can put their hand on their heart and honestly say that? You just can't put a price on it, can you?

charge the same. On many occasions the maker sold a product at cost price, or even at a loss, just to keep them, and their employees if they had any, in work. Actual profit was sometimes only possible with repairs and maintenance.

Ironically, things haven't changed much even today! We still have to overcome a few problems of public perception. While many people find the sight of a slightly rustic-looking craftsperson demonstrating their skills at a local county fair an endearing experience, and a pleasant way of spending some leisure time on a sunny weekend, they may still baulk at the price of the end product on sale. A handmade basket, for instance, will take the same amount of time to produce as an imported one would; the only difference being that the imported one is half the price, even though it has been transported from thousands of air-miles away. The reality is that a traditional craftsperson will work hard to earn just a quarter of the hourly rate of a plumber, for example, although he or she may be creating something beautiful that lasts a lifetime (rather than a temporary improvement in your water system).

But let us not forget that whilst being a craftsperson is not a way of making a good living – it is a good way of living.

We are not the ones commuting long distances to work, at great expense in crowded trains, tubes or buses, or sitting in polluting traffic jams. We do not work amongst hundreds of faceless others, sitting in identical chairs staring at identical computer screens all day. We do not have to suck up to our boss or engage in office politics. We are not working in a mind-numbing production line, operating noisy and dangerous machinery. It is we who are the lucky ones.

Author with 'Tipi' chair

At the same time as keeping the old traditions alive, the current generation of woodland craft people must also adapt to the modern day market – using light machinery to reduce repetitive production; developing our own products and designs to suite modern day needs and tastes; re-thinking production methodology to make more efficient use of our time; not being afraid to proudly justify the cost, and not feeling guilty about making a profit; and gladly passing down our knowledge to the next generation. With a bit of luck, they may be able to build on our achievements and even make a reasonable living, providing they can get this tricky mix right.

Being the modern day ambassadors of the rural crafts, we must always ensure that what we produce meets the highest possible standards, using best quality, local materials. It is not enough to offer a mediocre handmade product and expect a premium; we must set the benchmark for others to follow. The Shakers, renowned for their consistent supply of quality products had a saying along the lines of; 'make a product as if it will have to last for a thousand years, and you will die tomorrow.'

So, although the practice of woodland management and crafts will never be the same again, the skills and products are surviving, albeit in a vastly different world. By combining modern technology and marketing with older skills and practices, with respect for nature, trees and our proud tradition to produce high quality hand-made products, we are assuring, in our own small way, the continuation of our woodland heritage.

We are entering the age of the craftsman, where skills will be what matters. An age when the man who can grow asparagus will be more important than the man who can spell asparagus.

John Brown

Ash ladderback rocking chair with rush seat made by the author

Scots pine forest

CHAPTER 3

British woodland tree species

Silver birch

Native tree species of Britain

There are 33 recognised native tree species which naturally colonised Britain after the last ice age and before the formation of the English Channel. The list below represents the species in their order of arrival in Britain.

COMMON NAME	BOTANICAL NAME
Common Juniper	Juniperus communis
Downy Birch	Betula pubescens
Silver Birch	Betula pendula
Aspen	Populus tremula
Scots Pine	Pinus sylvestris
Bay Willow	Salix pentandra
Common Alder	Alnus glutinosa
Hazel	Corylus avellana
Small-leaved Lime	Tilia cordata
Bird Cherry	Prunus padus
Goat Willow	Salix caprea
Wych Elm	Ulmus glabra
Rowan	Sorbus aucuparia
Sessile Oak	Quercus petraea
Ash	Fraxinus excelsior
Holly	Ilex aquifolium
English Oak	Quercus robur
Hawthorn	Crataegus monogyna
Crack Willow	Salix fragilis
Black Poplar	Populas nigra
Yew	Taxus baccata
Whitebeam	Sorbus aria
Midland Hawthorn	Crataegus laevigata
Crab Apple	Malus sylvestris
Wild Cherry	Prunus avium
Strawberry Tree	Arbutus unedo
White Willow	Salix alba
Field Maple	Acer campestre
Wild Service Tree	Sorbus torminalis
Large-leaved Lime	Tilia platyphyllos
Beech	Fagus sylvatica
Hornbeam	Carpinus betulus
Box	Buxus sempervirens

Native British shrubs

Shrubs are often overlooked. A shrub is defined as the *understory* of woody plants, between three and 30 feet high, growing beneath the forest canopy; normally growing multiple stems, as opposed to a single stem.

They are as much a part of the British landscape as trees, and provide us with many culinary, medical and household applications.

SHRUB	LATIN NAME
Alder Buckthorn	Rhamnus frangula
Elder	Sambucus nigra
Dogwood	Cornus sanguinea
Rock Whitebeam	Sorbus rupicola
Sea Buckthorn	Hippophae rhamnoides
Spindle	Euonymus europaeus
Sallow, Goat Willow	Salix caprea
Grey Willow	Salix cinerea
Purple Willow	Salix purpurea
Common Osier	Salix viminalis
Eared Willow	Salix aurita
Guelder Rose	Viburnum opulus
Wayfaring Tree	Viburnum lantana
Privet	Ligustrum vulgare

Guelder rose

Naturalised trees

Naturalised species were *introduced* by humans *after* the formation of the English Channel. Good examples are Sweet Chestnut and English Elm, both introduced by the Romans and Sycamore introduced in Tudor times.

NAME	LATIN NAME	AREA OF ORIGIN
Maritime Pine	Pinus pinaster	Europe
European Black Pine	Pinus nigra	Europe
Norway Spruce	Picea abies	Scandinavia
European Larch	Larix decidua	Europe
European Pear	Pyrus communis	Europe
Plymouth Pear	Pyrus cordata	Europe
Cherry Plum	Prunus cerasifera	Europe
Sycamore	Acer pseudoplatanus	Europe
Norway Maple	Acer platanoides	Scandinavia
Sweet Chestnut	Castanea sativa	Europe
Holm Oak	Quercus ilex	Europe
Turkey Oak	Quercus cerris	Europe
Horse Chestnut	Aesculus hippocastanum	Europe
English Elm	Ulmus procera	Europe
Japanese Larch	Larix kaempferi	Asia
Lodgepole Pine	Pinus contorta	North America
Sitka Spruce	Picea sitchensis	North America
Black Spruce	Picea mariana	North America
Douglas Fir	Pseudotsuga menziesii	North America
Grand Fir	Abies grandis	North America
Western Hemlock	Tsuga heterophylla	North America
Western Red Cedar	Thuja plicata	North America
Lawson's Cypress	Chamaecyparis lawsoniana	North America
Monterey Cypress	Cupressus macrocarpa	North America

Sweet chestnut tree on the edge of a small wood

CHAPTER 4

The characteristics of broadleaf and conifer trees

Some people categorise trees as either hardwoods or softwoods. Other people refer to them as either broadleaf or conifer. Conifer literally means 'cone-bearing'. Defining trees as hardwoods and softwoods can be misleading because some hardwoods are softer than softwoods, and vice versa. Douglas fir, for instance, is a hard softwood, as are pitch pine and yew. Elm is a reasonably soft hardwood, and so are willow and balsa.

Broadleaf and conifer is a better way of differentiating between the two types, but explaining that conifers keep their leaves throughout the winter is OK until some 'clever' person reminds you that the larch (a conifer), actually loses its leaves/needles in winter. So, here are simple characteristics for you to peruse.

BROADLEAF	CONIFER
Generally harder wood than conifer	Generally softer wood than broadleaf
Angiosperms (covered seeds)	Gymnosperms (naked seeds)
Dendritic (tree form characterised by multiple branching from main stem)	Excurrent (tree form characterised by a straight, dominant main stem with subordinate lateral branching)
Leaves are flat	Needles instead of broad leaves
Deciduous (leaves fall in autumn)	Evergreen (needles don't fall in autumn)
Less fibrous than conifers	More fibrous than broadleaves
Non-resinous	Resinous
Quite a complex cell structure	Relatively simple cell structure
Evolved after conifers	Evolved before broadleaves
Less prone to insect and fungal attack	More prone to insect and fungal attack
Many broadleaf trees coppice well	Most conifers do not coppice well

Species:

Alder, ash, beech, birch, hornbeam, box, cherry, blackthorn, horse chestnut, sweet chestnut, elm, hazel, holly, lime, maple, sycamore, oak, plane, aspen, poplar, crab apple, hawthorn, whitebeam, walnut, willow.

Species:

Cedar, cyprus, fir, larch, pine, sequoia, spruce, yew.

Norway spruce trees in Iceland

The differing branch structures of broadleaf and conifer trees

When viewing the profile of broadleaf and conifer trees, each has a distinctly different structure. While broadleaves can sometimes be dual, or even multi-stemmed and their branches an array of multi-directional forms, conifers tend to grow straighter, with thinner, more uniform branch configurations.

Broadleaf trees put out branches upwards and outwards, the underside being supported at the junction of the trunk and branch with a bolster under compression.

Conifers put out branches downwards and outwards, the topside being supported like a suspension bridge with a top growth at the junction of the trunk and branch under tension.

Sunset clouds behind winter tree branches

CHAPTER 5

Wood characteristics by species

Listed in this chapter are the general characteristics of our most common trees. Specific properties and applications for these are to be found in later chapters.

Alder *Alnus*

When freshly cut, takes on a red/orange colour, turning creamy yellow/brown when seasoned. Fairly lightweight. Medium hardness. Easy to work. Coppices well. Cleaves quite well. Low resistance to decay outdoors unless kept continuously wet. Lasts very well underwater. Dries quickly with noticeable shrinkage.

Apple *Malus*

Mid to darker brown, hard, fairly tough and resists wear. Aromatic wood with close, fine grain. Easy to work, good for carving. Cleaves fairy well. Dries fairly slowly. Harder than pear.

Ash *Fraxinus*

Pale yellow to off-white. Tough, springy wood with occasional streaks of brown. Reasonably pronounced grain and distinct growth rings. Only a very thin layer of sapwood, so most of the surface area is useable. Can turn a temporary pinkish colour when worked unseasoned, known as 'Ash blush'. Olive Ash has a darker, beautiful butternut colour. Very durable and shock-resistant. Coppices well. Also cleaves and bends well. Low resistance to decay outdoors. Dries fairly quickly without much problem and stores well.

Alder trees in the Beaulieu River, New Forest

Beech *Fagus*

Light yellow/pinkish brown hard, tough wood occasionally with red/brown around the heartwood. Fine, close grained with even texture and little figure. Good for carving. Coppices reasonably. Cleaves and bends well. Low resistance to decay outdoors and to insects. Dries quite quickly.

Birch *Betula*

Light yellow/ brown hard, fine-grained, tough wood with occasional streaks of red/brown near the heartwood. No visible difference between the heartwood and sapwood. Coppices well when young. Good figuring. Cleaves and bends reasonably well. Low resistance to decay if exposed outdoors, but bark is waterproof. Dries fairly quickly.

Cherry *Prunus*

Light red/pink/golden brown, fairly hard and tough wood with red/brown streaks nearer the heartwood. Fine, close grain with distinctive growth rings. Easy to work. Popular with turners. Cleaves and bends reasonably well. High resistance to decay outdoors. Dries well.

Chestnut (sweet) *Castanea Sativa*

Orange/brown moderately hard, tough, durable and strong timber with a good grain. Very little sapwood so most of the wood is useable. Often used as a lighter and cheaper alternative to oak, having many of the same properties. Cleaves and steam bends well. Seasons slowly but prone to checking. High resistance to decay outdoors. Contains a lot of tannin.

Douglas Fir *Pseudotsuga*

Large, straight-growing softwood, resistant to decay and a fairly hard softwood.

Elder *Sambucus*

Rarely grows into a tree. When it does it will produce a hard, light cream, smooth wood.

Elm *Ulmus*

Rich red/brown hardwood with tough, erratic interlocking grain. Turns well. Dries and stabilises well. Strong. Resistant to splitting. Good resistance to decay outdoors. Can be used for underwater applications. Dries fairly quickly..

Avenue of English Elms, Fitzroy Gardens, Melbourne

Wych Elm *Ulmus Giabra*

Similar in colour to elm. Tough and supple wood favoured in boatbuilding. Inner bark (bast) excellent for chair seat weaving.

Hawthorn *Crataegus*

Light pinkish/brown hard, fine, close-grained, tough wood. Difficult to cleave. Good for carving, but very knotty. Coppices well. Dries fairly slowly.

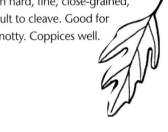

Hazel *Corylus*

Light brown medium hardwood not readily available in large diameters due to size of tree. Coppices, cleaves and bends well. Good resistance to decay outdoors, but small diameter rods prone to becoming brittle with time.

Hornbeam Tree in Barnet Gate Wood, London

Holly *Ilex*

Ivory coloured, reasonably tough-grained dense hardwood. Not readily available in large diameters due to the size of tree. Coppices well. Turns well. Dries quite slowly.

Hornbeam *Carpinus*

Ivory coloured, reasonably tough-grained dense hardwood. Not readily available in large diameters due to the size of tree. Coppices well. Turns well. Dries quite slowly.

Larch *Larix*

Distinctive red/orange/brown wood. A quite hard and durable softwood, fibrous and resistant to decay. The only conifer to lose its leaves in autumn.

Lime *Tilia*

Pale, straw-coloured lightweight wood. Very fine, soft textured, even grain. Excellent for carving. Coppices well. Low resistance to decay outdoors. Dries fairly quickly. Inner bark (bast) excellent for weaving and cordage.

Oak *Quercus*

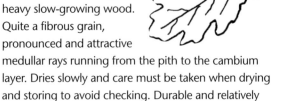

Ranging from light brown to red/brown. Hard, tough and heavy slow-growing wood. Quite a fibrous grain, pronounced and attractive medullar rays running from the pith to the cambium layer. Dries slowly and care must be taken when drying and storing to avoid checking. Durable and relatively insect resistant. Coppices, cleaves and bends well. High resistance to decay outdoors. Contains a lot of tannin.

Pine (scots) *Pinus*

Resinous, light cream soft wood turning into a yellow, red/brown patina with age. Not strong and doesn't rive well. Not durable outdoors

Poplar *Populus*

Low-density, and tough for its weight.

Rowan tree, also known as Mountain Ash

Rowan *Sorbus*

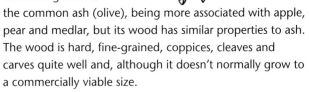

Known as the mountain ash but apart from similar leaves and wood characteristics, it is not in the same genus as the common ash (olive), being more associated with apple, pear and medlar, but its wood has similar properties to ash. The wood is hard, fine-grained, coppices, cleaves and carves quite well and, although it doesn't normally grow to a commercially viable size.

Sycamore *Acer*

Can vary in colour. Mostly pale yellow with light reddish/pink areas. Some streaked with red/brown and very occasionally pronounced, attractive figuring. Close grained, hard, reasonably tough wood good for turning. Coppices well. Cleaves fairly well. Low resistance to decay outdoors. Contains a very high moisture content, but dries fairly quickly and evenly and becomes quite lightweight when seasoned.

Norway Spruce *Picea*

Clean, white coloured softwood. Works well. Used outdoors with preservative as it is dimensionally stable.

Sitka Spruce *Picea*

Similar properties to Norway Spruce.

Walnut *Juglans*

Light to very dark brown, hard, tough, fine, figured grain and reasonably durable. The most beautifully figured grain can often come from the base of the trunk, so the tree would have to be dug out, rather than felled. Careful seasoning results in stable wood. Works and carves well.

Western Red Cedar *Thuja*

A lightweight, low density and low strength softwood. Resistant to fungi. Good for internal framing.

Willow *Salix*

Light colored, fairly soft open-textured wood but quite strong. Cleaves and bends well. Coppices well. Light and flexible. Low resistance to decay outdoors.

Yew *Taxus*

A hard, slow-growing softwood. Red/ orange/brown heartwood with an attractive close grain and off-white sapwood. Strong, durable and flexible. Good for carving, rives well, finishes well. High resistance to decay outdoors. Bends well in the round only.

Western Red Cedar. South Whidbey State Park, Washington, USA

Average Life Expectancy of British Trees *Source – British Hardwood Tree Nursery (BHT) and Hellis Tree Consultants*

SPECIES	AVERAGE LIFE EXPECTANCY (yrs)
Most Poplar, Willow	50 – 70
Aspen, Crab Apple, Hazel, Crack Willow, Whitebeam	70 – 100
Common Alder, Hawthorn, Silver Birch, Norway Spruce, Red Oak, Rowan, Wild Cherry	100 – 150
Ash, Beech, Norway Maple, Walnut	150 – 200
Elm, Wych Elm, English Oak, Holly, Hornbeam, Lime, Pear, Scots Pine, Sessile Oak, Sycamore	200 – 300
Larch, Austrian Pine, London Plane, Noble Fir, Horse Chestnut, Sweet Chestnut, Sitka Spruce, Yew	300 +

Angel wings

CHAPTER 6

The properties of wood by species

Tendency to warp during seasoning

All wood changes as it seasons, and will keep shrinking and swelling as the conditions around it change. Checking, cupping, bowing, twisting and kinking can all occur at various stages of seasoning wood. Although the inevitable shrinkage can be controlled to a great extent, subject to the ambient humidity, particularly when air-drying, it is worth bearing in mind that some woods are more stable than others during the seasoning process.

Stable	Fairly stable	Less stable
Alder	Birch	Beech
Ash	Elm	Sweet Chestnut
Aspen	Fir, Douglas	Sycamore
Cedar	Fir	
Cherry	Larch	
Some Pines	Oak	
Spruce	Some Pines	
Walnut	Willow	

Ability to cope underwater

The ability to be submerged and survive underwater. Typical underwater applications would be bridge and building pilings, lock gates and water pipes.

Excellent	Good
Alder	Beech
Elm	Oak
Scots pine	Larch
Yew	Norway spruce

Hardness and softness

Hardness in a wood makes it fairly resistant to dents and scratches. It also enables a clean saw cut and a very good surface finish after working with planes and spoke shaves. Softness in a wood enables it to be worked with less effort, to slightly less precision, but it is subject to grain tear-out and is easily dented and scratched.

Hard	Fairly hard	Fairly soft
Apple	Elder	Cedar,
Ash	Beech	Western red
Birch	Chestnut	Fir
Blackthorn	Fir, Douglas	Lime
Cherry	Hemlock	Pine
Elm	Spruce	Willow
Hawthorn		
Hornbeam		
Holly		
Larch		
Oak		
Olive		
Pear		
Sycamore		
Walnut		
Yew		

Bendability

The ability to bend into a curved form when steamed, or bent over a form and supported with or without straps. It is preferable if the wood is riven and contains no knots or other imperfections.

Good	Fair	Poor
Ash	Cedar, white	Alder
Beech	Chestnut,	Conifer, most
Birch	sweet	Lime
Cedar, Western	Elm	Poplar
red	Fir, Douglas	Sycamore
Cherry	Pine	Willow
Hazel		
Larch		
Oak		
Walnut		
Yew		

Toughness

Toughness is the ability to tolerate stresses, strains, shocks and general abuse.

Tough	Fairly tough	Fairly weak
Ash	Apple	Cedar,
Beech	Cedar,	Western red
Birch	Eastern red	Fir
Elm	Cherry	Lime
Hawthorn	Chestnut, sweet	Maple
Hornbeam	Fir, Douglas	Pine, (most)
Oak	Holly	Poplar
Walnut	Larch	
	Pear	
	Pine, (some)	
	Redwood	
	Spruce, sitka	
	Sycamore	

Decay resistance

The ability to withstand deterioration and decay outdoors if left untreated, especially when put in the ground (fence posts etc).

High	Intemediate	Low
Cedar (all)	Elm	Alder
Cherry	Douglas Fir	Ash
Chestnut sweet	Hornbeam	Beech
Juniper	Larch	Birch
Mulberry	Pine (some)	Lime
Oak	Hazel	Poplar
Walnut		Spruce
Yew		Sycamore
		Willow

Odour and taste

In certain applications, these properties are crucial. Species in the excellent category would have suitable uses in the preparation and storage of food, for example, or when coming into contact with the mouth or tongue, as with musical instruments.

Excellent	Acceptable	Undesirable
Apple	Oak, all	Cedar
Ash		Fir, Douglas
Beech		Larch, western
Birch		Pine, all
Cherry		
Chestnut		
Elm		
Fir		
Holly		
Lime		
Pear		
Poplar		
Spruce, all		
Sycamore		
Walnut		
Willow		

Cleaving/riving qualities

Ease and controllability for splitting down the grain.

Good to excellent	Fair	Poor
Ash	Alder	Elm
Beech	Apple	Eucalyptus
Cedar, western red	Birch	Hawthorn
Chestnut (horse & sweet)	Cedar, eastern red	Holly
Douglas Fir	Cherry	Hornbeam
Hazel	Lime	
Larch	Pear	
Oak	Pine (some)	
Pine (some)	Poplar (some)	
Spruce	Sycamore	
Walnut	Yew	
Willow		

Average annual tree girth increase

Trees in Britain increase their girth/circumference by an average of 2.5cm per year across the species (1.5cm if growing close together in a wood, or 2.5cm if the tree is free standing). Some species grow more quickly than others, and their growing conditions will vary from year to year. The list below is a broad representation of our most common trees.

This table can be useful when calculating the age of a live, standing tree.

Species	Annual girth/ circumference increase
Holly, Yew	1.25cm
Oak	1.88cm
Ash, Beech, Elm, Hazel	2.5cm
Sycamore	2.75cm
Pine, Spruce	3.13cm

Weeping willow

Average air-drying time

Approximate time taken to air dry hardwoods of 25mm (1in) in diameter from green (50% upwards moisture content) down to 20% moisture content (about the minimum level you can expect to reach by air-drying in the UK). Drying times depend on regional/local climate, time of year and how the wood is stored, but generally, wood only seasons in the warmer, summer months.

Species	Time taken to air dry (months)
Alder	3-9
Apple	6-15
Ash	4-10
Beech	4-10
Birch	4-10
Box	9-18
Chestnut (sweet)	6-15
Elm	4-10
Hawthorn	6-15
Holly	6-15
Hornbeam	6-15
Lime	4-10
Oak	9-18
Pear	6-15
Sycamore	4-10
Walnut	5-12

CHAPTER 7

Coppicing – from trees to workable wood

To make use of the natural resource growing in our woodlands, trees of different diameters can be coppiced – a practice originating thousands of years ago.

The word coppice derives from the French word couper, meaning to cut. Within a managed coppice woodland (typically under 10 acres), trees (or rods) of a suitable size are cut down during the winter months when the sap isn't flowing, to a stump left protruding from ground level, leaving the other trees of various diameters to grow up to the desired size until they in turn will also be cut down. Meanwhile the stools from the previous year will naturally shoot and re-grow into multiple poles again. When an area has been coppiced, it is usually fenced in for two or three years to prevent animals grazing on the new shoots.

Coppiced lime trees in South Ayrshire, Scotland

Willow pollards in morning fog, in Dulmen, Germany

Pollarding

The word pollard derives from the old English word 'poll', meaning 'head'. This procedure is done in situations where it is not practical or desirable to fence in a newly coppiced area. The same principles of coppicing apply when pollarding, the difference being that the tree is cut off at a height of approximately 2.5m (8ft) from the ground instead of cutting it at ground level. It can then re-generate multiple poles, out of the reach of grazing animals who would feed on the new shoots. Pollard rotation is every 10 to 20 years. Not all tree species respond to pollarding that well, but oak, beech and hornbeam are particularly suitable.

It is worth mentioning that conifers, with the exception of yew, do not coppice (this being technically re-growing from the same rooted, expanded stool into multiple poles). Conifer, if clear-felled will, eventually, germinate from old seeds and grow into new trees.

A renewable supply of wood

Cutting and leaving the trees to grow in coppice rotation allows a huge variety of end products to be made, with a continuous supply of renewable material every season. The trees may be left to grow for anything from 2 to 25 years, depending on the thickness of wood required. That, in turn, might vary from 2.5cm (1in) to 20cm (8in), depending on what the poles might be used for.

Coppicing also greatly extends the life of the trees (some ancient hazel stands date back approximately 1,500 years) while also encouraging biodiversity on the forest floor, allowing a plethora of wildlife, including some of today's endangered species, like the dormouse and certain butterflies, to flourish.

By comparison, the timescales for full rotation of mature tree stock could be anything from 65 to 150 years. It is almost as though coppicing is the 'fast food' of the woodland industry, giving a return on investment in a relatively short time.

In Britain, we mainly coppice ash, alder, birch, hazel, hornbeam, oak, sycamore and willow. Each tree has many possible applications after it is cut, depending on the local demands of the market and cutting rotation varies with species from 5 to 25 years. More than 20 different species of tree can be used in this manner, and estimates suggest that this can produce a staggering 200 possible end products.

Newly cut ash coppice stools

Coppiced ash stool re-growth after just six months – multiple stems reaching two metres high

43

Suitability of different species for coppicing and pollarding

Depending upon the location and soil types, the best rated species will re-grow reliably, over many years.

Species	Coppicing	Pollarding
Alder	Excellent	Reasonable
Ash	Excellent	Excellent
Beech	Good	Excellent
Birch	Good	Unsuitable
Poplar	Good	Excellent
Box	Unsuitable	Unsuitable
Cherry	Unsuitable	Unsuitable
Chestnut	Excellent	Reasonable
Elder	Unsuitable	Unsuitable
Elm	Unsuitable	Excellent
Eucalyptus	Excellent	Unsuitable
Hawthorn	Good	Reasonable
Hazel	Excellent	Unsuitable
Holly	Good	Excellent
Hornbeam	Excellent	Good
Juniper	Unsuitable	Unsuitable
Lime	Excellent	Excellent
Oak	Good	Reasonable
Pear	Reasonable	Unsuitable
Rowan	Good	Good
Scots Pine	Unsuitable	Unsuitable
Spindle	Unsuitable	Unsuitable
Sycamore	Excellent	Excellent
Willow	Excellent	Excellent
Wild Service	Good	Good
Wych Elm	Excellent	Excellent
Yew	Reasonable	Reasonable

Typical coppice rotation (depending on applications)

Species	Rotation (years)
Alder	15 - 25
Ash	12 - 30
Birch	8 - 16
Hazel	5 - 12
Hornbeam	12 - 30
Oak	20 - 30
Sweet Chestnut	15 - 25
Sycamore	15 - 25

Weaving a natural fence at Moreton Wood

Traditional coppice products

Product	Wood	Usual size
Barrel hoops	Ash, Hazel	1.2m - 2.1m (4ft - 7ft) x 3.8cm to 6.3cm (1.5in - 2.5in) diameter
Bark for tanning	Oak, Sweet Chestnut	From logs
Baskets	Ash, Oak, Willow	Cleft from logs
Bean poles	Ash, Birch, Chestnut, Hazel, Sycamore	2.1m (7ft) long x 2.5cm - 4cm (1in - 1.5in) diameter
Besom handles	Ash, Birch, Hazel, Sycamore	1m (3.5ft) long x 2.5cm (1in) diameter
Besom heads	Birch twigs	1m / 3ft bundle
Broom handles	Ash, Birch, Chestnut, Sycamore	180cm - 240cm (6ft - 8ft) long x 2.5cm (1in) diameter
Charcoal	Any	Logs
Chairs	Ash, Oak, Beech	Cleft from logs 15cm - 20cm (6in - 8in) diameter
Chair seat weaving	Wych Elm bast, Lime bast, Western Red Cedar bast.	Shaved from logs
Clothes pegs	Aspen, Beech, Birch, Sallow	Cleft from logs
Clothes props	Hazel	180cm - 240cm (6ft - 8ft) long x 5cm - 8cm (2in - 3in) diameter with a fork at the end
Ethering	Hazel	Rods up to 3.6m (12ft) x 3.8cm (1.5in) diameter
Faggots	Any brash	Bundles
Firewood	Most species	Logs
Fence posts	Chestnut	Cleft from logs 15cm - 20cm (6in - 8in) diameter
Flower/tomato stakes	Chestnut, Hazel	1.35m (4.5ft) x 2.5cm (1in) diameter
Hay rakes	Ash, Birch	Cleft from logs 15cm - 20cm (6in - 8in) diameter
Hedging stakes	Ash, Birch, Chestnut, Hazel, Sycamore	1.5m (5ft) x 2.5cm - 5cm (1in - 2in) diameter
Hop poles	Ash, Chestnut, Lime	4.8m - 6m (16ft - 20ft) long x 7.5cm (3in) diameter
Hurdles, gates	Chestnut, Elm, Sycamore	Cleft from logs 15cm - 20cm (6in - 8in) diameter
Hurdles, wattle	Hazel	1.8m to 3.5m (6ft - 12ft) long and up to 4cm (1.5in) diameter

Traditional coppice products

Product	Wood	Usual size
Horse jumps	Birch	1.5m (5ft) x 30cm (12in) diameter.
Lathes	Oak, Sweet Chestnut	Cleft from logs 15cm - 20cm (6in - 8in) diameter.
Longbows	Ash, Yew	Cleft from logs.
Mulch	Any	Everything.
Pale fencing	Chestnut	Cleft from logs 15cm - 20cm (6in - 8in) diameter.
Pea sticks	Chestnut, Hazel	1.5m (5ft) long, including side shoots.
Plant stands	Hazel	Rods up to 3.5m (12ft) high, approx 2.5cm (1in) at the base.
Rustic furniture	Any	In the round, up to 1.5m (5 ft) long x 2.5cm - 5cm (1in - 1.5in) diameter, or cleft from log.
Rustic garden framework	Chestnut, Elm, Hazel, Larch	All sizes of poles, and cleft from logs.
Rake handles	Ash, Chestnut	1.8m to 2.4m (6ft to 8ft) long.
Straw bale pins	Ash, Hazel	1.2m (4ft) long x 5cm (1.5in) diameter.
Straw bale staples	Hazel	1m (3ft) long x 2.5cm (1in) diameter.
Spelk/swill baskets	Oak	Cleft from log.
Staffs	Ash	Cleft from log.
Thatching spars	Hazel	60cm -75cm (2ft to 2.5ft)
Tool handles	Ash	Cleft from logs 15cm to 20cm (6in to 8in) diameter.
Tree stakes	Chestnut, Hazel	1.8m (6ft) long x 6.5cm (2.5in) diameter.
Trugs	Chestnut	Cleft from logs 15cm to 20cm (6in to 8in) diameter.
Walking sticks	Ash, Blackthorn Chestnut, Hazel, Holly, Rowan, Birch	90cm to 150cm (3ft to 5ft).
Wattle & daub panels	Chestnut, Oak, Hazel	Poles and cleft from logs.
Yurt poles (roof)	Ash, Chestnut	Up to 2.4m (8ft) long x 3cm to 5cm (1.5in to 2in) diameter.
Yurts	Ash, Hazel, Chestnut	1.8m (6ft) long x 2.5cm to 3.5cm (1in to 1.5in) diameter.

CHAPTER 8

A rough guide to measuring trees

Measuring the age, height and diameter of living, standing trees

Trees obviously get older every year, increasing their girth and height. Some species grow more quickly than others, and their growing conditions will vary from year to year, according to location and climate.

There are quite sophisticated and reasonably priced hand-held electronic devices on the market now for measuring trees very accurately, such as clinometers and hypsometers, and satellite management systems can tell you just about everything a tree is doing at any time of the day to a staggering degree of accuracy.

A few less complex traditional aids, like large wooden calipers, measuring sticks and flexible D-tapes for measuring the diameter are still widely used by professional tree specialists, but woodland people of days gone by measured trees by far simpler methods with surprisingly accurate results.

So, for the layperson who just wants to know the height of a trees in case it might hit their house if it falls down, or the diameter of a tree they may have planted years ago, the age of a particular tree that has caught their interest, or if you just want to drag the children away from their X-boxes for some fresh air and sunshine and natural fun, the methods listed next give you a fair idea of the measurement you want.

Calculating the age by counting the growth rings

The easiest and most accurate method is to count the annual growth rings, from the centre (pith) outwards, on the exposed end cross-section of the trunk after felling. One ring represents a year's growth. This method works

U.S. Economics Officer in Asadabad rough measuring age of a tree.

very well, but is a little drastic if the only reason for felling the tree is to see how old it is.

Calculating the age using a core sample

If a tree is to be left standing, another practice is to bore a small hole in the centre of the trunk at a height of about 1.5 metres (5ft) from ground level, with a hollow auger. The core sample, when extracted, will give a pretty accurate indication of the tree's age after the annual growth rings have been counted. This method is a humane and pretty reliable one, unless the tree turns out to have a hollow trunk. Of course, you must carefully replace the core sample after counting the growth rings and seal up the wound to avoid infection. Although the tree will heal itself internally, you would expect to see an unusual figuration if the tree were to be felled in the future and sawn up for boards.

47

Calculating the age from the girth of the tree

This method involves no harm to the tree. Choose a tree whose species you have previously identified. Measure up the trunk 1.5m (5 ft) from ground level, bearing in mind that true ground level may be below leaf mulch level in autumn/winter. If the tree is on a slope, is leaning from a bank, or has an unusually shaped bole, or has a split trunk, take the 1.5m (5 ft) measurement according to the diagrams below.

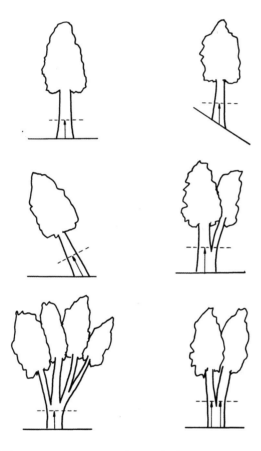

Taking a measurement up the trunk of a tree

Using a flexible tape, string or rope, measure the girth/circumference in centimetres. When the trunk splits in two or more trunks below 1.3m, measure the girth of the biggest trunk at 1.3m height. Do this also when two trees have been planted close together.

All tree species grow at different speeds, with the circumference increasing at a species average of roughly 2.5cm a year (1.5cm if growing close together in a wood, or 2.5cm if the tree is free standing). Use the following rough guide figures to include in your calculation.

Tree Species	Approximate Annual Girth/ Circumference Increase
Average	2.5cm
Holly, Yew	1.25cm
Oak	1.88cm
Ash, Beech, Elm, Hazel	2.5cm
Sycamore	2.75cm
Pine, Spruce	3.13cm

Take the circumference that you measured and divide it by the growth rate relating to your species of tree (from the table above). This will give you the age in years, which you can round off to the nearest whole number. For example:

If the a tree has a circumference of 220cm:

If the tree is an oak $220 \div 1.88 = 117$ years old
If the tree is a pine $220 \div 3.13 = 71$ years old

Calculating the height of a tree

If you are able enough to climb to the very top of a tree and dangle a rope down to ground level without crashing down to ground level yourself, you can measure the length of the rope to find your answer.

For the less adventurous, the following 4 methods work surprisingly well.

1. A very traditional method

This is allegedly an old North American Indian way. With your back to the trunk, walk away from the tree, occasionally stopping to bend down very low, and, with your hands gripping your knees to support you, look back up between your legs and see if the very top of the tree is in view. If not, stand back up straight and walk further away and look between your legs again. Repeat the exercise (without blacking out) until the top of the tree comes into view just below your crotch. Pace back to the base of the tree, counting the number of one-metre strides, or measure more accurately using a large flexible tape. This should be equivalent to the height of the tree.

2. A rule of thumb method

This works best if you can get a friend to help by standing by the base of the tree to be measured. Stand well back from the tree and extend your arm in front of you at eye level with your fist clenched and your thumb extending in a 'thumbs up', or pretend that you're a spectator in the Roman games giving your opinion on the fate of a defeated Gladiator – yes, you've got it.

Move back until the base of your fist is at the ground level, and the tip of your thumb is level with the top of the tree. Now, keeping the base of your fist very still, and your arm very straight, rotate your wrist anti-clockwise until your thumb has traveled 90 degrees (nine o'clock) and shout to your friend to start walking away from the tree to their right, until you shout at them to stop when they reach the tip of your thumb. Your friend can then pace back to the base of the tree, counting the number of one-metre strides, or measure more accurately using a large flexible tape, to give you the height of the tree.

3. The metre-long stick method

Take a stick about three feet or one metre long. Stand some way back from the tree and hold the stick horizontally. Place one end up to your eye, as if you were looking down the shaft of an arrow to see if it is straight, and extend either your left or right hand down the shaft until your arm is straight, then grip the stick with that extended arm.

Now, still holding the stick, turn it vertically so it points up, with your gripping hand at the base, keeping your arm straight, and your extended fist in line with the base of the tree. Move towards the tree or away from it until, when you hold the stick this way, the tip of the stick is in line with the top of the tree. From that standing point, pace back to the base of the tree, counting the number of one-metre strides, or measure more accurately using a large flexible tape.

4. The mirror method

If you have a small mirror, walk away from the tree, occasionally turning around and placing the mirror on the ground just in front of you, between you and the tree. Standing straight, if you can't see the top of the tree in the mirror's reflection, move further back until you can. When you can nearly see the top of the tree reflected back, shift slightly back, away from the mirror until you can. You will then need to take three measurements:

A - Height from the ground to your eye.
B - The distance that you are standing from the centre of the mirror lying on the ground (if any).
C - The distance from the centre of the mirror to the base of the tree, counting the number of one-metre strides, or measuring more accurately using a large flexible tape.

Add measurements A, B and C together to get the final answer.

How to measure the diameter of a living tree

If you need to know the volume of a tree, you will have to know the diameter. It's also handy to know the diameter of a tree for many other reasons. However, tree aren't ever perfectly round, and often grow more on one side if either located on a slope, or if one side gets more sun. This can make the trunk oval, which provides conflicting measurements depending on which direction you are measuring it from. The only accurate method of measuring the diameter of a tree, is to measure its circumference and then a do a bit of basic maths.

Stand next to the tree, wrap a piece of string tightly around the trunk 1.5m (5 ft) from the ground as if you were taking someone's chest measurement (see diagram above for how to measure up the trunk in awkward circumstances). Measure whatever the length of the removed string is, and divide this figure by 3.14 (π pi) to determine the diameter of the tree.

Formula:

$$\frac{\text{Circumference}}{\pi} = \text{diameter}$$

CHAPTER 9

Traditional common uses for wood by species

Does it matter if we aren't fussy about which species of wood we use to make things? Surely, it's all wood, isn't it?

Indeed it does matter which species of wood you use. If you suggested to a medieval bowman on the battle line that he should have bought an expensive European yew longbow instead of an inferior, cheaper elm or wych hazel practice bow that has snapped, just as he is drawing it against a thousand heavy cavalry charging down on him, he might have replied 'Now you tell me!' Or words to that effect.

Had Venice been built on ash pilings instead of those made of, amongst others, alder and yew, it wouldn't be one of the most popular tourist attractions in Europe today, having long since disappeared under water. Try getting a century against fierce Australian bowling aided by a heavy oak cricket bat instead of a beautifully balanced willow version, and you will be grateful that our forbearers passed down their tree wisdom to future generations.

In many cases, the wood used for a particular application will vary according to region and local availability. Different woods have similar properties too, but the tables below represent the common applications related to each tree species.

A

Alder, buckthorn – Fuse powder, superior charcoal.
Alder, common – Charcoal and gunpowder, underwater foundations, water pipes, lock sluice gates, clog soles, brush heads, hat-block moulds, tool handles, whistles, pipes, flutes, staves for herring casks, wainwrights' work, ancient warriors' shields, arrow shafts. Bark to tan hides. Carving, acoustic guitar necks and electric guitar bodies.
Apple – Carving, turnery, cogs for mills, spoons, saw handles, draughtsman's T-squares, golf club heads, woodcut blocks.
Ash – Barrel hoops, gate hurdles, tool handles, hay cribs, hay rakes, tent pegs, furniture, staircases, floorboards, charcoal, oars, hockey sticks, croquet mallets, baseball bats, polo mallets, snooker cues, cricket stumps, tennis racquets, walking sticks (particularly shepherds' crooks), snow shoes, skis, sledge runners, longbow staves, arrow shafts, spear shafts, jousting lances, shield handles, ladder sides and rungs, wheel felloes, wagon shafts, tops for gypsy caravans, police truncheons, drum rims, umbrella handles, rungs for

Willow bat, ash stumps at a cricket match at Kingswood School, Bath

ships' rope ladders, boat rigging hoops, splints for weaving, morris staves, wands, dowsing rods, laths, maypoles, yurt poles, church bell stops, parallel bars (gymnastics), trug handles and rims, aircraft wings

Aspen – Arrow shafts, clogs, paper, matches, fruit and vegetable boxes, interiors of saunas, veneer and plywood.

B

Beech – Furniture, spoons, chopping boards, butchers' blocks, kitchen utensils, darning mushrooms, bobbins, floorboards, mallet heads, tool handles, tent pegs, mauls, plane blocks, bellows, boat lasts, fishing floats, oars, granary shovels, bakers' peels, butter pats, clothes pegs, piano frames, hat boxes, brush heads, carving, turnery, barrel hoops, arrow shafts, sword scabbards, children's toys, shoemakers' lasts, boot trees, rifle stocks, textile rollers, carthorse collars, ox yokes, printing blocks, drum rims, sieve rims, dry barrel staves, toy hoops, gears and cogs, ladder rungs, wheel felloes, saddle trees, golf club heads, underwater piling. Leaves make excellent mattress stuffing.

A window and wooden wheel in the South Tyrol

Birch – Gunpowder, besom broom heads and handles, rake and axe handles, scythe snaiths, turnery, clogs, horse jumps, bobbins, charcoal, furniture, veneer, spoons, butter prints and house treen, smokers' pipes, barrel staves and bungs, roofing thatch, carving, bark containers, herring barrels, rune sets, wands, bark for writing paper, withes, walking sticks, arrow and spear shafts, plywood, aeroplane propellers, canoes, laths, ox yokes, bark for tanning, twigs for corporal punishment and beaters for forest fires, tipi poles, rope, saddle trees, window frames, flooring, maypoles, roofs for bush shelters.

Blackthorn – Walking sticks, shillelaghs, arrow shafts, whip

stocks, golf club heads, divination rods.

Box – Chisel handles and carving mallets, cleaves, pestles, chess pieces, hair combs, pulley blocks, woodcut and engraving blocks, musical instruments, smoking pipes, weaving shuttles, rolling pins, snuff boxes, rosary beads, buttons.

Broom – Broom heads.

Bullace – Furniture, turnery.

Rods for walking sticks leaning against an early 20th century bow wagon at Cotehele Mill

C

Cedar, western red – Roof shingles, external cladding, seat weaving, rope, aromatic panels in draws, bee hives, ladder sides, totem poles, barrel staves, arrows, dug-out canoes, ships' figureheads, garden furniture.

Cherry – Turnery, furniture, tobacco pipes, musical instruments, veneers, carving turning.

Chestnut, sweet – Fencing posts, gate hurdles and fence panels, furniture, roof shingles, walking sticks, yurt poles, charcoal, trug hoops and handles, beanpoles, paling fences, pea sticks, rake and broom handles, walking sticks, trug handles and rims, arrow shafts, mining pit props, railway sleepers, bark for tanning, ladder rungs, barrel staves, coffins.

Crab Apple – Carving, turnery.

D

Dogwood – Walking sticks, artists' charcoal, skewers, arrows, daggers, ramrods.

E

Elder – Carving, pipes, skewers, arrow shafts, wands, panpipes and flutes, pea-shooters, underwater pilings.

Elm, English – Chair seats, coffins, turnery, mallet heads, tools handles, cartwheel hubs, canoes, oar tips, ships' figureheads, water wheel floats/buckets, canal lock gates, water pipes, boarding for stables, keels and rudders for wooden ships, canal boat bottoms, fishing trawler boards, bellow backs, capstan blocks, chocks and wedges, withes, church bell stops, chopping blocks, anvil blocks, bowls and platters, dough troughs, cheese moulds, saw handles, Welsh short-bow shafts, external cladding.

Elm, Wych – Bark for seat weaving, rope, longbow staves.

Early 16th century water bucket raised from the Mary Rose

F

False Acacia – Fence posts, tool handles, turnery, walking sticks.
Fir, Douglas – Ships' masts, veneer, plywood, structural work, sea defences.

H

Hawthorn – Charcoal, walking sticks, wands, divination rods, rake teeth, mallet heads, ribs of rowing boats, veneers, wood block engraving, gear teeth. Blossom was the original wedding confetti.
Hazel – Basketry, charcoal for gunpowder, wattle hurdles, thatching spars, runners, ethers and pegs, wattle and daub walls, hedging stakes, basket rims, yurt poles, straw bale staples and pins, faggots, pea and bean sticks, clothes props, barrel hoops, besom handles, pheasant traps, lobster pots, eel and salmon traps, coracles, morris staves, fishing rods, whip handles, withes, divination rods, walking sticks, wands, rope, structures for bush shelters.
Hemlock – Barrel staves, roof shingles, bark for tannin.
Holly – Turnery, carving, inlays, woodcuts, cleaves, printing blocks, billiard cues, chariot shafts, shillelaghs, piano keys, mathematical instruments, knife handles, coffins, furniture, riding crops, whip stocks, walking sticks, spear shafts, net makers' needles, chess pieces, loom shuttles, wands.
Hornbeam – Wooden cogs, gear teeth, screws and pulleys, charcoal, mauls, bowls and butchers' blocks, ox yokes,

Half completed hazel screen by Moreton Wood Coppice Products

arrow shafts, skittles and balls, golf club heads, shoemakers' lasts, plane stocks, billiard cues, drum sticks, piano hammers, domino pieces.

L

Laburnum – Decorative work on musical instruments, veneer.
Larch – Outdoor posts and fencing, pails and churns, barrel staves, boat building, field gates, telegraph and tipi poles, underwater foundations, water pipes, bark for tannin, log cabins, pit props, flooring.
Lime – Superior gunpowder, carving, beehive frames, besom handles, chair seats, dug-out canoes, warriors' shields, dairy utensils, besom ties, inner bark used for seat weaving, rope (traditionally for church bells), netting, paper-making, hat blocks, piano keys and sounding boards, shoemakers' lasts, brush backs.

M

Maple – Turnery, violin backs, harps, guitars, carving, furniture, veneers, spoons, flooring.
Medlar – Carving.
Mulberry – Furniture, carving.

O

Oak, English – Boat building, cart wheel spokes, timber framing, gate posts and gates, gate hurdles, furniture, floorboards, swill/spelk basket lathes, roof shingles, trugs, lathes, ox yokes, barrels and hoops, wands, arrow shafts, jousting lances, wash tubs, malting vats, dagger handles, charcoal, ladder rungs, bark for tannin and wine corks, floor tiles, pit props, dug-out canoes, ships' figureheads, oar tips, waterwheelframes, gears and cogs, ladder rungs, coffins, roots for flower arranging and fish tanks.

P

Poplar – Shields, arrow shafts, floors, artificial limbs, wine cases, veneers, matchsticks, wooden pallets, baskets and boxes, bottoms for carts and barrows, brake blocks for horse-drawn vehicles, packing cases, clogs, timber frames, bowls, air drying stickers for sawn wooden boards.

Pear – Similar to apple.

Plum – Turnery, furniture.

R

Rowan – Similar to ash, even though it is not of the same species.

Guilder rose – Tobacco pipe stems, skewers.

Sussex trug made by Charlie Groves

S

Scots Pine – Turpentine, furniture, railway sleepers, telegraph poles, waterwheel axles, pit props, ships' masts, arrows, rope, woven baskets, roof timbers, underwater foundations, water pipes, dug-out canoes, ladder sides, roof shingles, barrel staves, washing tubs, log cabins.

Sallow and Aspen – Withes, bean rods, thatching wood, gate hurdles, scythe snaiths, clothes pegs, barrel hoops, hedge stakes, tool handles, rake handles and heads, charcoal, clog soles.

Spindle – Skewers, knitting needles, toothpicks, viola bows, pipe stems, artists' charcoal, bird cages, watch cleaning spills, chastity belt keys.

Spruce – Roofing shingles, venetian blind slats, violins, piano keys, barrel staves and hoops, sieve frames, cleft baskets, ships' masts, oars, ladder sides, air-drying stickers for sawn wooden boards, bushcraft shelters, log cabins.

Sycamore – Turnery, clogs, kitchen utensils, veneer, dairy bowls, spoons and ladles, furniture, favoured wood for musical instruments, especially harps and the backs of violins, walking sticks, textile rollers, rollers in mangles,

Timber frames have often been made from poplar

weaving shuttles, butter prints, chemists' pestles, table tops, shoemakers' lasts, cider presses, screws.

W

Whitebeam – Turnery, gun stocks, cog wheels, engraving blocks.

Wild Service – Wood cut blocks, gunstocks, mill shafts.

Willow – Gate hurdles, wattle hurdles, hay rakes and broom handles, tool handles, cricket bats, baskets and boxes, flutes and whistles, artists' charcoal, cart and barrow flooring, artificial limbs, divination rods, yokes, wands, harps, walking sticks, fish traps/lobster pots, thatching spars, coracles, rope, laths, furniture, toys, polo balls, catkin down for stuffing mattresses, biomass fuel, trug bodies, coffins, baskets, bush shelters.

Walnut – Veneer, gun stocks, propeller blades, panelling, furniture.

Y

Yew – Veneer, longbows, musical instruments (especially the lute). Underwater foundations.

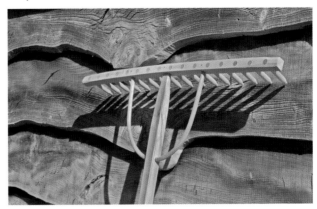

Hay rake made by Graeme Rudd

CHAPTER 10

Traditional common uses for wood by application

In many cases, the wood used for a particular application will vary according to region and local availability. Different woods have similar properties, but the lists below represent the normal applications related to each native and introduced British tree species, and, in general, list the preferred wood first.

A

Aeroplane structures, general – Ash, Birch, Spruce
Aeroplane propellers – Birch, Walnut
Aeroplane wings (Sopwith Pup & De Havilland Mosquito) – Ash
Air-drying stickers – Fir, Spruce, Poplar
Anvil blocks – Elm
Arrow shafts – Alder, Ash, Beech, Birch, Blackthorn, Deal, Dogwood, Elder, Hornbeam, Oak, Poplar, Sweet Chestnut, Pine, Cedar, Scots Pine
Artificial limbs – Poplar, Willow
Artists' charcoal – Dogwood, Spindle, Willow
Axe handles – Ash, Birch, Hickory

B

Bakers' peels – Beech
Balloon baskets – Willow
Bark containers – Birch, Elm, Cedar
Barrel bungs – Birch
Barrel staves – Oak, Birch, Chestnut, Douglas Fir, Poplar, Spruce, Scots Pine, Larch, Cedar, Hemlock, Beech
Barrel hoops – Ash, Beech, Hazel, Spruce, Yew
Barrow bottoms – Poplar, Willow

Baseball bats – Ash
Baskets (round rods) – Willow, Hazel, Poplar, Rowan
Baskets (cleft) – Willow (trugs), Oak (spelk), Scots Pine
Bassoons (musical) – Pear
Bean sticks – Ash, Birch, Hazel, Sweet Chestnut, Sycamore
Beater heads (forest fires) - Birch
Beehive frames – Cedar (western red), Lime, Pine
Bell stops – Ash, Elm
Bellow backs – Elm
Benders – Hazel
Besom binding – Ash bands, Lime bast, cleft Oak, twisted

Johan Olsen, one of the few remaining boat builders in the Faroe Islands

Hazel withe, Sweet Chestnut cleft bands, Willow twigs, shried brambles.

Besom broom heads – Birch, Heather, Willow
Besom horse jumps – Birch
Besom handles – Ash, Birch, Lime, Sycamore, Willow, Hazel
Bird cages – Spindle
Billiard cues – Ash, Holly, Hornbeam
Boat building – Douglas Fir, Oak, Larch
Boat lasts – Beech
Boat ribs – Hawthorn
Boat rigging hoops – Ash
Bobbins – Beech, Birch
Boot trees – Beech, Tulip
Bowls – Ash, Beech, Field Maple, Sycamore, Alder, Birch
Bows – Yew (most superior), Ash, Rowan, Wych Elm
Boxes – Poplar, Willow
Brakes (horse-drawn vehicles) – Poplar
Broom heads – Alder, Beech, Birch
Broom handles – Ash, Chestnut, Hazel, Willow
Brush heads – Alder, Beech, Broom
Brush backs – Alder, Beech, Birch
Buckets – Ash, Beech, Oak, Sycamore, some softwoods

Bushcraft shelters – Birch, Hazel, Spruce, Willow
Butchers' blocks – Beech, Hornbeam
Butter prints – Birch, Beech, Sycamore
Buttons – Box

Butter mould

C

Canal lock gates – Elm
Canoes – Birch, Elm, Cedar
Canoes (dug-out) – Oak, Cedar (western red), Scots Pine, Lime
Capstan blocks – Elm
Car bodies (Morgan & Morris Traveller) – Ash
Cart bottoms – Poplar, Willow
Cartwheel hubs/naves – Elm
Cartwheel rims (fellows) – Ash
Cartwheel spokes – Oak
Carthorse collars – Beech
Carving – Alder, Apple, Beech, Birch, Box, Cherry, Crab Apple, Elder, Holly, Juniper, Lime, Field Maple, Medlar, Mulberry, Rowan, Pear, Walnut
Chair frames – Ash, Oak, Beech
Chair frames woven – Hazel, Willow
Chair seats (solid) – Elm

Fireside stool made by the author, with help from Tilly

Chair seats (woven) – Cedar (bast), Wych Elm (bast), Lime (bast)
Charcoal – Alder, Ash, Beech, Birch, Sweet Chestnut, Hawthorn, Hazel, Hornbeam, Oak, Wild Service (Ash, Beech, Hornbeam, Hazel and Oak are preferred).
Charcoal, artists' – Dogwood, Spindle, Willow
Charcoal, gunpowder – Alder/Buckthorn, Hazel

Chariot shafts – Holly
Chastity belt keys – Spindle
Cheese moulds – Elm
Chess pieces – Box, Holly, Lime
Children's toys – Beech
Chisel handles – Box
Chocks – Elm
Chopping boards – Sycamore
Chopping blocks – Elm
Chopping boards – Beech
Churns – Sycamore, Larch
Cider press screws – Sycamore
Cladding – Cedar
Clarinets – Pear
Cleft baskets – Oak, Spruce
Clog soles – Alder, Beech, Birch, Poplar, Sycamore, Willow
Clothes pegs – Beech, Birch
Clothes props – Hazel
Coffins – Elm, Holly, Sweet Chestnut, Oak, Willow (woven).
Cogs and gears – Apple, Hornbeam, Pear, Oak, Beech, Yew, Whitebeam

Combs – Box
Confetti – hawthorn blossom
Construction – Oak, Scots Pine
Coracles – Hazel, Willow
Cordage – Scots Pine, Wych Elm, Lime and Cedar bast, Heather, Birch, Willow
Corn shovels – Beech
Cotton reels – Birch
Cricket bats – Willow
Cricket stumps – Ash
Croquet mallets – Ash
Cups – Lime, Yew

Pit and spur wheels with apple gear teeth at Cotehele Mill

D

Daggers – Dogwood
Dagger handles – Oak, Yew
Dairy equipment and utensils – Sycamore, Lime, Larch
Darning mushrooms – Beech
Door knobs – Box
Dominoes – Hornbeam
Dough troughs – Elm

Wooden pales and dough trough

Dowsing rods – Ash, Blackthorn, Hawthorn, Hazel, Rowan, Willow
Draughtsmen's squares – Apple, Pear
Draw panels – Cedar
Drinking tankards – Yew
Drum rims – Ash, Beech, Maple
Drumsticks – Ash, Hornbeam
Dry cooperage – Fir, Pine
Dug-out canoes – Oak, Cedar, Scots Pine, Lime

E

Eel traps – Hazel
Engraving blocks – Box, Holly, Hawthorn, Whitebeam
Ethers (thatching) – Hazel

F

Faggots – Birch, Sweet Chestnut, Hazel
Felloes (wheel rims) – Ash, Beech, Elm, Oak
Fencing panels – Cedar, Chestnut
Fencing posts – Oak, Chestnut, Acacia, Larch, Yew

Chestnut fencing by Moreton Wood coppice products

Fish traps – Willow
Fishing floats – Beech
Fishing rods – Hazel, Tonkin cane
Floorboards – Ash, Beech, Sweet Chestnut, Elm, Oak
Flutes – Alder, Box, Elder, Pear, Willow
Framing – Oak, Scots Pine
Fro handles – Ash
Furniture – Ash, Beech, Birch, Bullace, Cherry, Sweet Chestnut, Elm, Holly, Lime, Field Maple, Mulberry, Oak, Plumb, Sycamore, Wild Service, Yew
Furniture (garden) – Cedar (western red), Oak, Larch
Furniture (rustic) – Sweet Chestnut, Hawthorn, Hazel, Willow
Fuse powder – Alder Buckthorn

G

Gate hurdles – Ash, Elm, Sweet Chestnut, Sycamore, Oak, Hazel, Willow
Gate posts – Oak, Chestnut, Acacia, Larch, Yew
Gates – Oak, Larch, Ash
Gears and cogs – Hornbeam, Beech, Oak, Apple, Pear, Yew
Golf club heads – Apple, Beech, Blackthorn, Pear, Hornbeam
Golf club shafts – Ash, Hickory
Granary shovels – Beech
Guitar necks (acoustic) – Alder
Guitar bodies – Alder, Ash, Maple

Gunpowder – Alder, Juniper, Lime, Willow, Alder, Birch, Hazel
Gun stocks – Beech, Walnut, Whitebeam, Wild Service
Gypsy caravan roofs – Ash

H

Handles (tools) – Ash, Alder, Beech, Elm
Handles (rakes) – Ash, Willow
Harps – Sycamore, Maple, Willow

A Fender Telecaster guitar made from ash

Harpsichords – Hornbeam, Maple, Pear
Harpsichord hammers – Holly
Hat blocks – Alder, Lime
Hat boxes – Beech
Hay cribs – Ash
Hay rakes – Ash, Birch, Pine, Willow
Hedging stakes – Ash, Birch, Hazel, Sweet Chestnut,

Sycamore, Hazel
Herring barrels – Birch
Hockey sticks – Ash
Hoops (barrels) – Ash, Hazel, Chestnut, Rowan
Hoops (toys) – Beech
Hoops (boat rigging) – Ash
Hop poles – Ash, Lime, Sweet Chestnut
Horse jumps – Birch
Hurdles (gate) – Oak, Ash, Chestnut, Willow
Hurdles (wattle) – Hazel, Willow

I

Inlay – Holly

J

Jousting lances – Ash, Oak

K

Keels (ship) – Elm
Kitchen utensils – Beech, Sycamore
Knees (ship) – Oak, Larch
Knife handles – Holly
Knitting needles – Spindle

Wooden ladder in a fermentation room, Alsace, France

L

Lathes – Oak, Sweet Chestnut, Ash, Willow
Ladder sides – Ash, Scots Pine, Cedar, spruce
Ladder rungs – Ash, Beech, Oak, Sweet Chestnut
Ladles – Apple, Beech, Birch, Pear, Lime, Sycamore
Lobster pots – Hazel, Willow
Lock sluice gates – Alder, Elm
Log cabins – Larch, Pine, Spruce
Longbow staves – Yew (most superior), Ash, Rowan, Wych Elm
Loom shuttles – Holly
Lute bodies – Yew

M

Mallet handles – Ash
Mallet heads – Beech, Box, Crab Apple, Elm, Hawthorn, Hornbeam
Malt shovels – Beech
Malting vats – Oak

Mangle rollers – Sycamore
Masts – Douglas fir
Matchsticks and boxes – Poplar
Mathematical instruments – Box, Holly
Mattress stuffing – Beech leaves, Willow catkins
Mauls – Beech, Hornbeam
Maypoles – Ash, Birch
Mill wheel teeth – Apple, Pear, Beech, Oak, Hawthorn, Hornbeam, Yew
Morris staves – Ash, Hazel
Musical instruments – Cherry, Field Maple, Pear, Sycamore, Wild Service, Box, Laburnum

N

Nails (clinker-built ships) – Yew
Needles (net making) – Holly
Netting – Lime bast

O

Oars – Ash, Beech, Spruce
Oar blades – Redwood
Oar tips – Oak, Elm
Ox yokes – Birch, Oak, Beech, Hornbeam

P

Packing cases – Poplar
Palings – Sweet Chestnut
Pails – Larch
Pales – Oak, Chestnut
Pallets – Poplar
Panpipes – Elder
Paper – Birch bark
Parallel bars (gymnastics) – Ash
Pea shooters – Elder twigs
Pea sticks – Hazel, Sweet Chestnut
Pestles – Box, Sycamore
Piano frames – Beech
Piano hammers – Pear
Piano keys – Holly, Lime, Hornbeam
Piano parts – Beech, Holly, Spruce
Piano sounding boards – Lime, Spruce
Pill boxes – Lime
Pipes (musical) – Alder, Elder, Box
Pipes (tobacco) – Birch, Cherry, Elde, Box
Pipe stems (tobacco) – Spindle, Guelder rose (dogwood)
Pipes (water) – Alder, Elm, Larch, Scots Pine
Pit props (mining) – Oak, Sweet Chestnut, Larch, Scots Pine
Pheasant traps – Hazel

Plane blocks – Beech, Hornbeam
Platters – Elm
Plough beam – Ash, Oak
Plywood – Douglas Fir, Birch, Pine
Polo mallets – Ash
Polo balls – Willow
Posts and fencing – Oak, Larch, Sweet chestnut, Yew, Acacia
Printing blocks – Beech, Box
Propeller blades (aircraft) – Birch, Walnut
Pulley blocks – Box, Hornbeam

R
Railway sleepers – Oak, Scots Pine, Sweet Chestnut
Rake handles – Ash, Alder, Birch, Sweet Chestnut, Sycamore, Hazel, Willow, Pine
Rake heads – Ash, Birch, Willow
Rake teeth/tines – Ash, Birch, Hawthorn, Willow
Ramrods – Dogwood
Recorders – Pear
Riding crops – Holly
Rifle stocks – Beech, Walnut
Rolling pins – Beech, Box
Roof shingles – Oak, Cedar (western red), Sweet Chestnut, Spruce, Hemlock
Roof timbers – Oak, Scots Pine

Shingle roof

Roofing thatch – Birch
Rope – Birch, Scots Pine, Heather, Wych Elm (bast), Cedar (western red bast), Lime (bast), Willow, Bramble
Rope ladder rungs – Ash
Rosary beads – Box
Rounders bats - Ash
Rune sets – Birch, Rowan

S
Saddle trees – Beech, Birch
Salmon traps – Hazel
Saw handles – Apple, Elm
Screws – Hornbeam
Scythe snaiths – Ash, Birch
Seating (woven) – Cedar, Wych Elm, Lime bast.
Shepherds' crooks – Ash
Shields (warriors') – Alder, Lime, Poplar
Shillelaghs – Blackthorn, Holly
Shingles (roof) – Oak, Cedar (western red), Sweet Chestnut, Spruce, Hemlock, Scots Pine
Ships' figureheads – Elm, Cedar (western red), Oak
Ships' keels – Elm, Larch
Ships' knees – Oak, Larch
Ships' masts – Scots Pine, Spruce, Fir, Larch
Ships' rudders – Elm, Larch
Shoe heels (stiletto) – Beech
Shoe lasts – Alder, Beech, Birch, Lime, Sycamore, Hornbeam, Scots Pine

Wooden shoe 'lasts'

Sieve rims – Ash, Beech, Spruce
Skewers – Elder, Spindle, Guelder rose (dogwood)
Skis – Ash
Skittles – Hornbeam
Sledge runners – Ash
Snooker cues – Ash, Hornbeam
Snow shoes – Ash
Snuff boxes – Box
Spear shafts – Ash, Birch, Holly, Yew
Spelk/Swill baskets – Oak, Hazel
Spindles – Spindle
Spills – Spindle
Splints for weaving – Ash, Oak

spoons hand carved by the author from cherry

Spoons – Apple, Beech, Birch, Cherry, Pear, Maple, Sycamore
Stable boarding – Elm
Staircases – Ash, Oak, Pine
Staves – Ash, Rowan, Yew
Stickers (for air-drying boards) – Fir, Poplar, Spruce
Straw bale pins – Ash, Hazel
Straw bale staples – Hazel
Sword scabbards – Beech

T

Table tops (traditional) – Elm, Pine, Sycamore, Oak
Tankards, drinking – Yew
Tanning bark – Alder, Birch, Sweet Chestnut, Oak, Larch, Hemlock
Telegraph poles – Larch, Scots Pine
Tent pegs – Ash, Beech
Tennis racquets – Ash
Textile rollers – Beech, Sycamore
Thatch – Birch, Heather, Bracken
Thatching spars – Hazel

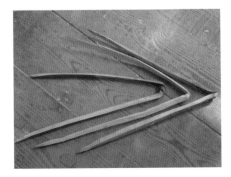

Hazel thatching 'spars'

Thatching runners and pegs – Hazel
Tight dry cooperage – Fir, Spruce, White Elm
Tipi poles – Larch
Tipi covers – Birch (bark)
Tool handles – Ash, Alder, Acacia, Beech, Elm, Elder, Rowan, Willow
Toothpicks – Spindle
Totem poles – Cedar (western red)
Toys – Beech
Treen – Sycamore, Beech, Birch, Elm
Trenails – British Oak, American Acacia and Locust
Tree Stakes – Chestnut, Hazel
Truncheons – Ash
Trug bodies/boards – Willow
Trug handles and rims – Ash, Chestnut, Willow
Turpentine – Scots Pine
Turnery – Acacia, Apple, Beech, Birch, Bullace, Cherry, Crab Apple, Elm, Holly, Juniper, Lime, Maple, Pear, Plumb, Sycamore, Yew

U

Umbrella handles – Ash
Underwater foundations – Alder, Beech, Elm, Oak, Scots Pine, Larch, Yew

V

Veneer – Birch, Cherry, Fir (Douglas), Oak, Sycamore, Walnut, Poplar, Hawthorn, Laburnum, Maple, Yew, Pear, Plane, Walnut
Venetian blinds slats – Spruce
Viola bows – Spindle
Violins – Maple, Sycamore, Spruce, Alder

W

Wagon bottoms – Poplar
Wagon frames and shafts – Ash
Walking sticks – Acacia, Ash, Chestnut, Hazel, Birch, Blackthorn, Dogwood, Hawthorn, Holly, Rowan, Sycamore, Whitebeam, Willow
Wands – Alder, Ash, Silver Birch, Elder, Hawthorn, Hazel, Holly, Oak, Rowan, Willow, Yew
Wash tubs – Oak, Scots Pine
Watch cleaning spills – Spindle
Water pipes – Alder, Elm, Larch, Scots Pine
Waterwheel floats/buckets – Elm, Oak, Larch, Scots Pine
Waterwheel frames and axles – Oak, Scots Pine
Wattle and daub panels – Chestnut, Oak, Hazel
Weavers' shuttles – Sycamore, Box

Wedges – Elm, Oak
Wet cooperage – Oak
Wheel hubs/ naves/stocks – Elm
Wheel rims / felloes – Ash, Beech, Elm, Oak

Wooden wheel under construction

Wheel spokes – Oak
Wheelbarrows – Ash
Whip handles/stocks – Hazel, Blackthorn, Holly, Yew
Whistles – Alder, Elder, Hazel, Willow
White cooperage – Ash, Beech, Chestnut, Elm, Fir, Oak,

Pine, Sycamore
Wine cases – Poplar
Withes – Birch, Elm, Hazel, Willow
Woodcut blocks – Apple, Pear, Box, Holly, Whitebeam, Wild Service
Writing parchment – Silver Birch (bark)

Y

Yoke (Ox and horse) – Hornbeam, Oak, Beech
Yurt poles, roof and walls – Ash, Hazel, Sweet Chestnut

Ash yurt frame made by Steve King

CHAPTER 11

Tool finder

Man is a tool-using animal. Without tools he is nothing, with tools he is all.

Thomas Carlyle 1795-1881

Green woodworking and woodland craft tools are specialised, so it will be no surprise to learn that there are only a limited number of manufacturers and suppliers in the UK.

Although the same supplier names crop up under many headings, it is for your convenience. This is to ensure that the listings are quick and easy to use, and can help you find a supplier in your area, or a particular brand of tool that you have been used to using, or have been recommended.

Also bear in mind that specialised quality tools can easily be obtained from overseas companies through the internet at very reasonable prices (depending on the current exchange rate), particularly from Germany and the USA.

Some specialist tools may not be produced any more – especially those used for barrel and wheel making, so hunting down old, used ones in boot sales, auctions or through small specialist traders in used tools may be your only choice. Alternatively, you may be able to find a local blacksmith who will make you a tool, providing you supply them with a photo or drawing of exactly what you want.

It can be very rewarding to make your own tools. Some specialist tool makers will sell you their handcrafted blades for spokeshaves, travishers and bush knives, along with the wood blanks for the handles and brief instructions on how to put the lot together.

What follows is a listing of the tools and who supplies them, along with the different brands they supply. There is then a list organised by brand name, so that if you are recommended a particular brand of tool, you can quickly find the suppliers who stock it. Chapter 12 provides contact information on the tool suppliers, as well as suppliers of used and refurbished tools.

French drawknife with wooden spokeshaves made by James Mursell

Listings by tool

A

Tool	Supplier	Brand
Adze	Axminster Tools	Henry Taylor
	John Beavis	own brand
	Bristol Design	
	Dave Budd	own brand
	Classic Hand Tools	Gransfors, Auriou, Pfeil
	Greenwood Direct	Gransfors
	The Old Tool Store	Gransfors
	Ben Orford	own brand
	Rutlands	Pfeil
	Alec Tiranti	
	Toolnut	Henry Taylor
	Woodland Craft Supplies	Hans Karlsson
	The Woodsmith's Store	Gransfors
Auger bits	Axminster Tools	
Augers, scotch eye	Woodland Craft Supplies	
	The Woodsmith's Store	
Axes, chopping, carving, side	Axminster Tools	Wetterlings
	John Beavis	own brand
	Bristol Design	Stubai
	Dave Budd	own brand
	Classic Hand Tools	Gransfors, Leonhard Muller, Pfeil
	Greenwood Direct	Gransfors
	Heinne Haynes	Hultafors
	The Old Tool Store	Gransfors
	Visa Tools	
	The Windy Smithy	own brand
	Woodland Craft Supplies	Gransfors, Stubai, Svante Djarv
	The Woodsmith's Store	Gransfors
Axe file	The Woodsmith's Store	Gransfors
Axe stones	Classic Hand Tools	Gransfors
	The Woodsmith's Store	Gransfors

B

Tool	Supplier	Brand
Bark peelers	Richmonds	
	Woodland Craft Supplies	
	The Woodsmith's Store	Morris
	The Old Tool Store	
Barking spoons (see spoons)		
Beading tools	The Woodsmith's Store	Ashley Iles
Besom clamps	The Woodsmith's Store	
Billhook	John Beavis	own brand
	Bristol Design	
	Dave Budd	own brand
	Woodland Craft Supplies	Morris
	The Woodsmith's Store	Morris
	Toolnut	Morris
Blade covers, leather	The Woodsmith's Store	
Block cutters	Toolnut	Ashley Iles
Bowl gouges (see gouges)		
Bowl hooks	The Woodsmith's Store	Ben Orford, Svante Djarv
Brace, hand	The Old Tool Store	
	Rutlands	
	The Woodsmith's Store	
Burnishers	Axminster Tools	Clifton, Kirschen, Veritas
	Classic Hand Tools	Clifton
	Toolnut	Clifton
Bushcraft supplies	Bison Bushcraft	
	The Bushcraft Store	
	Greenman Bushcraft	
	Finlay Primitive Crafts	
	Heinnie Haynes	
	Hunter's Bushcraft	
	Ronnie Shunshines	
	Outdoor Extreme	
	Strikeforce Supplies	
	Wild Stoves	
Bushcraft knives (handmade)	Ben Orford	own brand
	Gary Mills	own brand
	Stephen Wade Cox	own brand

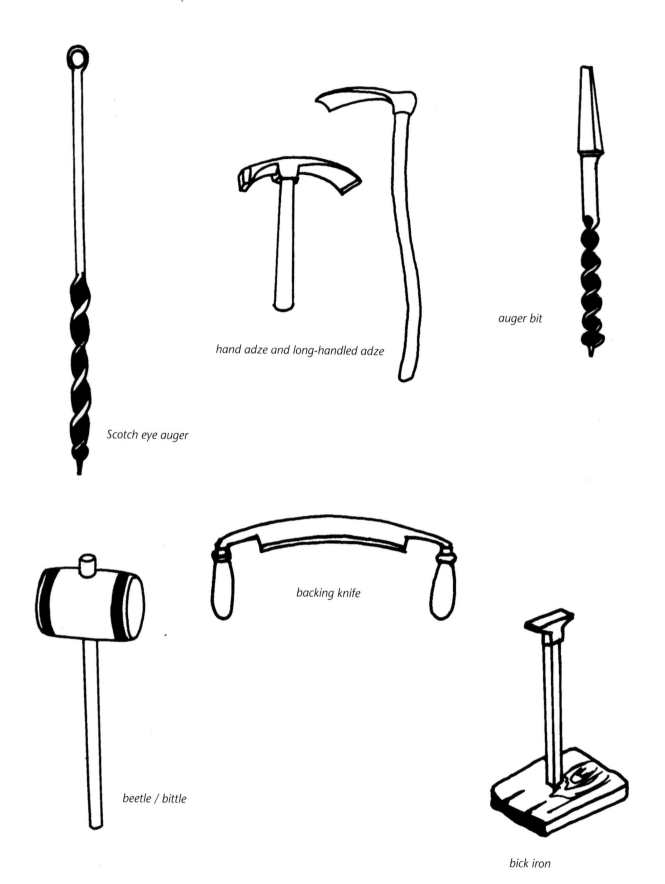

Scotch eye auger

hand adze and long-handled adze

auger bit

beetle / bittle

backing knife

bick iron

C

Tool	Supplier	Brand
Cabinet scrapers	Axminster Tools	
	Bristol Design	
	Classic Hand Tools	Clifton, Lie Nielson, Veritas
	Alec Tiranti	
	Toolnut	Clifton
Canes, chair seating	Relics of Whitney	
	Seat Weaving Supplies	
Cant hooks	Richmonds	
Carving chisels (see chisels)		
Carving gouges (see gouges)		
Carving knives (see knives)		
Carving mallets (see mallets)		
Charcoal retorts and kilns	Black Mountain Woodfuels	
	Carbon Compost Co	
	Carbon Gold	
	Pressvess Retort	
	The Woodsmith's Store	
Chisels, carving	Axminster Tools	Kirschen, Henry Taylor
	Bristol Design	
	Classic Hand Tools	Flexcut, Pfeil, Chris Pye, Veritas
	Rutlands	Pfeil
	Craft Supplies	Pfeil, Ramelson
	Alec Tiranti	Henry Taylor
	Toolnut	Ashley Iles
	Turners Retreat	Sorby, Ashley Iles
	Woodland Craft Supplies	Hans Karlsson
Chisels, general	Axminster Tools	Crown, Taylor, Kirchen, Lie Nielson
	Bristol Design	Crown
	Classic Hand Tools	Nielson, Blue Spruce, Sorby, Taylor
	Toolnut	Crown, Sorby, Henry Taylor
	Turners Retreat	Sorby
Chisels, Japanese	Axminster Tools	
	Rutlands	
	Classic Hand Tools	
Chisels, turning	Axminster Tools	Crown, Henry Taylor
	Ben Orford	own brand
	Bristol Design	Crown
	Thomas Flinn	Sorbey
	The Old Tool Store	Ashley Iles
	Turners Retreat	Sorbey
	Woodland Craft Supplies	Ashley Iles
	The Woodsmith's Store	Ashley Iles
Cooper's shaves (see inshave)		
Crook knives (see knives)		

D

Tool	Supplier	Brand
Danish cord	Seat Weaving Supplies	
Dogs, log	The Woodsmith's Store	Gransfors
	The Windy Smithy	own brand
Dog-leg gouges (see gouges)		
Dowel plates	Axminster Tools	Lie Nielsen
	Classic Hand Tools	Lie Nielsen
Drawbore pins	Classic Hand Tools	Lie Nielsen
	The Old Tool Store	Ray Iles
	Toolnut	
Drawknives	Axminster Tools	Crown, Flexcut, Mora
	Ben Orford	own brand
	Dave Budd	own brand
	Bristol Design	Crown
	Classic Hand Tools	Auriou, Flexcut, Ray Iles, Pfeil, Sorby
	The Old Tool Store	Ray Iles, Ashley Iles
	Rutlands	Pfeil
	Toolnut	Crown, Ray Iles, Sorby
	Turners Retreat	Sorby
	Woodland Craft Supplies	Arnaud, Sorby
	The Woodsmith's Store	Gransfors, Ray Iles, Svante Djarv
Drawknife sheaths (leather)	The Old Tool Store	

E

Tool	Supplier	Brand
End rounders	Ashem Crafts	own brand

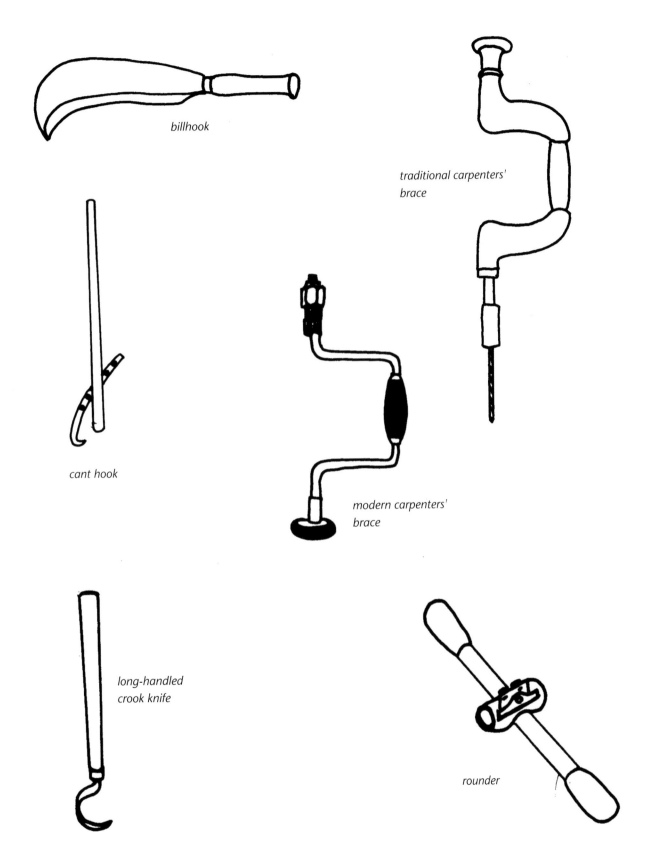

billhook

traditional carpenters'
brace

cant hook

modern carpenters'
brace

long-handled
crook knife

rounder

F

Tool	Supplier	Brand
Fencing tools	Visa Tools	
Forestry tools and equipment	Toolnut	
	Visa Tools	
	Richmonds	
Forstner bits	Axminster Tools	
Frame saws (wooden)	Thomas Flinn	
	Rutlands	
Framing pins	The Windy Smithy	own brand
Froes	Bristol Design	
	Classic Hand Tools	Gransfors
	Greenwood Direct	Gransfors
	The Old Tool Store	Ray Iles
	Toolnut	Ray Iles
	The Windy Smithy	own brand
	Woodland Craft Supplies	Gransfors, Ray Iles
	The Woodsmith's Store	Gransfors, Ray Iles
French straw	Seat Weaving Supplies	

G

Tool	Supplier	Brand
Gouges, bowl	The Woodsmith's Store	Ashley Iles
Gouges, carving	Axminster Tools	Henry Taylor, Kirschen, Victor
	Bristol Designs	
	Woodland Craft Supplies	Hans Karlsson
	The Woodsmith's Store	Ashley Iles, Svante Djarv
Grasshooks	Visa Tools	
Groundwork tools	Visa Tools	

H

Tool	Supplier	Brand
Hollowing planes	Bristol Design	
	Hollow shoulder tools	
	Ashem Crafts	
Honing guides	Axminster Tools	
	Toolnut	Veritas
Honing paste	Bristol Design	
	The Woodsmith's Store	
Honing stones	Axminster Tools	
	Bristol Design	
	Classic Hand Tools	Norton
	The Old Tool Store	
	Alex Tiranti	
	Toolnut	
	The Woodsmith's Store	
Honing strops	Bristol Design	
	Alec Tiranti	
	The Woodsmith's Store	
Hookgates	The Woodsmith's Store	Sorby

I

Tool	Supplier	Brand
Inshaves	Ben Orford	own brand
	Bristol Design	
	Classic Hand Tools	Ray Iles
	Rutland	Pfeil
	Woodland Craft Supplies	Ray Iles

J

Tool	Supplier	Brand
Japanese tools	Axminster Tools	
	Classic Hand Tools	
	Rutlands	

K

Tool	Supplier	Brand
Knives, carving	Andy Eyles	own brand
	Ben Orford	own brand
	Dave Budd	own brand
	Axminster Tools	Mora, Flexcut
	Bristol Design	
	Woodland Craft Supplies	Sloyd, Svante Djarv
	The Woodsmith's Store	Svante Djarv
Knives, Bushcraft	Axminster Tools	Mora
	Ben Orford	own brand
	Gary Mills	own brand
	Stephen Wade Cox	own brand
	Dave Budd	own brand
Knives, Crook	Ben Orford	own brand
	The Woodsmith's Store	Frost
	Dave Budd	own brand
Knives, folding	Axminster Tools	Various
	Heinnie Haynes	Various
	Woodland Craft Supplies	Opinel
	The Woodsmith's Store	Opinel
Knives, spoon	Ben Orford	own brand
	Dave Budd	own brand
	Woodland Craft Supplies	Sloyd, Svante Djarv
	The Woodsmith's Store	Svante Djarv

L

Tool	Supplier	Brand
Lathes, pole	The Woodsmith's Store	
Log dogs	Classic Hand Tools	Gransfors
	Richmonds	
	The Woodsmith's Store	Gransfors
	Dave Budd	own brand
Log house drawknives	Classic Hand Tools	
	The Old Tool Store	
	Greenwood Direct	
	Richmonds	
	Woodland Craft Supplies	
	The Woodsmith's Store	
Log scribes	Classic Hand Tools	Gransfors
	Richmonds	
Log splitters/axes/mauls	Visa Tools	
	Richmonds	
Log splitters, hydraulic	Visa Tools	
	Richmonds	
Logging tools and equipment	Toolnut	
	Richmonds	
	Visa Tools	

M

Tool	Supplier	Brand
Mallets, carvers	Axminster Tools	
	Bristol Designs	
	Craft Supplies	
	Alec Tiranti	
	Toolnut	Ray Iles, Marples, Veritas
	Classic Hand Tools	Blue Spruce, Pfeil, Veritas
Mallets, rawhide	Axminster Tools	Thor
Mallets, rubber	Axminster Tools	

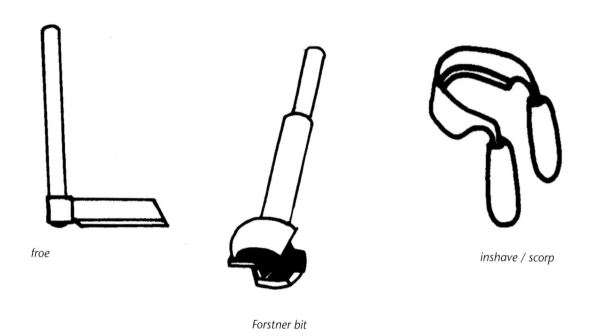

froe

Forstner bit

inshave / scorp

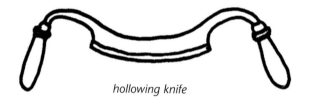

hollowing knife

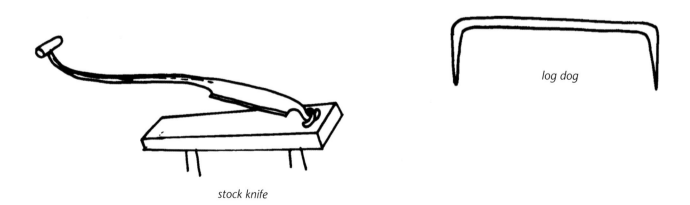

log dog

stock knife

O

Tool	Supplier	Brand
Oil, gun	Napier of London	
Oil stones	Axminster Tools	
	Bristol design	
	Classic Hand Tools	Norton

P

Tool	Supplier	Brand
Peeling knives	The Windy Smithy	own brand
Pole lathes	The Woodsmith's Store	
Pole lathe components	The Woodsmith's Store	
Post diggers	Visa Tools	
Post drivers	Visa Tools	
Post hammers	Visa Tools	
Post hole borers/augers	Visa Tools	

R

Tool	Supplier	Brand
Range kettles	The Kelly Kettle Company	
	Ghillie Kettle Company	
Rasps	Axminster Tools	Vallorbe
	Classic Hand Tools	Auriou
	Craft Supplies	
	Alec Tiranti	
	Turners Retreat	
	Rutlands	
Reamers	Axminster Tools	
	Classic Hand Tools	Veritas
Refurbished woodworking tools	Bristol Design	
	The Old Tool Store	
	Second Hand Tools	
Rifflers	Axminster Tools	
	Craft Supplies	
	Classic Hand Tools	
	Alec Tiranti	
Ring tools	The Woodsmith's Store	Ashley Iles
Rounders	Ashem Crafts	
	Craft Supplies	
	Toolnut	
Rounding planes	Ashem Crafts	Fred Lambert
	Bristol Design	
	Classic Hand Tools	Ray Iles
	The Old Tool Store	Ray Iles
	Toolnut	Ray Iles
Rush, real, fibre	Relics of Whitney	
	Seat Weaving Supplies	

S

Tool	Supplier	Brand
Saws, Japanese	Axminster Tools	
	Classic Hand Tools	
	Rutlands	
Saws, turning (wooden)	Thomas Flinn	
Saws	Thomas Flinn	
Saws, two-man	Thomas Flinn	
	Woodland Craft Supplies	
	The Woodsmith's Store	
Saws, silki	Axminster Tools	
	Brimarc Tools	
	Classic Hand Tools	
	Turners Retreat	
Scorps	Bristol Design	
	Classic Hand Tools	Pfeil
	The Old Tool Store	Ashley Iles
	Rutlands	Pfeil
	The Woodsmith's Store	Ray Iles
	Toolnut	Ray Iles
Scrapers, chairmakers'	Axminster Tools	Veritas
	Toolnut	Veritas
Screw thread boxes	Turners Retreat	
	Rutlands	
Scythes	Axminster Tools	
	Visa Tools	
Seagrass	Relics of Whitney	
	Seat Weaving Supplies	
Shaker tape	Ashem Crafts	
Sharpening stones, tools & accessories	Axminster Tools	
	Bristol Design	
	Classic Hand Tools	
	Craft Supplies	
	Rutlands	
	Turners Retreat	
Sharpening systems	Axminster Tools	Tormek, Jet
	Brimarc Tools	Tormek, Jet
	Classic Hand Tools	Pro-edge, Tormek
	Robert Sorby	Pro-edge
	Turners Retreat	Pro-edge, Tormek
Shave horses	The Woodsmith's Store	
Slashers	Toolnut	Morris

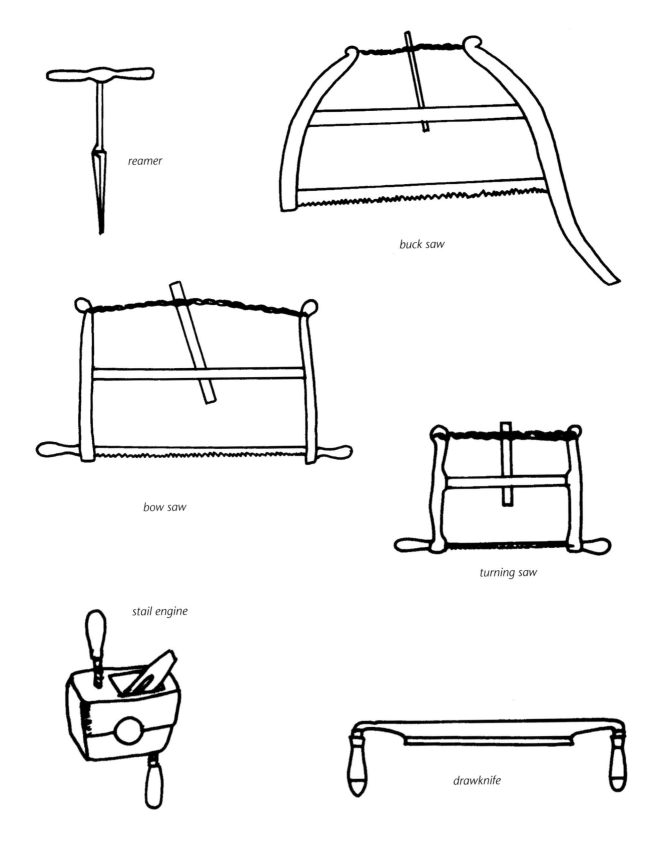

reamer

buck saw

bow saw

turning saw

stail engine

drawknife

S

Tool	Supplier	Brand
Slash hooks	Axminster Tools	
	Visa Tools	
	John Beavis	
Spar hooks	Toolnut	Morris
Splitting wedges	Axminster Tools	
	Bristol Design	
	The Windy Smithy	
Spokeshaves	Axminster Tools	Clifton, Lie Nielson, Veritas
	Bristol Design	Clifton
	Classic Hand Tools	Clifton, Nielson, Veritas, Woodjoy
	The Old Tool Store	Clifton, Kunz
	Toolnut	Clifton, Veritas
	Woodland Craft Supplies	Clifton, Veritas
	The Woodsmith's Store	Clifton
Spokeshaves, wood bodied	Bristol Design	
	Old Tool Store	
	The Windsor Workshop	
Spokeshaves, DIY kits	The Windsor Workshop	
	Hock Tools (USA)	
	Veritas Tools	
Spoon bits	Bristol Design	Clico
	Thomas Flinn	Clifton
	Classic Hand Tools	Clifton
	Toolnut	Clifton
Spoons, barking	Richmonds	
	Woodland Craft Supplies	
	The Woodsmith's Store	Morris
	The Old Tool Store	
Spoon knives (see knives)		
Stail engines	Ashem Crafts	
Storm kettles	The Kelly Kettle Company	
	Ghillie Kettle Company	
Strops, leather	Bristol Design	
	Alec Tiranti	

T

Tool	Supplier	Brand
Tenon cutters	Ashem Crafts	
	Classic Hand Tools	Veritas
	Woodland Craft Supplies	Ray Iles, Veritas
Tine cutters	Woodland Craft Supplies	
	The Old Tool Store	
Tool edge sheaths	The Woodsmith's Store	
Tool rolls	Axminster Tools	
	Alec Tiranti	
	Turners Retreat	
Trapping planes	Ashem Crafts	
Travishers	Bristol Design	own brand
	The Old Tool Store	Ray Iles
	Classic Hand Tools	
	The Windsor Workshop	own brand
	The Woodsmith's Store	Ray Iles, Tom Thackray
Travisher DIY kits	The Windsor Workshop	
Trug runners (see gouges)		
Turning chisels (see chisels)		
Turning accessories	Axminster Tools	
	Classic Hand Tools	Sorby
	Craft Supplies	
	Turners Retreat	
Turning saws (wooden)	Thomas Flinn	
Twybils	The Old Tool Store	Ashley Iles
	Woodland Craft Supplies	Ashley Iles
	The Woodsmith's Store	Ashley Iles
	Dave Budd	own brand

W

Tool	Supplier	Brand
Waterstones	Axminster Tools	
	Bristol Design	
	Classic Hand Tools	
	Craft Supplies	
	Turners Retreat	
Wedges, splitting	Axminster Tools	
	Bristol Design	
	The Windy Smithy	

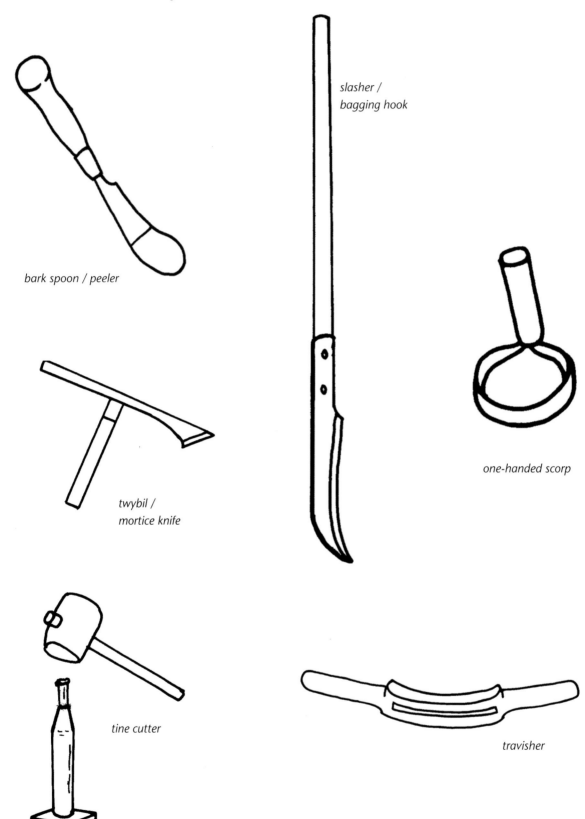

bark spoon / peeler

twybil /
mortice knife

slasher /
bagging hook

one-handed scorp

tine cutter

travisher

Tool listings by brand

To use these listings, find the brand in bold type (ordered alphabetically), and suppliers are listed underneath.

Arkansas benchstone
Alec Tiranti
Toolnut
The Woodsmith's Store

Arnaud
Classic Hand Tools
Woodland Craft Supplies

Ashley Iles
The Old Tool Store
Toolnut
Woodland Craft Supplies
The Woodsmith's Store

Auriou
Classic Hand Tools

Blue Spruce
Classic Hand Tools

Buckingham Woodstation
Terry Buckingham

Chris Pye
Classic Hand Tools

Clico
Axminster Tools
Bristol Design
Thomas Flinn

Clifton
Axminster Tools
Bristol Designs
Thomas Flinn
Classic Hand Tools
The Old Tool Store
Turners Retreat
Woodland Craft Supplies
The Woodsmith's Store

Crown
Axminster Tools
Toolnut
Thomas Flinn

Flexcut
Axminster Tools
Brimarc Tools
Classic Hand Tools
Craft Supplies
Turners Retreat

Gransfors
Classic Hand Tools
The Old Tool Store
Greenwood Direct
Woodland Craft Supplies
The Woodsmith's Store

Hans Karlsson
Woodland Craft Supplies

Henry Taylor
Axminster Tools
Classic Hand Tools
Alec Tiranti
Toolnut

Hultafors (axes)
Heinnie Haynes

Jet
Axminster Tools
Brimarc Tools

Kunz
The Old Tool Store

Leonard Muller
Classic Hand Tools

Lie Nielsen
Axminster Tools
Brimarc Tools
Classic Hand Tools

Marples
Toolnut
Thomas Flinn

Mora/Sloyd
Axminster Tools
Woodland Craft Supplies

Merknife
The Windy Smithy

Morris
Toolnut
Woodland Craft Supplies
The Woodsmith's Store

Norton
Classic Hand Tools

Opinel
Axminster Tools
Heinnie Haynes
Woodland Craft Supplies

Pfeil
Classic Hand Tools
Craft Supplies

Pro-edge
Robert Sorby
Turners Retreat

Ramelson
Craft Supplies

Ray Iles
Classic Hand Tools
The Old Tool Store
Toolnut
The Woodsmith's Store
Woodland Craft Supplies

Robert Sorby
Axminster Tools
Classic Hand Tools
Thomas Flinn
Toolnut
Turners Retreat
Woodland Supplies
The Woodsmith's Store

Silki saws
Axminster Tools
Brimarc Tools
Classic Hand Tools
Turners Retreat

Sloyd/Mora
Axminster Tools
Brimarc Tools
Woodland Craft Supplies

Stubai
Bristol Design
Woodland Craft Supplies

Svante Djarve
Woodland Craft Supplies
The Woodsmith's Store

Thor
Axminster Tools

Tom Thackary
The Woodsmith's Store

Tormek
Axminster Tools
Classic Hand Tools
Craft Supplies

Veritas
Axminster Tools
Brimarc Tools
Classic Hand Tools
Craft Supplies
Rutlands
Woodland Craft Supplies

Wetterlings
Axminster Tools
Rutlands

Woodjoy
Classic Hand Tools

CHAPTER 12
Tool suppliers

Carol Horsington's basket weaving tools at Cornish Willow

Green woodworking and woodland craft tools are more specialised than those used in general woodworking, so the suppliers are not generally known. There are a comparatively small number of them dotted around the country and they all tend to offer quite a comprehensive generic range of very similar tools, from various manufacturers. Invariably, they will be practitioners of these crafts and therefore offer a very informative and helpful service.

Ashem Crafts
Worcester • 01905 640070
www.ashemcrafts.com
Rotary planes, tenon cutters.

Ashley Iles Ltd
East Kirkby • 01790 763372
www.ashleyiles.co.uk
Maker of carving/turning chisels.

Axminster Tool Centre
Axminster – 01297 35058
High Wycombe – 01494 885480
Nuneaton – 02476 011402
Sittingbourne – 01795 437143
www.axminster.co.uk
Huge range of tools including good
green woodworking selection.

John Beavis
Wiltshire • 07795 433993
www.olivemeadforge.co.uk
Beautiful hand-forged hedging and
bushcraft tools. Fantastic range of axes,
drawknives, adzes, billhooks and slashers.

Bison Bushcraft
Battle, East Sussex • 0845 8387062
www.bisonbushcraft.co.uk
Bushcraft supplies.

Black Mountain Woodfuels
www.blackmountainwoodfuels.co.uk
Charcoal retorts and kilns, including
the specialised coppice stove.

Brimarc Tools and Machinery
Axminster, Devon
0333 240 6967
www.brimarc.com
A large range of tools and machinery.

Bristol Design (Tools) Ltd
Bristol • 0117 929 1740
www.bristol-design.co.uk
Specialist woodworking, green
woodworking and woodland craft tools.
Also used tools.

Dave Budd
0776 4742569
www.davebudd.com
Hand-forged tools.

The Bushcraft Store
Enfield, Middlesex • 020 8367 3420
www.thebushcraftstore.co.uk
Bushcraft supplies.

Carbon Compost Co
Devon • 01392 431454
www.biocharretort.com
Suppliers of the Exeter Charcoal Retort.

Carbon Gold
www.carbongold.com
The biochar kiln.

Classic Hand Tools
Ipswich • 01473 784983
www.classichandtools.com
Green woodworking and woodland
craft tools.

Craft Supplies Ltd / Turners Retreat)
Nottinghamshire • 01302 744344
www.turners-retreat.co.uk
Specialising in wood-turning and
wood-carving tools and equipment.

Diefenbacher Tools
USA • (720) 502 6687
www.diefenbacher.com
An international range of quality,
specialist tools at very reasonable
prices, depending on exchange rates.

Andy Eyles (Wildwood Knives)
www.wildwoodknives.com
enquiries@wildwoodknives.com
Specialist maker of hand-forged chip-
carving knives with natural, ergonomic
handles.

A. Finlay Primitive Crafts
Ayr • 01292 531885
www.a-finlay-primitive-crafts.co.uk
Bushcraft supplies.

Thomas Flinn & Co
Sheffield • 0114 272 5387
www.flinn-garlick-saws.co.uk
Saw and hand tool manufacturers.

The Ghillie Kettle Company
Redditch, Worcestershire
01527 66217
www.ghillie-kettle.co.uk
Makers of a version of this legendary
water boiler that has a whistle.

Greenman Bushcraft
Essex • 01245 201002
www.greenmanbushcraft.co.uk
Bushcraft supplies.

Greenwood Direct
01249 782100
www.greenwood-direct.co.uk
UK distributors of Gransfors Bruks axes.

Heinnie Haynes
Barry, Vale of Glamorgan
033 0300 0400
www.heinnie.com
Axes, knives, bushcraft supplies.

Hock Tools
USA • (707) 964 2782
www.hocktools.com
Specialist manufacturer of cutting
blades for planes, spokeshaves and
chip-cutting knives.

Hunter's Bushcraft
Newhaven, East Sussex
0800 875 8040
www.hunterscampingandbushcraft.
co.uk
Bushcraft supplies.

Joce Metal
East Sussex • 01892 782000
www.jocemetal.co.uk
The Buckingham Woodstation, for
cutting fire logs

The Kelly Kettle Company
Co Mayo, Ireland
+353 87 607 5483
www.kellykettle.com
Makers of the famous outdoor water
boiler.

Gary Mills
07747 315412
www.gmhandmadeknives.co.uk
Specialist maker of hand-forged
bushcraft knives.

The Old Tool Store
Horncastle • 01507 525697
www.oldtools.free-online.co.uk
New and used woodworking tools.

Ben Orford
Herefordshire • 01866 880410
www.benorford.com
Specialist maker of hand-forged
carving and bushcraft knives, green
woodworking and turning tools.

Outdoor Extreme
Ayr • 01292 531675
www.outdoor-extreme.co.uk
Bushcraft supplies.

Pressvess Retort
West Midlands • 01384 400088
www.pressvess.co.uk
Charcoal retorts and kilns.

Relics of Whitney
Whitney, Oxfordshire
01993 764611
www.relicsofwitney.co.uk
Seat-weaving materials and tools.

Richmonds
Haslemere, Surrey • 01428 658487
www.richmondsgroundcare.co.uk
Suppliers of forestry, arboricultural and
groundwork equipment.

Ronnie Sunshines
Beckhamstead, Herts
01442 872829
www.ronniesunshines.com
Bushcraft supplies.

Rutlands
Derbyshire • 01629 815518
www.rutlands.co.uk
Supplies a large range of quality tools.

Seat Weaving Supplies
Dorset • 01202 895859
www.seatweavingsupplies.co.uk
Seat weaving materials.

Robert Sorby
Sheffield • 0114 225 0700
www.robert-sorby.co.uk
Manufacturers of woodworking
chisels, turning chisels and accessories.

Strikeforce Supplies
Frome, Somerset • 01373 469900
www.strikeforcesupplies.co.uk
Bushcraft supplies

Alec Tiranti Ltd
Berkshire • 0845 123 2100
www.tiranti.co.uk
Carving tools and equipment.

Toolnut Ltd
East Sussex • 01424 422954
www.toolnut.co.uk
Green woodworking and woodland
craft tools.

Turners Retreat (see Craft Supplies)

Veritas Tools
Canada and the USA
613 596 1922
www.veritastools.com

Visa Hand Tools Ltd
Leeds • 0113 2869245
www.visatools.co.uk
Forestry and groundworks equipment.

Stephen Wade Cox
www.swc-handmade-knives.com
Specialist maker of hand-made
bushcraft knives and kits.

Wild Stoves
Dorset • 01308 426499
www.wildstoves.co.uk
Suppliers of rocket stoves.

The Windsor Workshop
West Sussex • 01798 815925
www.thewindsorworkshop.co.uk
Own brand spokeshaves and travishers.

The Windy Smithy
Collumpton, Devon
07866 241783, 07756 100681
www.windysmithy.co.uk
Specialist maker of hand-forged tools
for timber framing and woodland crafts.
Also excellent woodburning stoves.

Woodland Craft Supplies
Peterborough • 07736 308475
www.woodlandcraftsupplies.co.uk
Green woodworking and woodland
craft tools.

The Woodsmith's Store,
Tyne and Wear • 0191 252 4064
www.woodsmithstore.co.uk
Green woodworking and woodland
craft tools.

Antique billhooks at Ludlow market, Shropshire

Dealers of used and refurbished tools

Buying used tools can be a very good idea, not only if you're just starting out, but also if you want to find a specialised tool which is no longer made. One advantage of an old tool is the steel, which in some cases can be superior to that used in a new tool. Used tools also look and feel good too – old boxwood or beech-bodied spoke shaves are very tactile and a pleasure to use. Old hand-forged axes and drawknives have a character and feel to them, and a well-used billhook just feels right in the hand.

Tracking down used tools at boot sales, markets and local shows can be a good way to acquire tools, but for sheer convenience, a used tool dealer's website is a shortcut to hidden treasure.

The dealers of used tools in this list provide fair coverage of the UK.

Bristol Design (Tools) Ltd
Bristol
www.bristol-design.co.uk

Leeside Tool Shop
West Sussex
www.leeside tools.com

Old Schools Tools
Merseyside
www.oldschooltools.co.uk

The Old Tool Shed
East Anglia
www.theoldtoolshed.co.uk

Old Tools Ltd
East Sussex
www.oldtools.co.uk

The Old Tool Store
Lincolnshire
www.oldtoolstore.com

Second Hand Tools
Seaton, Devon
www.secondhandtools.co.uk

Timeless Tools
Web-based and good selection of hedgelaying and woodland tools.
www.timelesstools.co.uk

Tool Bazaar
Perthshire
www.toolbazaar.co.uk

The Tool Box
Colyton
www.thetoolbox.org.uk

The Tool Shop
Suffolk
www.antiquetools.co.uk

The Tool Shop
Stafford Road, Wallington, Surrey
0208647 0773
No website

CHAPTER 13

Tool blades and sharpening angles

Ancient Japanese woodworkers were said to spend the first hour of the working day meditatively honing their cutting tools before starting any work.

Abraham Lincoln apparently commented that if he were given six hours to cut a tree down, he would spend the first four sharpening the axe.

The most common mispractice of a woodworker is to use dull tools. We are all familiar with the phrase "use the right tool for the right job", but perhaps we should add "and make sure that it's very sharp."

Using dull edged tools makes them harder to use, causes fatigue, lengthens the time it takes to do the job, leaves an inferior finish on the wood, decreases the control of a cut, increases the risk of an injury if the blade slips, and can put

The correct blade will leave a beautiful finish

the operator in a bad frame of mind. All negative effects.

A blade with the correct bevel angle, honed to a fine finish, is a pleasure to use. The cut will be controlled and effortless and the job will be completed quickly, leaving a beautiful finish on the wood. The operator will derive pleasure and pride from the job and the edge on the blade will be long-lasting, requiring little maintenance. All positive effects.

The most important things to know about edge tools are the hardness/toughness, the bevel angle, and the blade finish. You may also consider the difference between a stainless steel and a high carbon blade.

Hardness/toughness

The 'hardness' of steel is measured on the Rockwell C scale. Conceived in the early 20th century, the Rockwell C test involves the depth of penetration of an indent made on a piece of metal made by a diamond cone dropped from a specific height with a weight attached, and measured in HRC. Typically, HRC 55-66 in knives and HRC 40-45 in chisels and axes. 'Toughness' is the steel's ability to withstand fracture, so making a blade harder will reduce its toughness. When heat-treating a blade, the correct balance between hardness and toughness must be achieved. Too hard and it could break under use, too soft and it won't hold an edge.

Bevel angle

Basically, the lower the bevel angle is (say, 10-15 degrees) the sharper the edge will be. However, a low bevel angle results in a less durable edge, which could be prone to chipping under heavy use. A higher bevel angle (25 degrees plus), will be more able to withstand heavier use and the edge will keep sharper for longer.

A 10-20 degree bevel angle (left) compared to a 30-35 degree bevel angle (right)

Blade finish

Smooth edges are best for cutting with a straight push and are ideally suited to surgeons' and barbers' tools, and of course, general woodworking tools.

Blades left with a rough edge, sharpened with 20 to 30 grit, for example, will cut aggressively, especially with a low

bevel angle on a thin blade. This is because if you look at it under a microscope, you will see micro-serrations similar to, and acting like a saw blade. Whilst this would be perfect for slicing fibrous materials like rope, the disadvantage would be that the edge would become dull sooner, as the micro points would wear or bend under use.

So, a smooth edge, sharpened using a finer abrasive, will take more effort to sharpen, but less effort will be required to cut with it and it will last longer.

A rough edge, sharpened on a coarser abrasive, needs less effort to sharpen, but it will take more effort to cut with it and it won't last as long.

Stainless steel and high carbon blades

A stainless steel blade will not tarnish and rust. However, it will require more effort to put a good edge on stainless steel.

The higher the carbon content in a blade, the easier it is to sharpen and hold a very sharp edge. Because of the carbon however, the blade is subject to tarnishing and rust if not properly looked after.

Summary

By getting the balance right between hardness, toughness, bevel angle and finish, a cutting blade will do the job perfectly and last a long time. Obviously, the manufacturers get all of this right when they make a tool for a particular application, (thick, softer blade with a high bevel angle and medium finish for a chopping axe; thin, hard blade with a low bevel angle and fine, polished finish for a surgeon's scalpel) but understanding the basic principles of blade design and finish will greatly help you achieve the right combination when sharpening and honing your cutting tools in the workshop.

This chapter is concerned with the basic geometry and materials used for cutting blades, and does not attempt to tell you how to sharpen them. There are many good books about the subject of sharpening a blade, including the one recommended at the end of this chapter.

The edge of a drawknife

Bevel angle	Typical application	Qualities
Under 10 degrees	Surgical blades and razors.	Best for cutting soft materials, as they will not damage the edge.
10 to 17 degrees	Filleting and paring knives, some razors.	Best for cutting slightly thicker materials.
18 to 25 degrees	Most kitchen, carving and small penknives.	Durable and sharp cutting edge.
25 degrees	Turning chisels used on green wood on a pole lathe.	Best combination for working green wood on a foot lathe.
25 to 30 degrees	Hunting, sports, bush and pocket knives, bench planes, paring and chopping chisels, drawknives.	Durable and versatile blade with good toughness and cutting edge.
30 degrees	Drawknife.	Durable and sharp.
30 to 35 degrees	Axes, cleavers, machetes.	Very durable, reduced cutting edge, but more force can be used.
40 to 70 degrees	Turning chisels used on seasoned wood on a power lathe.	Best combination for wood and machine.

CHAPTER 14

The axe and the knife

The axe

Go back a million years and a flint hand axe was used by our ancestors for general cutting and the scraping of animal hides. These early tools were teardrop shaped and fitted snugly in the palm of the hand. Stone and slate was also favoured for hand axes, each with their own functional merits. Along the way, the axe head was eventually tied to the end of a stick, greatly increasing the power of the tool. The longer the handle, the more the power increased.

Axe heads from the Stone, Bronze and Iron Ages

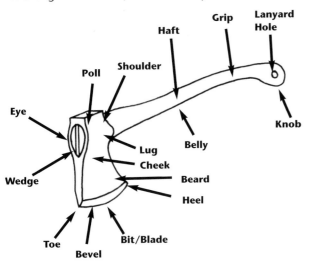

The anatomy of an axe

The bronze-age was a major evolutional leap forward in many ways, and the crude stone axe was replaced with a superior bronze, or copper version. It wasn't until

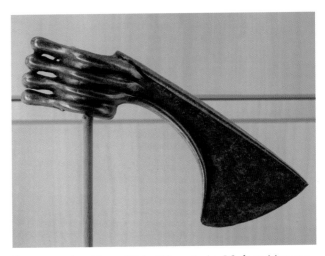

Bronze axe-head from 9th to 8th centuries BC, from Museum of Fine Arts Lyon

the iron-age however, that the axe as we know today manifested itself, with a larger, broader bladed head containing a hole in it to accommodate a fitted wooden handle. The rest is history.

The basic generic design of a metal head with a hole in it to take a wooden handle has stood the test of time throughout world cultures. The axe has undergone many hundreds of sophisticated designs based upon the simple principle of a stick with metal at the end, and has proven to be one of the most singularly versatile and useful tools ever to have been made.

Throughout the world, the axe has played a dual role in the history of humankind. On the one hand, the axe has been an extremely portable and versatile tool. Depending on its design and the size and length of its handle, it can be used in the heaviest of work, such as in chopping down trees, or in the fine art of carving a spoon. On the other hand, like many other inventions, the axe has proven to be a very effective and devastating weapon, used in one form or another by warriors throughout the world, most notoriously during the Viking period c 800-1100 AD.

This icon of design has been revered since it was first held in the hand. The axe is a symbol of power. An extension of the capabilities of humankind. A reminder of our past, and a reassurance that if we were forced to

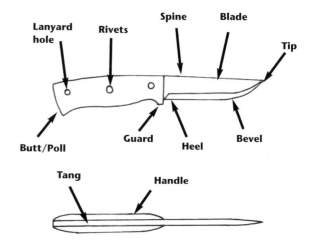

The anatomy of a knife

have to live in the wild again and fend for ourselves, a medium-sized forest axe would be a most indispensable aid to survival.

The knife

Go back even further through time and we discover that another irreplaceable icon of design and functionality.

Gransfors Bruks small forest axe, carving side axe and fro

Knife blades from late neolithic France, in the Museum of Toulouse

Just as the earliest axe was honed out of a palm sized piece of flint, slate or stone, the early knife predates the axe significantly by about a million years, and is just a smaller and thinner version.

The materials for the blade developed through the bronze and iron-age and attachment to a bone or wooden handle occurred in time (as with the axe).

Many thousand versions of the knife have been designed, and like the axe, the knife is both a tool and a weapon. However, it has a third, more modern function – this being an aid to eating. In earlier times, it was used to cut up large servings of meat into mouth-sized pieces whilst eating with ones hands. Curiously, the knife is a relatively recent western aid to the actual mechanical cutting and manipulation of our food used in conjunction with a fork.

Many cultures throughout the world deem modern day cutlery superfluous, having always used their hands to supply their mouth with food. In fact, if you consider it, massive populations in the East tuck in heartily to their daily meals with their hands, whilst we (sophisticated) Europeans go through the daily ritual of laying the table with eating irons, using them with the correct protocol, and adding them to the pile of washing-up afterwards. One could be forgiven for re-thinking our Western eating habits.

Curiously enough, despite our dazzling array of cutlery, we still haven't designed a piece capable of dealing with eating the formidable pea. It is a very dexterous person indeed who can sit through a whole meal involving these slippery green spheres without losing the odd one from the precariously balanced pile on our fork, or resorting to stabbing them in a most uncivilised manner. Using a spoon during the main course to deal with the problem just isn't etiquette.

(Top to bottom) Excellent Mora utility knife, classic Opinel folding knife, Mora carving knife and Mora blade and tang for fitting into a handle

Now, having wandered off track somewhat, we must return to the true knife. Being less bulky and conspicuous than the axe, the knife has always been the preferred tool of choice to carry on our body, either concealed, or prominently displayed. Whilst there are an infinite number of knife designs, from fixed blade to pocket folding knives, some involving very elaborate blade engraving, handle materials and scabbard materials, this book is concerned with highlighting the generic design of the versatile, fixed blade bush, or hunting knife, used by millions of people worldwide on a daily basis.

Carry a legally permitted sharp folding knife (maximum 3 inch/7.62cm blade) with you every day for a couple of months, and you will be so impressed with the versatility and usefulness of this tool, that you will never want to be without one again.

CHAPTER 15

Green woodworking – A fusion of mind, body and spirit

A tree is our most intimate contact with nature.
George Nakashima

Bodging in the woodland

In 1978, Baltimore chairmaker John Alexander (now Jennie Alexander) had a book published entitled *Making a Chair from a Tree – an introduction to working green wood*. This publication, now currently out of print, was a landmark in revealing the methods of post and rung chairmaking starting with unseasoned wood, and was responsible for inspiring many of our current practitioners, on both sides of the Atlantic.

In his book, the phrase 'green woodworking' was coined, and possibly adopted afterwards as the definitive phrase associated with a wide range of traditional woodworking

practices involving a skilled craftsperson and freshly felled wood. However, the use of the phrase 'green' wood has been well understood by tradesmen for at least a century. In his excellent and personal recollections of being a wheelwright in the late 19th century, George Sturt, in his book *The Wheelwright's Shop* published in 1923, mentions 'green timber' (that is, timber with some sap left in it, imperfectly seasoned).

Working with unseasoned wood has been practised since man first shaped a stick with a shard of flint to fashion the first spear point. After the discovery that fire and metal

Guy Mallinson's woodland crafts training workshop, Dorset

could be combined to produce basic cutting and shaping tools, surprisingly little has changed in basic blade design and use. The generic properties and characteristics of different tree species haven't changed either; so working with green wood is, therefore, one of the oldest crafts in existence.

Hands on

Green wood craftsmanship, in its most basic form, is the practice of working with freshly felled, unseasoned wood in its rawest state, whilst relatively soft, using only basic hand tools.

Unlike our modern day carpenters, joiners and cabinet makers, the green wood craftsperson becomes involved with wood from the very beginning when it is still a standing tree. Once the tree is felled, the craftsperson performs every subsequent process, right up to the finished product. This close proximity with nature tends to rub off, transferring a compassionate understanding of trees and a healthy respect for nature and the environment – one of the very positive side effects of this wonderful craft.

When producing component parts, it is important to understand that they are all obtained naturally by splitting (riving) the timber along the grain which separates the natural fibres without actually cutting into them, ensuring that every component part is extremely strong – far more so than any machined equivalent.

Wood in its unseasoned state is relatively soft to work. With a few sharp tools you can shape green wood easily and efficiently with little wear and tear on your meticulously honed cutting edges. Green wood joinery, or wet/dry joinery, allows for the natural shrinkage of wood to produce incredibly strong structures with built in longevity, without the need to use glue, screws or nails. This type of joinery combines relatively dry and relatively wet components, assembled under deliberate tension, with grains aligned in such a way as to allow for natural shrinkage and subsequent expansion as ambient moisture fluctuates.

Fortunately, the green wood craftsperson does not need expensive, noisy and potentially dangerous machinery to process the wood, or a large workshop in which to accommodate it. All that is required are a few specialised hand tools and a place to work undercover. If a component needs a curve, it is easily bent by using steam instead of cutting from a solid blank, which leaves a lot of waste wood.

The basic principles of how trees grow and react after

felling, how wood will dry differently according to species, and how each species has unique individual properties, underpin the work of all the woodland trades. It is evident from examining the handiwork of our knowledgeable ancestors, that they had a very comprehensive understanding of these things, and it influenced the way they practiced their respective trades for hundreds of years.

General carpenters, wheelwrights, coopers, thatchers, weavers, bodgers, rake and hay fork makers, bowl and platter turners, and, in fact, all of the essential trades of the woodlands, had a thorough understanding of their wood and how to work it, and employed their skills with a pride

Cleft, steam bent dining chairs made by the author

and professionalism that modern day methods do not allow.

We seem to find ourselves in a situation now, with all manufacturing, where a vastly disproportionate amount of time is spent on looking at ways to cut costs of production and basic materials, and, of course, the cost of labour. All of which is to the detriment of the quality and longevity of the end product.

One of the pinnacles of the craft of working green wood has to be the creation of a chair. Two of the best known classic handmade chairs are the Windsor (in which vertical spindles form the back of the chair), and the Ladderback (where horizontal spindles or slats – like a ladder – form the back), also known as a post-and-rung chair. Although very different in construction, both share similar joinery techniques and employ every skill and technique required of an experienced green wood crafts person. These chairs are well designed, comfortable (if skilfully made), aesthetically pleasing and constructed to last for generations.

A way of life

The beauty and reward of using traditional hand tools on newly felled timber derives from the sound, smell and vision – the swish of the cut, the aroma of freshly worked unseasoned timber and the sumptuous curves of the newly exposed grain. An ambience of contemplation, connection and creativity – it's more a way of life than a job. It requires a degree of natural talent, a positive attitude and most importantly, love, passion and respect for wood, nature and how you can work with it. It is a liberating journey involving the mind, body and spirit. Psychologists are of the opinion that of all the trades, working with wood is the most perfectly balanced between mental, physical and aesthetic.

By understanding nature and working in partnership with it, instead of exploiting and manipulating it, we can achieve stunning results. A very important and poignant message for everybody, perhaps?

CHAPTER 16

The bodgers of the woodlands

He is absorbed in the worth of the work, contemplating the habits and constitution of the woods, reading the ways of nature like a sage poring over an old folio....

But not only does the craftsman work in the same way as nature without hurry or against the grain of things, but he is also in a special relation to it from which he never deviates. This relation is a symbiotic one, which simply means that he uses without misusing his natural material to the mutual benefit both of nature and himself....

Though he rarely objectifies this emotional sense, much less give it a name, all making for him has a sacramental meaning and his very touch upon the works of nature expresses a life-service towards a creative universal of which he is intuitively aware....

Guard him, woods and heaths and hills of creative nature, for in your midst is creative man, once ordinary man and now a rarity!

H.J. Massingham 'The English Countryman' 1942

Of all the trades associated with woodland crafts, the bodger seems to be the best known. Yet despite the term bodger, or chair bodger, being frequently voiced, there seems to be a common misconception of what a bodger actually was. The Concise Oxford Dictionary has no definition of bodger, but does categorise 'bodge' as a 'Var. of Botch – (make a) clumsy patch; spoil(t) or bungle(d) work; repair badly'.

To put the records straight, the bodger associated with chairs was actually a very skilled green wood craftsperson.

How the bodgers worked

A census of Buckinghamshire in 1798 revealed 58 chairmakers (small factories) located in and around High Wycombe with reports of 'some work done outside chair shop', which referred to 'bodgers'.

In the early 19th century, bodgers made whole chairs from green timber, as well as stools, cleft tent pegs, bowls, spoons, platters, and so on (the latter collectively known as treen), which they sold locally. By the late 19th century

Group of bodgers and their encampment

however, it was easier and more profitable to specialise in producing basic chair components for sale to factories who employed people to make chairs from them.

Thus, the bodger worked (and occasionally lived) in the woods during the spring and summer, under temporary shelters known as 'hovels'. These were made of poles lashed together in a triangular structure, with a waterproof roof and enclosed sides made from woven materials. Although some lived in these shelters, in truth, the majority of them lived relatively nearby to the

Three bodgers in front of a pole lathe hut in Hampden Woods c 1900

woodlands and 'commuted' by foot or bicycle each day.

Mostly self-employed, they purchased (or had the factories purchase) areas of beech woods and ash coppice every year through auction. They then felled and worked on a selective rotation of trees, leaving the smaller trees to grow on and seed naturally. Coppicing ensured a renewable source of quality material for centuries.

A few simple and specialised tools were used to produce legs and stretchers from logs that were cleft (split along the grain to retain the natural fibres), shaped with a side axe and shaved with a drawknife on a shaving horse (a foot-operated gripping device with origins in the 16th century). The rough billet would then be mounted on a pole lathe (a foot-powered lathe with origins dating back to 300 BC) and turned into the finished cylinder, which was then stacked and left to dry in the open air.

All figures vary of course, but in the early 20th century, a skilled bodger could produce up to 144 components, comprising of rungs and stretchers, in a day, (yes – a day!), averaging out at about 800 units a week. Earliest records from the 1900s show that they would receive five shillings in payment from the local chair-making factories for each gross (144) of chair parts. Considering

Freshly produced chair legs and stretchers air-drying in woodland c 1902

production line. Large quantities were shipped off to London and sold through dealers at low prices to working class families, inns, restaurants and other public places, and exported abroad within the British Empire. These cheaply produced, expendable utility chairs were not used by the upper classes, who favoured the rather more prestigious seating on which to park their posh bottoms. They did, however, buy them for their servants to use ('them downstairs').

Rather than employ specialist chairmakers, the responsibility for producing a chair in the factory from the basic components supplied by the bodgers was divided up between people known then as bottomers, benchmen, benders, framers and finishers – each person specialising in a skill which contributed to the end product.

The factories eventually cut corners and produced legs and stretchers 'in-house' from sawn and turned planks which were, of course, vastly inferior to those produced by the bodgers from cleft wood. In 1850, there were a reported 100 pole lathes being worked in the Chilterns, but by 1930 the recorded number was down to just nine. By the late 1950s, the woods were virtually empty of these itinerant craftsmen and as they died, their craft,

that they had to work so hard for their money, under all weather conditions, this was a very modest wage.

In Great Britain, bodgers are mostly associated with High Wycombe in Buckinghamshire. They would work in the surrounding beech woods in the Chiltern Hills and sell the week's produce to the nearby factories, where the 'English Windsor' chair was mass-produced on a

Two members of the Stevens family in their workshop in Lacey Green c 1900

once so locally vital and unique, died with them.

Thus it was that when Owen Dean of Great Hampden, and Samual Rockall of Summer Heath, the last of the original bodgers in Britain, passed away in 1960 and 1962 respectively, 500 years of tradition came to an end.

An independent chairmaker, even in those days, was a specialised and very skilled craftsman who drew on a multitude of green woodworking skills. Most often, everyday rural chairs and stools were made by the local wheelwright or carpenter to order, without patterns, drawings or jigs. This so very often resulted in uniquely colloquial designs of varying construction and quality.

Carrying on the tradition

Most chairs today are still mass-produced in factories, and lack the character, individuality and longevity of a traditionally handmade chair. They have no soul.

Thankfully there are still a handful or two of individual chairmakers to be found around Britain, tucked away in their workshops, producing heirloom pieces from cleft, local, sustainable wood, keeping alive the methods and skills of the rural green wood craftsman and combining them with a chairmaker's specialist 'know-how'. These people are the real deal, so seek them out and buy your chairs from them. There is no substitute.

Although the days of the bodger have sadly long since disappeared, their spirit still lives on in the chairs that survive to this day, and in the practitioners who have found new ways to apply these ancient skills.

English comb-back Windsor armchair made by James Mursell

CHAPTER 17

The shaving horse and pole lathe

No two green woodworking devices have ever been bettered for their simplicity, ease of manufacture, portability, reliability and their immediate ease of use in any location, without the need for electricity. The shaving horse and pole lathe are icons of design, beautiful to behold, deceptively efficient, and a pleasure to use.

The shaving horse

This ingeniously simple and indispensable device has been used by craftsmen for centuries. It has stood the test of time. The basic design remains virtually unchanged, and is still in daily use all over the world in one form or another, by tens of thousands of craftspeople.

Essentially a foot-operated quick-release wooden clamp, the shaving horse is designed to hold a piece of wood securely, while leaving the operator, who sits astride the device (as astride a horse), with both hands free to work the piece of wood with an edge tool, usually a drawknife.

The basic structure is simply a horizontal plank of wood 4 to 5 feet (120 - 150 cm) long, supported by three or four legs. It stands approximately chair seat height 17 to 18 inches (43 - 46 cm) off the ground, with a second H-shaped structure pivoted vertically through the plank or around it in an H-shape. When this H-shaped structure is pushed forwards by the feet of the operator it presses firmly down onto the wood that is being worked on performing an impressively efficient and strong clamping function.

Although two different versions of the shaving horse evolved, they essentially remain the only ones used today. The oldest version, with official records dating back to 1556, (although even earlier references would suggest circa 1485), is the Continental, sometimes referred to as the Mule, or Dumb-head design. The second variant, known as the English shaving horse, seems to have appeared as recently as the late 18th century, although it may have been used in one form or another earlier than that but not recorded.

Continental shaving horse

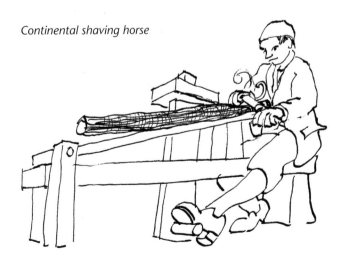

Continental shaving horse

The Continental

The Continental started its life as a sort of table with a slot cut in it to accommodate the vertical shaft running through it, attached to the table with a pivot pin. Above the table, a horizontal chunk of wood known as the dumb head was attached to the top of the shaft to grip the wood being worked on, while a horizontal footrest attached to the bottom of the shaft below the table. Depending on the height of the table, this style of shave horse was used either with the operator standing at the table or sitting on a stool. Later, the continental was adapted to a low, long slim bench (similar to the English design) so the operator could conveniently sit astride it. It is this design that we now use today.

The English

Instead of a table, the English shaving horse started out as a low, long, slim bench with a vertical 'H-shaped' shaft, consisting of two pieces, one either side of the bench (rather than going through it), with a pivot pin holding them to the bench. Two more horizontal pieces were added to the 'H', above and below the bench, to provide the clamp and foot pedal respectively. The operator sat astride the bench.

Records seem to suggest that whilst the continental was (and still is) the preferred design in Europe, the English version is the one most widely used within Britain and America, probably due to the self-levelling and even pressure synonymous with the design of the clamping structure.

Irrespective of the version used, this wonderfully effective device, with its instant clamping and unclamping function is an all-time classic piece of kit, used by coopers, wheelwrights, chairmakers and the like, for shaping a billet of wood with a drawknife.

English shaving horse

Freedom of design

Despite a loosely generic design, the shaving horse still remains a 'shop-made' device, meaning that they are built by the woodworkers themselves in their workshops. They are often constructed from inexpensive scrap wood, and as a consequence, no two horses will be identical - the design and manufacture being a matter of personal taste and requirement.

Little wonder then that throughout the world there exist hundreds of thousands of subtly different designs, each with their own functional quality, each projecting their own sculptural statement from the most basic rustic horse, hewn by axe from a log, to the most refined versions machined from kiln-dried boards, the shaving horse remains one of the most personal hand-made devices in existence.

The shaving pony

In recent years, woodworkers with limited space have adopted a simple design made to be bolted onto the side of a work bench. The shaving pony simply has a much longer pivot assembly, reaching almost down to the ground, and a head design somewhere between the Continental dumb head and a European horse. The user sits in front of it on a stool and works in exactly the same way as one would on a conventional horse. These devices are very portable and can be a very effective clamp to have at the end of your bench.

Author's bench shaving pony

The symbiosis of tool and device

To work green wood with a drawknife, you ideally need a shaving horse. A drawknife requires both hands to control, and some sort of clamp. A standard carpenter's vice simply cannot fit the bill. So, while a shaving horse is essentially just a pile of scrap wood on its own, when brought together with the drawknife, there is a symbiosis of tool and device, representing the most longstanding partnership in the history of wood crafting. Just add man.

The pole lathe (or spring pole lathe)

Pole Lathe

Earliest records would suggest that the pole lathe was in use, in one form or another, as far back as 3,000 BC in Ancient Egypt. It was certainly widely used by the Romans and the Saxons, and by the early twelfth century, it was firmly established, enabling mass production of wooden components and artefacts. Such was the importance of this icon of design, that in the 16th century, even Leonardo Da Vinci had a go at designing a version that enabled continuous rotation.

In England, records show that the spring pole lathe was

used for wood turning from the 4th century onwards. In 1180, a Turner's Guild was established in Cologne, Germany, and London followed with the London Company of Turners in 1360. Later, in 1591, wood turners established a Guild in London, offering apprenticeships. By 1720 the London Guild of Wood Turners had 40 members.

The principles of design

A spring pole lathe is designed to hold a piece of wood and rotate it so that the wood worker can shape the piece, using various cutting tools. A length of twine is wound around the work piece, one end of it attached to a foot pedal at one end, and the other end to a long flexible pole above the device. With the operator pushing down on the foot treadle, the work piece spins one direction. When the treadle has reached its full depression downwards and is released, the flexible pole will spring back up, spinning the work piece back in the other direction.

Spring pole lathe

It is important to understand that this very simple reciprocal motion will cause the work piece to rotate in different directions as the foot treadle is depressed and released – rotating towards the operator when depressed and backwards away from the operator on release; thus, the cutting tool can only be engaged on the down stroke and withdrawn on the upstroke.

Other operator-powered lathes

As the name suggests, the 'pole' lathe derives its name from the pole used to obtain the 'spring' required to provide the energy. A nearby thin, springy tree bough is also very effective and is very easy to set up if you position your lathe under one. Early designs like this were usually only suitable for outdoor use, although, to allow some protection from wind and rain, bodgers often used to leave the pole outside and build a rough shelter around the lathe, with the line running through a gap in the front.

The most commonly used set-up for indoor use would be to attach a flexible cord (or a bungee) to a roof timber, or to fix a wooden upright either end of the lathe bed with another length of flexible cord tied horizontally between the two uprights at approximately 8 feet (245 cm) high, attached to the driving cord. It is this flexible cord that provides the 'springiness' required. This could, perhaps be described as the 'overhead treadle lathe'. In some cases, a wooden bobbin is added to the overhead horizontal rig and is therefore described as the 'bobbin lathe'.

In the 16th century, Leonardo Da Vinci came up with a design for a continuous rotation lathe powered by a foot treadle. The sound theory behind this is that it enabled continuous rotation of the work piece (as in modern day electric lathes) thus making the operation more efficient as there would be no need to withdraw the cutting tool on each reverse cycle. Continuous rotation still requires the operator to use some sort of a foot pedal, and in Da Vinci's case, the driving mechanism consisted of connecting cams and belts, much like the old Singer foot-powered sewing machine.

Another successful and fairly recent version is the wheel and pulley lathe, which is particularly useful for turning large diameter, heavy work pieces like the elm hub of a wooden wagon wheel. A large metal wheel is positioned at right angles to the lathe bed, usually some way behind the operator. A large belt runs from this to a considerably smaller wheel connected to the lathe poppets. This set-up

Bowl turning demonstration by Paul Moreton on an overhead lathe to a spellbound young audience

enables very efficient continuous rotation, but does require a second person to continuously turn the large driving wheel. This job would inevitably fall to the craftsperson's apprentice, or at a push, anyone unlucky enough to be found unoccupied at the time.

A partnership of devices

Typically, an unseasoned log is split down the grain to a rough billet, shaped with a hand axe to close to the dimensions required, and then further refined with a drawknife, while held in a shave horse. It is then mounted in the pole lathe for turning into the final component.

It is these two devices, inevitably found together in both indoor and outdoor work sites, that can turn rough wood into beautiful items. They have formed a faithful and long-lasting partnership through the ages, and as long as green woodworking is practised, this partnership will no doubt be one that remains unchanged.

Where do I get a shave horse or a pole lathe?

Make one yourself!

I have purposely avoided including a generic design for a shave horse or a pole lathe, because I am trying to make a point here.

Working with green wood is a very personal thing, and also, in many cases, a life choice. You could be sitting on a shave horse, or using a pole lathe, for most of the day. So why not make them according to your personal aesthetic taste? There are no rules. You will be looking at it, and using it every day. It is almost like a marriage!

Yes, of course, you can purchase one or the other from people who make them out of sawn timber (at quite unreasonable prices), which will just 'sit' there and 'function'. But to buy one of these 'flat pack' items will suggest that you are missing the point.

To get started, you could go on a specialised green woodworking course (usually two days), or surf around the numerous websites available and find a design. There are many books published that include designs and dimensions for these two devices. Of course, we are all different sizes and shapes, so our first effort may not be perfect for us. Make, try, adjust, re-design, enjoy!

Green woodworking is fun. As long as you understand that and apart from the obvious fact that you have to learn 'the knowledge', the rest is up to your own imagination.

Author's shaving horse in woodland workshop

CHAPTER 18
Wood burning

Burning logs to heat your home results in far lower CO_2 emissions than using coal, oil, or gas.

Moreover, if you burn sustainably grown wood, the CO_2 that the tree took in from the atmosphere is released again, but because sustainably grown wood is a continual process (the tree that was cut down to give you wood will already have been replaced by another which is absorbing and locking in CO_2 again), there is no overall increase in CO_2 levels.

OK, the processing and transportation of the wood usually results in some emissions, particularly if the firewood isn't seasoned properly (adding unwanted extra weight from the high water content in the logs), so although wood burning is not totally carbon neutral, it is a very low-carbon form of heating. Wood smoke also emits fewer sulphides when burning than coal does.

Seasoned wood

It cannot be stressed enough that firewood should be well seasoned – that is, allowed to dry thoroughly – before

Forest firewood stack

burning. It is said that a few native hardwoods can be burned when unseasoned (or 'green') – ash, holly and birch, but they will give a far superior burn when seasoned well.

It is really not advisable to burn unseasoned wood. Freshly cut wood has a high moisture content — typically 60-70% of the weight of the tree. The moisture content must be reduced to below 25% before you burn it – ideally 5 to 10%. If the moisture content is above this, particularly if well above this, most of the energy required to burn the log will be used to evaporate the moisture within it, before the wood fibres can start to burn. You will actually hear the log hissing in the fire – a tell-tail sign of unseasoned wood attempting to burn. The moisture in the wood is effectively trying to 'put out' the fire, resulting in a hard to burn, smoky, cool fire giving out very little heat. If half the fire's energy is being used to boil out the water in the wood it will result in the log only burning at 50% efficiency.

In short, if you burn unseasoned wood in your fire, you are not only wasting your time, energy and money, but you are also going to have to put up with a pretty troublesome and pathetically inefficient, smoky mess in your fire grate. Wood burned at 5-10% moisture content will produce approximately 1,000 kw per tonne more of extra energy than wood seasoned down to just 20% moisture content.

If you pick up an unseasoned log, it will feel damp to the touch and smell musty. It will also feel unusually heavy in your hand due to the high water content, and sound dense if you tap it. Conversely, when you pick up a well-seasoned log, the weight will be substantially less than the unseasoned equivalent. It will feel dry. You will see splits in the end grain and if you smell it, you will smell wood, rather than a musty, peaty aroma of dampness.

Burning unseasoned wood can result in the build-up of

Properly seasoned logs burning cleanly

dangerous tar deposits in your chimney which can reduce the life of your stove, flu pipe and chimney. These deposits are also a major contributor to chimney fires, which can be life-threatening.

Tar is the condensation of unburned, very flammable particles present in the exhaust gas (smoke). The actual cause of tar condensation is determined by the surface temperature of the chimney or flue which the gas comes into contact with. Like hot breath on a cold mirror, if the surface temperature of the chimney or flue is cool, it will cause the vaporised carbon particles in the gas to solidify. This condensation is the tar build-up.

If the wood you burn is wet, the fire will smoulder, burn cool and inefficiently and tar will build up rapidly in your chimney or flue. If the wood you burn is dry, the fire will burn faster, hotter and more efficiently. A hot fire means a hot chimney, and hot chimney means considerably less tar build-up.

Contrary to what is normally said, soft woods/conifers are perfectly suitable for burning and will burn efficiently and safely (some more than others) so long as they are well seasoned (18 months to 2 years). In fact, most have a higher calorific value than hardwoods when burnt, although they tend to burn quite fast and some are prone to spitting.

Remember – well seasoned wood burns hot and fast. It is not the tar in the wood that causes all the problems; it is the water in the tar.

Lastly, it cannot be stressed enough that sweeping your chimney or flue a minimum of once every season (or year) is essential. Tar will always collect in it over a prolonged period, so even if you only burn the best, well-seasoned firewood,

remember to have the chimney or flue swept. Tar deposits are highly flammable and can cause chimney fires. Either sweep it yourself, or get someone in to do it – but just do it.

For those people using wood burners, (a much more efficient method of heating a room), exactly the same rules apply regarding firewood. The stainless steel flues also need sweeping every year, and you should also check the rope seal on the inside of the doors and replace when necessary. Wood that is prone to spitting is best burnt in a wood-burning stove with the doors shut.

Harvesting

For the majority of us, buying firewood from a local supplier and having it delivered is the easiest option. In the recent past, this has always been a bit of a gamble initially until you find a reliable person who regularly supplies you with a good measure of well-seasoned firewood of the right kind. We have all experienced a delivery consisting of a dubious mixture of various musty smelling, unidentifiable species interspersed with the odd dry oak or beech log. The volume you buy (or more correctly, the volume actually delivered) tends to vary on the day.

What is 'a load' anyway? Some say it's a pick-up truck filled (they all vary in volume), other say it's an open back van, or lorry 'load'. The truth is, all 'loads' vary, unless the firewood merchant is going to meticulously stack the logs into a cubic metre container, or calculate the weight of a pile of logs at a certain moisture content.

Thankfully, the industry standard seems to have settled on units of a cubic metre and you can expect to be quoted a standard price per cubic metre of firewood.

With the unprecedented increase in the use of wood-burning stoves, in response to the price of gas and oil, the firewood industry is experiencing a boom. This means, unfortunately, that everybody is jumping on the bandwagon to supply firewood, so you need to be even more careful when choosing a supplier. Here are a few tips to assist you:

- Choose a local supplier who has been recommended to you.
- Ideally choose one who is as near to you as possible.
- Order your logs well in advance of winter, as even good local suppliers tend to run out of good, well-seasoned logs as winter progresses.
- Do your best to allocate a big enough area outside your house to store your firewood for the winter and have it delivered in one go, to keep transport costs down. If you

are ordering several cubic metres, you may get a discount.

- Order a minimum of a cubic metre, as although it is often possible to buy half a cubic metre, it will cost you more.
- If you have enough space, it is a very good idea to order unseasoned logs from your supplier and keep them alongside your seasoned ones. This can make a big difference to the price, for example, if a cubic metre of seasoned logs is, say £80, you will probably get the same volume of unseasoned logs for £60.
- If you have the time, tools, trailer and energy, you may consider buying your unseasoned wood direct from tree surgeons or forest managers, who will be felling timber all year round and would be only too happy to sell you small buts and branches at a very reasonable price, as long as you collect at ride or roadside. You will, of course, have to chop it into firewood yourself, and although you will probably burn as many calories processing it as you receive when it is burnt, you will be kept warm by the glow of inner smugness you feel at having got such a good deal in the first place.

Alternatively, for those lucky enough to own or rent a woodland, or who participate in a local community woodland management enterprise, or for those who are friendly with a local farmer who wants his hedgerows maintained every year in return for the wood, here are a few helpful guidelines.

Ideally, wood should be felled in the early winter months (November onwards) when the sap ceases to flow, but in practice, obtaining wood for burning is an all year round process. Just make sure to keep track of when each stack was felled, split and stored.

Trunks and limbs should then be processed into logs and kindling as soon as possible, as it is easier to split when green, which exposes and increases the surface area, enabling the log to dry quicker. Wood cells don't lose much moisture through the bark. Most moisture escapes from the end grain and through any severed fibres, so when the wood is left in the 'round' with the bark on, it dries very slowly, especially if it is left in long lengths. If you have to keep logs in the 'round' with the bark on, chop them into lengths of around 30cms (12in) or less.

Storing

The logs should be stacked off the ground (old wood pallets are ideal and allow for an airflow underneath) in a structure with a roof and open sides. Leave a minimum of 30cms (12 in) between the top of the stack and the roof to allow some airflow at the summit and ideally, fix horizontal planks of timber up the sides with generous gaps in between to allow air circulation and wind into the stack. Do not cover a firewood stack with a tarpaulin as this will inhibit moisture evaporation.

The logs should be left for at least one summer and used the following year. As a general rule of thumb, 12 months seasoning is good, but 18 months to two years (two summers of seasoning) will result in superior burning wood. Some wood seasons quicker than others, so be aware of this and try to have a good mix (see the table *Average air-drying time for green wood by species* in Chapter 6) but remember that the drying time in the table refers to wood of one inch diameter, so multiply up according to the diameter of your firewood logs. In general, split your logs into quarters so that you only leave one side of the triangle with bark left on. The smaller the surface area of the log, the quicker it will season.

It is also useful to know that different woods burn faster than others. Some woods give out better heat than others, some spit excessively, and some woods just aren't worth bothering with as a heat source, because you would burn more calories processing it than you would get back in the heat output. So, in the ideal world, you should have a good variety and thicknesses of slow and fast burning woods, seasoned for 18 months, and stored within easy access to your fireplace or wood burner.

A stack of firewood in the South Tyrol

Burning

Now we know that trying to burn wood with a high moisture content is a waste of time and money, and potentially dangerous. It is just as important to understand that how you burn your wood can also affect tar build-up in your chimney or flue. We need to learn some basic fire-craft.

The best way to get a point over is to give an example. Someone I know had a very old 10KW wood burner installed in a small room in his house measuring 12ft x 12ft. Being such a large capacity fire, burning wood to anywhere near full capacity would make it unbearably hot, so, on the odd occasion when he decided to light the fire, it was only at best, just ticking over, producing a small amount of heat.

One night there was a great WHOOSH! He had a chimney fire. After the fire brigade had put it out, they asked him if he had been burning unseasoned wood. He replied no. His moisture meter told him it was down to 20% moisture content, so on the face of it that should have been OK. Despite this, the reasons why he had the chimney fire are twofold. Firstly, he only lit a fire occasionally, and secondly, he never burnt it hot enough.

In the winter time, days, or weeks in between fires will leave the chimney or flue subject to coldness and the build-up of natural condensation, which as previously explained, will trap tar from the burning wood. If the fire is not burning hot enough, irrespective of low moisture content in the wood, the chimney will never heat up enough to keep it free of tar deposits. That's why it is so important in the case of open fires and wood burners, to get a roaring fire as quickly as possible after lighting, and to maintain it so you always have flickering flames. If you install a wood burner, ensure that it has the right capacity for the size of your room. Incidentally, my friend has now installed a 4KW wood burner in his room, which he burns at full capacity (hot) to make his small room very cosy (and safe) in the winter.

So, here are a few very basic fire-craft rules to help you safely enjoy your log fire.

- Choose your firewood merchant carefully.
- Try and obtain your firewood well in advance. Buying unseasoned wood in bulk is the most economical way, but you need somewhere to store it for a year or two before you burn it.
- Store in a dry, ventilated area within easy reach of the house.
- Never try and get away with burning unseasoned wood. It just doesn't work.

Roaring fire in a woodburning stove

- Understand the burning properties of each species of wood and mix them together where appropriate.
- Ensure that your wood burner is the correct capacity for the size of your room.
- Have your chimney or flue swept at least once a year, especially in the autumn when you will start to burn fires again.
- Become skilled at starting a fire efficiently and quickly. Get it up to a roaring, red heat and then maintain the flames throughout the burn.
- Be patient and wait until you really need to add logs to a fire. Wait until all the wood is burning red before adding more logs. Don't just dump a load on top of the flame. This will immediately reduce the heat drastically and can even put out the fire completely. Just add one or two new logs at a time, leaving sufficient air gaps in between for the flames to take.
- Shutting down the wood burner air adjustment to 'keep-in' a fire overnight is a debatable practice. This will have the effect of producing more smoke than is usually desirable and will result in a less than warm burn. If you do shut down your fire regularly, just ensure that you have the flue swept even more regularly.
- Get to know the more aromatic woods and keep them for special occasions like Christmas, friend and family gatherings, or when you just want some quiet quality time on your own with a good book and a glass of hedgerow wine. Try adding well dried pine cones, eucalyptus and bay leaves or dried orange peel to a hot fire for a delightful aromatic twist.

Fire is considered to be a Hindu God in India. Such is the power of the flame, that a couple can say their marriage vows in front of a fire, without witnesses and receive the blessing of Agni.

The Yule Log

The origin of the Yule log takes us back to the Pagan Celts. Yiaoul was the God of sun, or fire. The Celtic Druids professed to maintain perpetual fire. Once a year, the people ritually extinguished their fires and re-kindled them from the sacred fire of their Druid leaders.

The Yule log, by tradition is oak or ash, and put on the Christmas fire for a while before removing to prevent it burning fully. This charred log is reserved and used to re-kindle the following year's Christmas fire in a ritual re-enactment of the Celt's practice of renewing their ancient hearths with the sacred fire of the Druids.

So, what is the best wood to burn? See the tables below, or learn the old way:

The Firewood Poem

Beechwood fires are bright and clear
If the logs are kept a year,
Chestnut's only good they say,
If for logs 'tis laid away.
Make a fire of Elder tree,
Death within your house will be;
But ash new or ash old,
Is fit for a queen with crown of gold

Birch and fir logs burn too fast
Blaze up bright and do not last,
it is by the Irish said
Hawthorn bakes the sweetest bread.
Elm wood burns like churchyard mould,
E'en the very flames are cold
But ash green or ash brown
Is fit for a queen with golden crown

Poplar gives a bitter smoke,
Fills your eyes and makes you choke,
Apple wood will scent your room
Pear wood smells like flowers in bloom
Oaken logs, if dry and old
keep away the winter's cold

But ash wet or ash dry
a king shall warm his slippers by.

Lady Celia Congreve
Published in the Times 1930

Logs to Burn

Logs to burn, logs to burn,
Logs to save the coal a turn.
Here's a word to make you wise,
When you hear the Woodman's cries,
Never heed his usual tale,
That he's splendid logs for sale
But read these lines and really learn
The proper kind of logs to burn....
Oak logs will warm you well,
If they're old and dry.
Larch logs of pinewoods smell
But the sparks will fly.
Beech logs for Christmas time,
Yew logs heat well,
'Scotch' logs it is a crime
For anyone to sell.
Birch logs will burn too fast,
Chestnut scarce at all,
Hawthorn logs are good to last
If cut in the fall.
Holly logs will burn like wax,
You should burn them green,
Elm logs burn like smouldering flax,
No flame to be seen.
Pear logs and apple logs,
They will scent your room,
Cherry logs across the dogs
Smell like flowers in bloom.
But ash logs all smooth and grey
Burn them green or old,
Buy up all that come your way
They're worth their weight in gold.

Honor Goodhart
1926

Suitability for burning by species

Name	Star rating	Grade	Comments
Alder	**	Fair	Easily split but little heat produced. May spit too.
Apple	***	Good	Splits reasonably well. Burns slowly with good heat and a pleasant smell.
Ash	*****	Excellent	Splits well. Can be burned green but best seasoned. Good, long burn and heat with little smoke and pleasant smell. Good all-rounder.
Aspen	*	Low	Burns quickly with little heat.
Bay	****	Very Good	Burns well and aromatically.
Beech	*****	Excellent	Season fully. Splits well. Medium burn with good heat and little smoke. Good all-rounder.
Birch	****	Very Good	Splits well. Burns fast so mix with elm or oak. Good heat. Occasional spitting. Bark excellent for fire lighting.
Blackthorn	****	Very Good	Burns slowly with very good heat.
Box	****	Very Good	Good burn and heat.
Cedar	****	Very Good Season well.	Splits well. Good heat with a pleasant smell. Some smoke. May spit.
Cherry	***	Good	Burns slowly with reasonable heat and a pleasant smell.
Dogwood	***	Good	Burns well but smells a bit like a damp dog!
Elm	****	Very Good	Sometimes difficult to split. Slow burner, good heat with some smoke and good embers. Mix with faster burning wood and season thoroughly before use.
Eucalyptus	****	Very Good	Best split immediately after felling. Season well. Burns hot. Pleasant smell. Spits a bit. Bark makes excellent fire-lighters.
Fir	**	Fair	Be sure to season very thoroughly. Mix with a good hardwood.
Hawthorn	*****	Excellent	Burns slowly and very hot.
Hazel	***	Good	Season well. Burns fast with nutty aroma. Mix with slower burning wood.
Holly	***	Good	Best well-seasoned. Hot burn. Smells a bit so best in wood burners.
Hornbeam	****	Very good	Burns well and hot but hard to split. Very little smoke.
Horse Chestnut	**	Fair	Splits well. Reasonable heat but not very aromatic aroma. Spits a bit too.
Juniper	****	Very Good	Burns well with good heat, almost no smoke and a fragrant smell
Laburnum		WARNING!	Burns well with good heat, but it's poisonous, so only burn outdoors and avoid the smoke.
Larch	**	Fair	Burns well but spits quite a lot. Season well.

Suitability for burning by species (continued)

Name	Star	Grade	Comments rating
Laurel		WARNING!	Burns OK but it's poisonous, so only burn outdoors and avoid the smoke.
Lime	*	Low	Splits well but low quality firewood with unpleasant smell.
Maple	***	Good	Good heat and burns with little smoke.
Oak	*****	Excellent	Long lasting and slow burning. Splits well. High heat with little smoke and pleasant smell. Season thoroughly.
Pear	***	Good	Burns slowly with good heat and a pleasant smell.
Pine	**	Fair	Can spit and smoke. Short burn with medium heat. Season thoroughly.
Plane	***	Good	Useable firewood.
Poplar	*	Low	Lesser quality firewood. Hard to light, spits and smokes with low heat. Season thoroughly.
Rhododendron		WARNING!	Burns OK, but is poisonous. Only burn outside and avoid the smoke.
Rowan	***	Good	Burns well.
Spruce	*	Low	Low quality firewood. Smokes and spits with low heat. Season thoroughly.
Sweet Chestnut	**	Fair	Splits well. Burns well, but spits excessively. Not for open fires.
Sycamore (maple)	***	Good	Splits well. Burns quite well but quickly, with good heat.
Walnut	***	Good	Burns well with good heat and smell. Season well.
Willow	**	Fair	Season well. Short burn and smoky if not well seasoned. Unusual smell.
Yew		WARNING!	Useable and burns very well, but it's poisonous so only burn outdoors and avoid the smoke.

CHAPTER 19

Woodburning stoves for workshops

The following are specialist suppliers, who stock various kinds of wood-burning stoves suitable for use in workshops, sheds, cabins, boats, yurts and tipis.

Arada Ltd
Axminster, Devon
01297 35998
www.aradastoves.com
Acorn range of small stoves.

Axminster Tool Centre
Axminster, Devon
www.axminster.co.uk
Supply small stoves and workshop heaters. Nationwide availability.

Chase Heating Ltd
Worcestershire
01386 555333
www.chaseheating.co.uk
Nice little Villager Puffin stove.

Chilli Penguin Stoves
The Fire and Stove Showroom, Cardiff
02920 811478
www.chillipenguin.co.uk
Manufacturers of wood-burning stoves ideal for canal boats.

Four Dog Stoves
USA
www.fourdog.com
According to many yurt makers and users, this US company makes the very best yurt stoves for heating, cooking and hot water.

Hot Spot
Uttoxeter, Staffordshire
01899 565411
www.thehotspot.co.uk
Suppliers of Relax range of sawdust and wood offcut-burning workshop stoves.

KP Stoves
Lancashire
07764 813867
www.kpwoodburningstove.co.uk
Affordable. quality stoves, 18-80kW.

Natural Heating
Lanarkshire
01698 821111
www.naturalheating.co.uk
Large range of small stoves.

The Old Tool Store
Lincolnshire
01507 525697
www.oldtools.free-online.co.uk
Stock a unique, portable Frontier stove, featuring a hotplate for boiling water or cooking, with folding legs and detachable flue which stores inside the stove. There is even a carrying handle.

Salamander Stoves
Devon
01626 363507

www.salamanderstoves.com
Supplier of the Hobbit stove.

Stoves Online
Dartmouth
0845 2265754
www.stovesonline.co.uk
Wide range of small stoves and masses of helpful info on wood burning.

The Windy Smithy
Cullompton, Devon
07866 241783
www.windysmithy.co.uk
Nicely made and efficient small to medium sized, wood-burning stoves including two sizes of stoves/ovens and fire saucers.

Wood Burning Stoves Ltd
Ayrshire
01560 483966
www.woodburningstoveslimited.com
Nice range of small, affordable stoves.

Workshop Stoves
Dartmouth, Devon
0845 2265754
www.workshopstoves.co.uk
Greenheart and Bruno sawdust and wood off-cut burning stoves ideal for busy workshops.

CHAPTER 20

Twenty useful things to do with wood ash

Anyone who burns wood as a source of heat will be familiar with the grey ash residue left after the logs have burnt, but rather than being considered a waste product to be disposed of, think of wood ash as a multi-tasking asset, because wood ash contains:

lime, calcium, potassium, aluminium, magnesium, iron, phosphorus, manganese, sodium, nitrogen, arsenic, boron, cadmium, chromium, copper, lead, mercury, molybdenum, nickel, selenium and zinc.

Here are a few old and new uses for this versatile bi-product. (*Obviously, any addition to soil or compost should be based upon the current pH of your particular soil*).

1. **Compost additive** – sprinkle a thin dusting of ash on top of each layer of natural compost as you are building it up.

2. **Compost toilet flush** – keep a bucket of ash with a trowel handy in a compost toilet and sprinkle down the hole when you've done your business.

3. **Fertiliser** – used sparingly, wood ash increases the alkalinity of your soil. Calcium loving tomatoes will benefit from a quarter cupful of ash thrown in the hole when you're planting them.

Use ash to 'flush' compost toilets

4. **Slug and snail repellent** – place an unbroken line of ash around your fruit and vegetable plots. Replace regularly, particularly after rainfall.

5. **Moss killer on lawns** – a light dusting directly onto it.

6. **Controlling pond algae** – one tablespoon of ash per 1,000 gallons of pond water adds enough potassium to strengthen aquatic plants that compete with algae, and slow it down.

7. **Weevil repellent** – female weevils lay eggs inside dried goods like nuts, grains and dried beans. The larvae eat the inside and bore out. Something in ash discourages them doing this so the dry goods used to be packed in ash and the food would keep in good condition, particularly during long-term transportation.

8. **Soap** – soak ash in water, then mix it with animal fat and boil. Adding salt makes it harden as it cools. The end product is called Lye.

Ash can be used with fat to create soap

9. **Abrasive cleaner** – dip a damp rag into ash and rub it into silverware, brass or glass. Very effective on the inside of glass fireplace doors.

10. **Gritting** – sprinkle on slippery patches of ice on steps and drives. Ash helps to actually break down the ice. Keep a container of ash in the boot of your car in case you get stuck on icy roads. Just sprinkle ash in front of your front or back wheels and drive out over it.

11. **Spillage** – keep a bucket of ash handy in the garage and sprinkle onto any oil spillages.

12. **Tooth cleaner** – used before commercial toothpaste was available.

13. **Dehumidifier** – larger, half-burnt lumps of black ash (charcoal) can be put in a tin punched with holes. Helps absorb and reduce moisture in damp areas.

14. **Dust bath** – If you keep chickens, or if you encourage wild birds to visit your garden, put a small pile of ash on the ground (in the case of chickens) or in a suitable receptacle positioned well above the ground (for wild birds). A dust bath controls mites, lice etc, and the birds seem to have a lot of fun too.

Chickens taking a dust bath

15. **Odour control** – put some ash in an old (clean) sock and leave in trainers or sports kit bags to draw in the aroma. Rub a handful into your dog's coat to make it less whiffy.

16. **Water filter** – Probably only of use in bush craft circles, but lumps of black charcoal left over from an open bonfire can be crushed and used to filter river or stream water.

17. **Natural wall material** – Mix in with your straw, clay and cow dung when making cob walls.

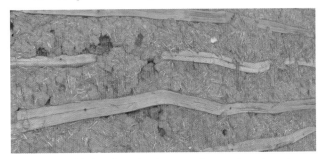

Ash can be added to the mix when creating a cob wall, such as this one

18. **Pottery glaze additive** – Used as a flux within a glaze, introducing silica to the glaze recipe. Firing at stoneware temperature produces subtle textures and colours.

19. **Base layer insulation for log fires** – If you are burning only logs in a fireplace or wood burner, a two inch deep layer on the base works well. After a burn, the next day, within the layer of ash, small hot coals sometime remain, sufficient to start a new burn even after twelve hours.

20. **Papier mache additive** – Add to the standard mix of PVA glue and water to obtain a textured finish; particularly attractive if you are painting afterwards.

CHAPTER 21

Charcoal burning – An ancient craft with a promising future

For over 5,000 years, man has been burning wood under controlled conditions until it carbonises into charcoal. Bronze Age smiths used charcoal to smelt bronze and iron as no other substance, when re-burnt, could reach the temperatures required to work metal and to melt it for casting. Weapons, artefacts and items of personal decoration were produced using charcoal as the primary heat source.

By-products from charcaoal's manufacture are recorded back in Roman times. They include pitch used for caulking clinker-built ships and waterproofing for timber exposed to wet conditions, such as pillars for buildings and bridges. The ancient Egyptians distilled pyroligeneous acid from the charcoal-making process which was an essential liquor used in the practice of embalming. They weren't short of sand either, and as charcoal can reach temperatures exceeding 1100 Celsius, it enabled them to fuse sand, sodium ash and limestone to make glass.

Later, the Chinese made gunpowder and fuse powder derived from alder, buckthorn and willow. Artist's charcoal is the result of burning de-barked willow.

More recently, the bi-products of charcoal production have been used in agriculture, horticulture, and the textile industry, where they play a part in solvents, oils, acids, insecticides and fertilisers. Charcoal is also used in the making of penicillin, vacuum flasks, artificial silk, paints and plastics, for sugar and metal refining, and in insulation in batteries and fridges. It is even included in certain foods. The list goes on. Charcoal is not just for barbecues and to draw with.

The incomplete burn

The basic principle of producing charcoal is to heat the wood in a controlled environment. By inhibiting the air in the processes, and eliminating all moisture, there is insufficient oxygen to cause complete combustion, and the wood is transformed into a solid block of black carbon.

In England, the traditional method of achieving this was to level the ground on a convenient forest site at a safe distance away from other trees (being careful not to include any animal burrows), clearing away all natural combustible growth around the perimeter and overhead.

First stack in a ring kiln

A wooden stake was driven into the ground representing the middle of the burn site and a string tied to it to mark out the circumference, giving a diameter of about 4.5m (15ft).

Round wood was used for the burn, the best being alder, buckthorn, oak and chestnut (although many other woods can be used nowadays such as ash, beech, hazel and hornbeam) after being allowed to season for at least six months.

The wood, up to 150mm (6in) in diameter, or split from larger stock, was cut into lengths of 1-1.22m (3 to 4 foot) and stacked upright, leaning at an angle against the central stake. Above this first layer, the remainder of the exposed stake was cut off and a sharpened stick, known as a motty-peg was driven into the top of the central stake to provide a rest for the second and third stacks which, when completed, would form a dome-like structure, 1.5 - 1.8m (5 to 6ft) high and 4.5m (15ft) across. The whole wooden stack was then completely covered in dried straw, leaves and small brash and bracken, which in turn was covered with the residues of previous burns and fine earth, rendering the structure air tight.

When ready to burn, the motty-peg was removed and the resulting hollow shaft (chimney) was filled with burning charcoal to ignite the stack. After a few hours, damp patches would appear around the walls, telling the burner that combustion had been achieved successfully and moisture was being forced out of the wood. The motty-peg hole was then sealed, after which the slow-burning stack was constantly monitored and repaired as small cracks appeared, particularly at the base.

The burning wood would initially emit thick white smoke, consisting mostly of water vapour, turning to a hazy blue, and disappearing altogether as the burn eventually became complete and the stack gradually subsided to one third of its original size.

Variations on this English method exist throughout Europe and the rest of the world, but as long as the basic principles are adhered to, the result is much the same.

In the past, the need for charcoal employed thousands of people throughout the woodlands of Europe during the summer season – cutting and stacking the wood at the end of each season and burning it April to November. Some were itinerant seasonal workers – whole families living in the woodland in temporary turf-covered huts, hired by woodland owners and fuel merchants. Others, already living nearby, would agree areas of woodland to work under contract and would then employ these workers. A lucky few were employed by the Crown. Fourteenth century records show burners were paid three pence per man per day. In the early 20th century, a man could earn up to thirty shillings a week – similar to other skilled artisans at that time.

Today, the dramatic decline of woodland produce and the use of other heat sources has left our woodlands virtually empty of charcoal burners. But, thankfully, a slow revival of the crafts and products of the woodland is starting to take root and charcoal is part of that.

Making use of our woodland resources

An article in The Times in June 1995 commented that 'the deciduous woodlands that supply the raw materials for charcoal should benefit from this gradual cottage industry

A traditional stack of charcoal beginning to burn

revival. Britain in particular has a vast resource of broadleaf woods that have received little if any management for more than half a century. Ancient coppice stools, formerly cut to the ground on a regular seven to fifteen year cycle, have towered into high, dense, unkempt canopies. Overgrown coppice woods may provide a valuable haven for rare insects and fungi, but they also inhibit the growth of young trees and exclude many spring flowers and butterflies. So, providing sufficient areas are left untouched, cutting down the excess growth for charcoal will help restore the balance of woodland ecology'.

Yet much of the charcoal used in Britain, which is widely used as filters or in chemical processes, as well as in agriculture and horticulture, is being imported. An estimated 90% of the approximately 70,000 tons (*Forestry & British Timber* March 1996) of charcoal used in Britain is imported from as far away as Indonesia, South America and West Africa. Some comes from precious Indonesian mangrove forests which are not sustainably managed. Their crude method of production is so inefficient that barely over 50% reaches pyrolisation – the other 50% (still unconverted wood) just emits clouds of smoke into our atmosphere.

Birds Magazine (Oct 1995), pointed out that "British charcoal, by contrast, is of a higher quality, with a carbon content of up to 90% and there is enough coppice woodland in south-east England alone to supply the whole of the barbecue charcoal market with a superior product. British native hardwoods produce excellent lumpwood charcoal, which requires no lighter fuel and gives a good heat within 15-20 minutes. Even the dust residue is in demand for high grade steel production."

So why import? The *British Charcoal Group* points to the 90 million cubic metres of Britain's broadleaved standing resource, which is estimated to grow at around two million cubic metres per annum and only half of which is used by the manufacturing industry. 'It would seem therefore million metres of broadleaved timber is available each year for uses that could include charcoal'. (*Forestry & British Timber, March 1996*).

Starting the burn in a ring kiln

In addition, with so much overstood coppice in our woodlands, and given the fact that modern designs of charcoal burners can now produce good charcoal from low quality wood, if we were to re-introduce coppicing as a viable practice for small woodland businesses and wood fuel, the sheer glut from the initial re-coppicing operation would get us off to a flying start.

New designs of burners

Just as the wood-burning stove has evolved in design in recent years, so have charcoal burners, becoming much more efficient and easier to use.

Nobody burns charcoal using the stack method any more, unless for training or demonstration purposes, preferring to use metal ring kilns with lids. Recent innovative designs of non-industrial sized charcoal burners (known as retorts) reduce the wood to charcoal conversion rate from around 7:1 (7 tons of wood to produce 1 ton of charcoal) to 4:1. A modern day retort is a quite sophisticated burning chamber, typically double-walled and insulated, easier to load than the metal ring kilns, and capable of efficiently converting lower grades of timber into high quality charcoal. They emit much less smoke and up to 75% fewer pollutants, and can approach 100% pyrolisation with little to no ash or waste. Being easier to load reduces time, and there are no special skills required to operate them. Each burn of a typically-sized retort reduces the time from the 48 hours

British charcoal, produced by Steve King

a traditional metal ring kiln would take, to just 24 hours. The traditional 'stack' method required 72 hours to complete the cycle.

In the past, it has been normal to site a woodland kiln in a convenient position and cut and transport the logs to the burn site. Some modern retorts are designed to be mounted on a trailer and transported to wherever they are required. Like portable saw mills, the mobile retort has greater flexibility and enables sharing by neighbouring charcoal producers, potentially reducing the production overheads and encouraging nearby woodland owners to produce their own charcoal.

New networks for distribution

Now there are over 300 producers of charcoal in the UK (2011 figures), as opposed to a mere handful a decade ago. Charcoal makers are seeing the advantages of co-operative marketing, and actively sell and distribute their excellent product on a regional basis using shared websites. Many make their products available in their local area, from petrol stations, farm shops, garden centres and recreational activity sites, which not only keeps the cost of transport and pollution to a minimum, but promotes local product loyalty, and creates a few more jobs in the area.

Charcoal retorts in Poland

So, perhaps in its own small way, British charcoal production and distribution could provide another example of how enterprising people can successfully re-introduce a traditional woodland craft while revitalising our dormant woodlands, discouraging unnecessary imports, providing local employment and promoting a sense of local awareness and community.

CHAPTER 22

The hedgerows of Britain

At least ten different kinds of berries hung on the branches where I stood. There were the blackberry, and the common hawthorn. There was the elderberry which makes such good wine, and alongside is the scarlet seed-cases of the wild rose. There were the black clusters of the privet and the buckthorn, and the juicy crimson of the guelder rose. Crab apples grew nearby, and the spindle-tree hung out its pink fruit. Over them all twined the black and white bryony, each with its crimson berries. It was a wonderful sight, that patch of hedge, with everything on it glistening in the sun after a morning shower.

Robert Gibbings – *Sweet Thames Run Softly* (1940)

Hedge sparrow nest

Hedgerows provide the structure of our British landscape. They are unique, vibrant, natural ecosystems that have provided shelter, food, medicine and wood to mammals, birds and insects since they began to be planted as early as 4000 to 2500 years BC.

Collectively there are estimated to be up to half a million miles of them in the British Isles, playing host to a wide diversity of plant and wildlife. It is also thought that a staggering 1.8 million trees and shrubs occupy our hedgerows – a third of them over a century old. About 25 species of tree and shrub can be found in them (600 plant species in total), while 65 species of bird, 40 species of butterfly and 20 types of mammal make hedgerows their home.

Apart from forming natural fencing to enclose livestock and provide them with shelter from the wind, hedgerows also play a substantial and often overlooked role in stabilising our environment by storing up to 800kg of CO_2 per kilometre of new hedgerow, locking it in for decades. They also help to prevent soil erosion (despite the studious efforts of dear little fluffy rabbits to decimate our hedgerow banks).

Dr M. Hooper devised a rule of thumb method in the

A hawthorn hedge in the early stages of the hedge-laying process

1960s for dating the age of an established hedgerow. Pace out a 30 yard length and then count the different number of 'woody' species in it. Then multiply the number by 110 to estimate the hedgerow's age.

A very brief history

The word 'hedge' comes from the old English *haga*, meaning enclosure, which is derived from the Anglo Saxon word for hawthorn fruit.

Written evidence of their existence can be found as far back as the 12th century. The Romans – already planters of hedgerows in their native Italy – instigated the planting of vast amounts of them after they turned up and decided to occupy Britain for a while, although there is strong evidence of pre-Roman hedgerow existence, and post-Roman planting continued with the Anglo Saxons.

The enclosures act resulted in the common people being literally thrown off the land they had collectively cared for for generations. This overwhelmingly benefitted the rich landowners, who gave over the enclosed fields to intensive farming of crops and livestock. This also saw the planting of an additional 200,000 miles (4.5 million acres) of new hedgerow over the 18th and 19th centuries, effectively doubling those planted in the previous 500 years, according to Oliver Rackham in his book *Trees and*

Woodlands in the British Landscape.

The 1950s saw massive grubbing out of hedgerows as fields became larger, and modern machinery, requiring more space to manoeuvre, replaced the horse. Dutch Elm disease decimated this quintessentially British species in the 1970s and 80s and with the sharp decline in true hedgerow management in Britain, including traditional hedge laying and dry stone walling, the future of hedgerows may be in doubt. Despite this, the hardy British hedgerow still survives, and there is some encouraging interest in them being re-kindled, aided by many very good organisations dedicated to their wellbeing, working in partnership with farmers, landowners and the public.

Since this book is predominantly about trees, below is a list of typical British trees and shrubs to be found in our wonderful hedgerows.

British hedgerow trees and shrubs

Ash	Wild Cherry	Hawthorn	Privet
Alder	Crab Apple	Hornbeam	Spindle
Aspen	Elm	Hazel	Dog Rose
Buckthorn	Gorse	Lime	Wayfaring Tree
Beech	Dogwood	Holly	Goat Willow
Birch	Elder	Field Maple	Wild Service
Blackthorn	Guelder Rose	Oak	Yew

CHAPTER 23

The hedgerow superstore

Traditional applications for hedgerow, trees and shrubs

Not so long ago, the common country people of Britain relied heavily upon the natural resources of the local hedgerows for their medicinal, culinary and artistic needs. For hundreds of years, this wisdom was passed down through generations. Now, this knowledge is all but lost to most people. The following is a guide to some of the historical uses of the hedgerow.

Note: Many of these uses, particularly related to food and medication, are ancient and should not be used for these purposes now, unless you are in full possession of recipes, proportions, toxicity and application information from an expert source.

Species	Latin name	Some traditional uses
Alder	Alnus glutinosa	Fresh leaves are a natural insect and flea repellent. Bark and leaves used to combat cold symptoms, sooth burns, inflammation and some skin conditions, sore throats, mouth ulcers, bruises and swellings. Dye from bark, fruit and leaves.
Apple	Malus	Leaves and fruit. Poultices for sore eyes, asthma and lung congestions, laxatives, tea, juice and alcoholic drinks. Pectin for setting jellies and jams. 'Verjuice' produced to treat scalds and strains.
Ash	Fraxinus excelsior	Bark for yellow dye and arthritis and rheumatism, medication for leprous or scabby heads. Leaf for poultice to protect against adder bites, as a laxative, liver and spleen cleanser, apparently good for the immune system. Seeds (keys) make chutney.
Bay	Laurus nobilis	Leaves for bruises, coughs and colds, dandruff, muscle sprains and stiffness, indigestion and flatulence and famous condiment in cooking.
Beech	Fagus sylvatica	Nuts for human and pig consumption and vegetable oil. Young leaves distilled to make a liqueur, or eaten in salads. Oil and tar for antiseptic, coughs and skin diseases.
Birch, Silver	Betula pendula	Aspirin is derived from the bark and oil of the bark for an insect repellent. Tea from leaves effective against rheumatism, kidney and bladder stones, an antiseptic gargle and inhalant. Sap used for a shampoo and in wine making.

Juniper berries

A walnut on the tree

Hazelnuts in Yerevan, Armenia

Hawthorn flowers

Species	Latin name	Some traditional uses
Blackthorn (sloe)	Prunus spinosa	Berries for blue and brown colouring and for sloe gin and wine. Leaves for antiseptic mouthwash, eye lotion. Bark for a relaxing tea. Permanent ink.
Wild Plum	Prunus domestica	Fruit for jams and jellies.
Bullace (wild damson)	Prunus domestica insititia	Purple dye. Jam, jelly, damson gin.
Buckthorn	Rhamnus spinosa	Bark for blue and green dye.
Cedar	Thuja Plicata	Used by ancient Celts to preserve the heads of enemies taken in battle.
Cherry (wild)	Prunus avium	Resin used as chewing gum and in syrup and cough mixture. Bark utilised in rum and brandy as well as for colds, fevers, worm infestations, wounds, burns and headaches.
Chestnut (sweet)	Castanea sativa	Nuts for flour. Leaves for diarrhoea, rheumatism, whooping cough and menstrual bleeding.
Chestnut (horse)	Aesculus hippocastanum	Seed and sometimes bark used for bruises, varicose veins and skin toner.
Crab Apple	Malus sylvestris	Fruit for jellies, jams and cider.
Dogrose	Rosa canica canina	Petals for jwine, tea, brandy, vinegar, honey, Turkish delight, jelly, jam and crystalised fruits. An excellent source of vitamin C, usually as rosehip syrup.
Elder	Sambucus nigra	Berries for jam, sauces, wine and a source of vitamin C. Bark and flowers for green, black and purple dye. Flowers for drinks and fritters. Decoctions of bark, leaves, berries or flowers for the complexion, as a diuretic and for bruises and sunburn, shampoo, ear drops, a laxative and relief from headaches and colds.
Guilder Rose	Vibernum Opulus	Sauces and drinks. Jam. Bark used to treat cramp.
Hawthorn	Crataegus monogyna	Flowers, fruits, leaves. Sauces and drinks from the berries. Leaves used for salad vegetables and a soothing tea which aids circulation. Liquor from flowers. Berries for jellies, wines, liqueurs and a sort of ketchup. Blossom is the original wedding confetti.
Hornbeam	Carpinus Betulas	Yellow dye from bark.
Hazel	Coryllus avellana	Nuts for food and to cure coughs and sore throats. Leaves for salad. Also used for diarrhoea, bruising and varicose veins.
Heather	Calluna Vulgaris	Flowers for perfume, migraine and menstrual relief, honey, beer.
Holly	Ilex aquifolium	Leaves and bark for poultices, and stimulating the body, cleansing drink and winter fodder for cattle. Roots for coughs and tuberculosis. Berries dried and powdered to dust over bleeding wounds.
Juniper	Juniperus communis	Berries for jam and flavouring for game dishes and spirits. Incense. An antiseptic, easing flatulence, coughs, cramps, gout, rheumatism and sore throats. General pain relief. Expels worms. Treats sores and scabs.
Laurel	Lauraceae	Treatment for kidney and bladder stones, pancreas, spleen and liver problems. Insect bites and stings, sore throats and lung problems.

Species	Latin name	Some traditional uses
Larch	Larix	Bark for chest infections, leaves and bark for headache treatments.
Lime	Tilia	Edible leaves for salads, flowers for medicinal tea and honey. Leaf infusion good for colds and flu, relaxation, stress relief, reduces cholesterol. Bark good for stomach, diarrhoea and urinary problems.
Maple	Acer	Depending on species – sap for wine, skin care products and syrup from sap. Bark for colds and coughs, cramps, diarrhoea.
Medlar	Mespilus germanica	Wine
Mulberry	Morus nigra	Jams and wines
Scots Pine	Pinus sylvestris	Antiseptic tars and oils, protection of cell damage, blocked sinuses and respiratory disorders, antiseptic.
Pine	Pinus	Oil from needles to treat asthma, bronchitis. Also used as scent in cleaning fluids and fresh air spray. Disinfectants.
Plum (wild)	Prunus domestica	Bark for dye.
Rowan	Sorbus aucuparia	Berries for jam, wine. Bark an antiseptic and astringent, relieves diarrhoea and sore throats. A good source of vitamin C, once used against scurvy.
Sessile Oak	Quercus robur	Acorns an astringent, skin cleanser and antiseptic. Also used for flour and coffee substitute. Bark for tannin. Juice from leaves an antiseptic, as is the bark. Acorns and bark combined as an antidote to poison and relief from menstrual cycle discomfort. Bark for diarrhoea, haemorrhoids and wounds.
Sycamore	Acer pseudoplatanus	Wine from sap.
Privet	Ligustrum vulgare	Yellow and green dyes.
Vine	Vinea	Grapes for dried fruit, coughs and chest disorders, wine and brandy, sore mouths, poultices, kidney and bladder stones.
Walnut	Juglans regia	Nuts for oil and pickle, Unripe nuts for worm infestations. Leaves for wine, skin conditions, insect repellent and constipation relief. Bark used as a toothbrush, fights plaque, bacteria and gum disease.
Willow	Salix atrocinerea	Yellow dye from bark, also aspirin is derived from the bark, for relief of pain and inflammation. Leaves used for effective dandruff shampoo. Sap and leaves for antiseptic gargle, eye lotion and inhalant for sinus and catarrh.
Witch Hazel	Hamamelis virginiana	Distilled water for sores, grazes and stopping bleeding. Eyewash, sore throats, bleeding gums, haemorrhoids.
Yew	Taxus baccata	***Warning – All parts are poisonous***. Recently used as a cancer drug. Native American and Himalayan dwellers however, used it (albeit in very small quantities) for rheumatism, bronchial complaints, heart problems, cramps and stomach disorders.

CHAPTER 24
Hedgerow liqueurs

Our native trees and shrubs are a veritable larder of raw produce just waiting to be enjoyed. The most common alcoholic drink made from this bountiful free fare is wine, which, although documented in numerous publications, can be notoriously tricky to get right. Sometimes the end result, after many months of diligent processing, ranges between the absolutely sublime and the buttock-clenching, mouth-puckering opposite.

The best tip is that – like everything natural and fabulous – it takes time. A good homemade wine will require at least 18 months before reaching maturity. Let nature takes its course and you will be rewarded with an end product that has real character and subtle flavour. In the meantime, why not try some recipes from the native woodlands and hedgerows that require very little time and skill to produce, yet nevertheless deliver quite astonishing results?

Elderflower champagne and cordial are best made and consumed fresh. The beauty of some of our seasonal ingredients lies in the fact that we can only harvest, process and consume them during the season in which they live, when they are at their very best, intensifying our expectation and enjoyment of them. So, in my opinion, elderflower champagne and cordial – being representative of the summer – should not be preserved for consumption outside of it.

Beech, sloe and elderberry liqueur, meanwhile, benefit greatly from slow marinating. They should be made in quantity when the fruit is at its best and then left alone for

Elder flowers

at least a year. When it's time to make some the following season, you can drink some of last year's stock and keep the remainder to mature a further year. This way you build up a superb stock of varying vintages over a period of years. Remember, the longer you keep it, the better it gets. Remember – willpower!

Elderflower cordial

Aromatic, thirst quenching – a versatile summer classic. Harvest the fresh, creamy white sprays in June or July when they are firm, and before any of the small flowers start to discolour and drop.

20 to 30 whole fresh sprays of elderflowers
zest of 2 unwaxed lemons and 1 orange
2 litres (3 pints) water
caster sugar
fresh lemon juice
about an inch fresh ginger, grated (optional)

Put the elderflower sprays into a large plastic container (a clean bucket, perhaps) with the lemon and orange zest, add 2 litres of boiled water, cover and leave overnight.

Strain the liquid through muslin and measure the amount of liquid you have. Transfer to a large pan, adding 175g caster sugar and 55ml (2fl oz) lemon juice for every 570ml (1 pint) of liquid. At this stage, you can also add the grated ginger, to give it a subtle, back-of-the-throat warming tang. Heat and bring to a simmer, then leave to cool. Skim off any scum on the surface. Filter through muslin into a clean container.

Filter again into clean bottles though a funnel and seal with corks or screw tops. This will keep for several weeks in the fridge, but if you want it to last longer you will need to add a teaspoon of tartaric acid when you add the sugar and lemon juice and make sure that the bottles are properly sterilised.

Serve chilled with still or carbonated water (1 part cordial to 5 to 8 parts water, according to taste) and ice. Alternatively, add gin or vodka, tonic, ice and a slice of lemon for a seriously refreshing, grown-up drink.

Elderflower champagne

A very lively, refreshing, mildly alcoholic summer drink. Harvest the fresh, creamy white sprays in June or July when they are firm, and before any of the small flowers start to discolour and drop.

20-30 whole fresh sprays (or heads) of elderflowers
1 kg sugar
the juice and zest of 2 unwaxed lemons
10 litres water
2 tablespoons of white wine vinegar

Boil two litres of water and pour into a clean plastic bucket. Add the sugar and stir to dissolve. Add the remaining 8 litres of water together with the rest of the ingredients and give it all a good stir. Cover and leave for 24 hours, gently stirring about three times a day.

After 24 hours, if the brew is NOT frothing on the surface (natural fermentation) stir in one tablespoon of baker's yeast dissolved in warm water. Leave for five days, stirring gently from time to time.

Strain liquid through muslin into suitable clean containers, either plastic screw top bottles, or genuine Cava or Champagne bottles with stoppers and wires, which you can buy from a homemade wine supplies shop.

Leave for eight days, during which time the champagne will continue to ferment in the bottle. If you have used plastic screw top bottles, gently let out excess gas if you see the bottles expanding too much.

The champagne is now ready to refrigerate and serve. If using proper champagne bottles, opening them is just as spectacular as opening a bottle of real champagne.

Serve chilled in champagne flutes.

Beech leaf liqueur

This is a very unusual, eyebrow-raising, delicious drink. Who would have thought that leaves could taste so good! Harvest the young leaves in the early spring.

2 - 3 large handfuls of beech leaves
570ml gin
150g caster sugar
boiling water
1 - 2 tablespoons brandy

Pack a Kilner jar or suitable lidded container two-thirds full of young, green, fresh beech leaves. Fill nearly up to the top with a good quality gin and leave for three weeks in a cool dark place. Shake every day.

Filter the gin through muslin into a clean container and discard the leaves. For every 570ml (1 pint) of gin, add 150g (5oz) caster sugar, dissolved in 285ml (half a pint) boiling water. Mix together, and add a tablespoon of good quality brandy. Taste and add another tablespoon or two of brandy if desired.

Leave for at least a month. Strain through muslin into bottles and leave for as long as you can before drinking. It will benefit from being left for a year or more.

Delicious chilled, on its own or with tonic water, and a slice of lemon or lime.

Variations:

Beech leaf liqueur with vodka
As above but replace gin with vodka.

Lime leaf liqueur
As above, but use lime leaves in a vodka marinade!

Sloe berries on a blackthorn hedge

Sloe gin (or vodka)

Traditionally, gin is used, but if you don't particularly like gin, vodka is a great alternative. Harvest the sloes in September or October, or whenever you find them plump and ripe. This recipe works well with damsons as well as sloes.

1kg (2lb) ripe sloes
225g to 350g (8 to 12oz) sugar according to taste
1.5 litres (3 pints) good quality gin or vodka

Apparently it is advisable to harvest the sloes just after the first frost, but with our ever changing climate it's best to harvest them when they are plump and ripe and then freeze them before use. The freezing will simulate the frost.

Wipe the sloes and prick them several times with a cocktail stick and put them in a preserving jar or suitable lidded container. Ok, it's fiddly and time consuming, but there really is no substitute for the slow release of the sloe juice.

Alternatively, if you can't be fussed with such a fiddly job, freeze the sloes then remove and very lightly crush before putting them into the container. I say very lightly crush, because if you smash them to a pulp, you'll end up extracting all the tannins as well and it won't taste as fantastic.

Add the sugar and gin or vodka, mix thoroughly and seal tightly. Leave in a cool, dark place for a minimum of three months, shaking regularly. Filter through a double layer of muslin into a clean container and taste for sweetness. Add extra sugar dissolved in a little hot water if required. Filter through muslin into bottles and put down to rest for 1 to 5 years.

Elderberry gin (or vodka)

A delightful, tangy alternative to sloe gin using elderberry in a vodka or gin infusion. Harvest the elderberries in September or October, when ripe and plump, before the birds beat you to it.

1 kg elderberries
225g sugar – Muscovado can be nice
1 teaspoon (unwaxed) lemon zest
2 tablespoons lemon juice
1 cup water
1.5 litres good quality vodka or gin

Elderberries in the hedgerows

Lightly crush the berries and sugar together and put into a lidded preserving jar. Add the lemon zest, juice and good quality vodka or gin. Mix thoroughly and seal. Age a minimum of one month in a cool, dark place, shaking daily. Filter through a double layer of muslin into a clean container and taste for sweetness. Add more sugar, dissolved in a little hot water if desired. Leave one week. Filter through muslin into bottles.

Age for at least one year before drinking. Drink chilled.

Other wild fruit liquers

Put the ingredients for each recipe into a Kilner jar or lidded container, stir and seal. Leave for 2-3 months, shaking daily for the first month or so, and then weekly. Strain through double muslin into clean, glass screw-top bottles.

Blackberry Gin/Vodka
2lb (1kg) blackberries
8oz (225g) sugar
1.5 pints (750 ml) gin or vodka

Blackcurrant Gin/Vodka
12oz (350g) blackcurrants
2oz (50g) raspberries
1 clove
½ inch (12mm) cinnamon stick
8oz (225g) sugar
2 pints (1ltr) gin or vodka

Raspberry or Strawberry Vodka
Fresh raspberries or strawberries to half fill your Kilner jar
Enough good vodka to almost fill up the jar

Blackberry Cordial
(from Mary Norwak's *The Complete Book of Home Preserving* (1978) – Ward Lock Ltd)
This is a bit like a whisky mac. You could also drink it warm for a comforting winter nightcap.
6lb (2.5kg) blackberries
6oz (150g) sugar
1oz (25g) grated root ginger
Rind of 1 unwaxed lemon
3 pints (1.5ltrs) whisky of your choice

Damson Cordial
(from Mary Norwak's *The Complete Book of Home Preserving* (1978) – Ward Lock Ltd)

Depending on the size of kilner jar you use, half fill it with damsons, add 4oz (100g) sugar, 1 vanilla pod, 2 inches/5cm unwaxed lemon peel, a small piece of cinnamon stick and root ginger to each 1lb of fruit. Fill up with brandy and seal. Leave for 6 months. Filter through double muslin into clean, glass screw cap bottles.

CHAPTER 25

A natural woodland palette

Dye colours derived from tree parts

Woodland trees, plants and herbs have long been a good free source of natural dye for colouring wool, linen and silk, and for making writing inks; and have provided a reliable supply. Vegetable, plant and tree dyes benefit from the addition of mordant – a metallic salt substance which, after it is applied to the fabric, allows the dye to be absorbed.

Wool coloured by natural dyes

Species	Colours obtained							
	Root	Bark	Wood	Leaf	Shoots	Fruit	Seed	Nut
Alder		red	pink		yellow		green	
Alder Buckthorn		yellow brown						`
Apple		yellow						
Pear		yellow						
Ash		yellow						
Cherry		yellow				blue grey		
Elder		black		green	blue lilac violet			
Juniper					olive brown			
Larch				brown				
Oak		black brown purple yellow						
Pine							red yellow	
Plum		red brown				blue		
Privet				yellow		blue green		
Rowan		black				blue		
Spindle						red yellow green		
Walnut	brown			brown				brown
Willow	purple red							

CHAPTER 26

Tree folklore and myth

There's something in a noble tree –
What shall I say? A Soul?
For 'tis not a form, or aught we see
In leg or branch, or bole.
Some presence, though not understood,
Dwells there always, and seems
To be aquatinted with our mood,
And mingles in our dreams.

Samual Valentine Cole

Much is believed, felt and spoken of trees.

Considering the sheer magnificence of these most important living things, it is little wonder that since ancient times, folklore and myth have been attached to trees wherever they grow upon our planet.

That they have a presence is unquestionable. That they have a spirit? The Celts thought so. Druids based their magic around them and venerated trees as the link between heaven and earth. The very word druid derives from dru (oak) and -wid (truth or knowledge). Witches also take trees as the centre of their magic. Many of those who work and live in the woodlands have felt a presence in the trees, often referring to it as genii or faeries.

A better name for the spirit life force of a tree could be dryad, perhaps, which originates in Greek mythology. In his book *Wandlor*, Alferian Gwydion MacLir describes "Dryad as in the tree, growing within it and a trans-temporal and trans-spatial force living simultaneously in the astral dimension and our known world, representative of the four elements, earth, fire, water, air combined into a quintessence that is a living organism."

Some believe that when a tree branch falls off, or is cut, the dryad spirit is still in the wood and will remain in it. Others say that the tree withdraws its spirit from the branch when it senses the impending loss, although there is general agreement that the spirit remains in the branch to some degree and can be awoken by enchantment after it has been crafted into a wand.

The *Green Man* is a legendary pagan deity found in many cultures throughout the world, also known as *Green Jack, Jack-in-the-green*, or *Green George*. Represented by a face surrounded by, or including leaves, vines and branches, sometimes sprouting from the nose, mouth and nostrils, the Green Man appears in drawings, carving and sculptures as a generic symbol representing rebirth, renaissance, and the cycles of natural growth each spring.

The Daghdha (day-a) is the Celtic god and guardian of the trees, whom you must thank after communicating with tree spirits, aided by your Ogham stick, a carved stick used in many Celtic rituals.

In Scottish folklore, the *Ghillie Dhu*, a 'dark haired man', is a shy faerie guardian spirit of the trees, similar to the Green Man in England and Wales. He is clothed in leaves and moss, with a particular liking for birch trees.

In Japan, they have a word, kodama, for the 'spirit of a tree', involving a feeling of special kinship with the heart of the tree.

Roger Deakin's excellent book '*Wildwood*' informs us that woodland people can tell the species of a tree from the rustling sound it makes in the wind.

We still traditionally buy, decorate, and place presents around our Christmas pine, spruce or fir trees, and have heard of the Yule log, even though most of us don't really know where the practices originated from. Actually, the Christmas tree thing originated in Germany, and the Celts are responsible for the Yule log.

Finally, although woven willow may now replace the traditional elm box, most of us depart into the cosmos encased by wood!

Apple

The apple is the oldest cultivated tree in Europe. The original native tree for England was the crab apple, *malus sylvestris*. The common variety as we know it today was introduced by the Romans, via Western Asia. The apple is generally known as the forbidden fruit in the Garden of Eden, which gave Adam and Eve their knowledge of good and evil, but the original fruit referred to may have been a fig or a pomegranate, and it was only as the tale travelled to Western Europe that it became an apple.

Apples also appear in many myths from around the world. In Norse tradition, the goddess *Lounn* provides apples to the gods to give them eternal youthfulness and fertility. In Greek mythology, *Heracles*, as part of his 12 labours was required to travel to the gardens of *Hesperides* and pick the golden apples off the *Tree of Life*. The Greek goddess of discord, *Eris*, used one such golden apple to indirectly cause the Trojan wars.

Cut through the centre, the core of the apple creates a five-pointed star shape, which druids and witches have used in rituals as a natural pentagram. Mistletoe, the druids' most sacred plant, is often found on apple trees (see the section on Misteltoe in this chapter).

In the Gaelic festival, *Samhain*, which falls between the autumn equinox and the winter solstice (around the end of the harvest), apples were often a part of the customs. It was said that if a young maiden peeled an apple in front of a mirror and threw the continuous peel over her left shoulder, she would be able to see the initial of her future husband made by the peel on the floor.

We have all heard that 'an apple a day keeps the doctor away', which is perhaps not surprising, as apples contain vital vitamins, minerals and antioxidants, which balance digestion, stimulate blood production and the metabolism of fats, and cleanse the system. Less well known is the advice that to eliminate a wart, you can rub the two halves of an apple on it, and then bury the apple halves.

Alder

Probably derived its name from the Old English word *ealdor* meaning *chief* or the Old German word *elawer* meaning *reddish-yellow,* referring to the colour ranges of the wood.

The alder is sacred to the mythological Celtic hero *Bran the Blessed* and is associated with the Roman god *Saturn*.

Because its pith is easily removed from small twigs, alder wood makes good whistles, pipes and flutes for use in music and magic ceremonies. Several shoots bound together and trimmed to the desired length, produce a note suitable for summoning, controlling and banishing air elementals, hence the old phrase 'whistling up the wind'.

Celts also favoured the wood to make shields, possibly because of its striking orange-red colour when worked.

Ash

The name 'ash' may relate to fire, as this tree, like oak, is said to attract lightning.

Ash's Latin name *fraxinus* and old English name *aesc* are both names for spear. Not surprisingly, ash wood has always been the first choice for spear shafts and *Odin, Poseidon* and *Thor* each wielded a spear of ash.

The wood is also sacred to the Welsh sea god, *Llyr,* and the Greek goddess *Nemesis* carried an ash wand as a symbol of divine justice.

Ash is the tree from which the hanged man is suspended in Tarot decks.

Irish folklore warned that shadows from an ash tree would damage crops.

In Europe, it was believed that ash leaves, or a circle drawn with an ash branch repelled snakes.

The ash tree also features very strongly in Norse mythology. It was known as the World Tree and considered a good omen. It was believed that a fermented mead known as 'The Mead of Inspiration', derived from ash, would turn the drinker into a scholar.

There are also many old sayings and practices associated with the ash tree and its leaves. For example, it was believed in certain parts of northern England that if a woman placed an ash leaf in her left shoe, she would immediately meet her future husband.

Even Ash, even Ash,
I pluck thee off the tree;
The first young man that I do meet
My lover he shall be.

A season's rainfall was forecast by which species showed its spring leaves first – oak or ash. Usually, oak is first.

Oak before Ash, we're in for a splash;
Ash before Oak, we're in for a soak.

A wart can be removed in magic by sticking a pin in it that has previously been thrust into an ash tree while chanting:

Ashen tree, Ashen tree,
Pray take these warts off of me.

The pins are then stuck back into the ash tree and left.

In Saxon times, it was believed that splitting a young Ash, holding it open with wedges and passing naked, diseased children through the aperture would assist in a cure – particularly if the tree survived after it was bound back together. New born babies were often given a small spoonful of ash sap.

A more macabre medieval practice existed involving the boring of a deep hole in an Ash trunk, pushing in an unfortunate live shrew-mouse and plugging up the hole. After a few incantations, this humble tree would be venerated by all and be referred to as a Shrew-ash.

The explanation for this pre-RSPCA ritual lies in the fact that it was long thought that wherever a shrew-mouse crawled over sleeping livestock, the poor animal would become afflicted with anguish, and the potential loss of the use of the limb on which the timid, innocent shrew had inadvertently walked upon. Whenever a limping cow, sheep or horse was discovered, a trip to the Shrew-ash would provide a blessed branch with which to brush gently over the afflicted limb to alleviate pain and affect a cure. (Source – *The Forest Trees of Britain* – Rev. C.A.Johns)

Aspen/Poplar

Known as the 'shivering tree' due to the apparent continuous trembling of its leaves. The Greek word *kepkis* which means shuttle, was given to the tree because of the action of the leaves which quiver back and forth continuously.

O woman! In our hours of ease,
Uncertain, coy, and hard to please,
And variably as the shade,
By the light, quivering Aspen made!
Sir Walter Scott

Bay

In ancient Greece, the bay tree was dedicated to the god *Apollo* and his son *Aesculapius* and was seen as sacred. Aesculapius was the god of medicine and the bay was believed to have curative powers. People used to carry a branch of a bay tree above their heads in a thunderstorm to protect against lightening.

Beech

Beech is known as the lovers' tree because the smooth bark is very suitable for carving initials and other such graffiti.

If a beech stick is carved with your greatest wish, some say that it will come true.

Oh Rosalind! These trees shall be my books,
And in their barks my thoughts I'll character;
That every eye, which in this forest looks,
Shall see thy virtue witnessed everywhere,
Run, run, Orlando; carve on every tree,
The fair, the chaste, and unexpressive she.
As you like it – **William Shakespeare**

Birch

The birch is sacred to the Norse god Thor and Roman goddess *Diana*, as well as appearing frequently in Gaelic folksongs, often in association with death, faeries or returning from the grave.

Birch wood is used to make Rune sets, divination rods and wands.

The birch is the national tree of Russia and the State tree of New Hampshire USA.

In Russian forests, Forest Devils, or the *genii* of the forest preferred the birch tree. Cutting the branches and placing them in a circle with the points toward the centre was said to enable the genii to appear. Placing a birch branch above the door of a house protected against evil spirits and misfortune.

The birch bark has long been used for writing on due to its smooth and durable surface and texture. Many ancient fossilised examples have been found across the world.

Not so long ago, in 20th century England, birch tree twigs were bound in bundles for 'birching', a form of corporal punishment.

Cherry

In European folklore, you repeat this is a chant when counting the number of cherry stones you have left on your plate to determine when you are to marry:

1 stone – this year
2 stones – next year
3 stones – sometime
4 stones – never
......and so on (repeat)

If the owner of a cherry tree allowed a woman who had recently given birth to her first child to eat the first cherry to ripen, he would be assured of a good crop that season.

Danish folklore believed that Demons lived in Cherry trees.

In Serbian folklore, the *Vila* are beautiful female creatures, similar to fairies and elves who live in the hills amongst cherry trees. These mythical creatures have long flowing hair and are clad in white. They love to sing and dance and when travelling through the woodland, they make a similar sound to that of a woodpecker.

Folklore has it that should a parent discipline a child and say that they have a devil in them, or should be sent to him, the Vila would have the right to take the child, perhaps to protect it.

Cherry! Dearest Cherry!
Higher lift thy branches
Under which the Vilas
Dance their magic roundels.
Unknown

Elder

The name derived from the Anglo-Saxon word *aeld* meaning *fire*. The hollow branches of elder were used to kindle fires by blowing through them. The hollow twigs were no doubt also used by mischievous children as the very first peashooters.

Linked with death, birth and rebirth, branches of the elder tree were often used for funeral pyres.

The elder was sometimes thought to exude negative forces. A being known as the Elder Mother (*Hylde-Moer*) guarded the elder tree and her permission had to be sought before cutting one down. Even then, some foresters of old would avoid them, not even daring to touch them for fear of stirring the Hylde-Moer's wrath.

The elder has also been associated with witches. It was believed that they could turn themselves into elder trees, and the wood was said to be the most suitable wood for a witch's broomstick.

Elves are said to come and listen to music played by flutes made of elder wood.

In Sicily, elder was the preferred wood for driving out serpents and warding of thieves. It is also said that St Patrick used a branch of elder like a sacred rod to remove all the serpents from Ireland.

Elm

Sacred to *Dana*, the mother of all gods and goddesses in Celtic mythology.

The elm has its dark side – often linked with death and the underworld. It is not advisable to linger under an elm, due to their nasty habit of dropping a large, heavy bough, even though it looks perfectly healthy and it is a calm, dry, windless day.

Elms sometimes throw out a strong side branch, which in the past was eminently suitable as a gallows tree. It is associated with certain death rituals in Britain and Greece, where they are planted in graveyards. Elm wood was also favoured for coffins.

Hawthorn

The Greeks and Romans considered it to be a symbol of hope and marriage. In Greece, wedding couples traditionally wore crowns of hawthorn blossom. Irish folklore considered it unlucky to cut

down a hawthorn. Doing so would risk offending the faeries that inhabited it. Hawthorns guard wishing wells in Ireland where shreds of clothing – *clouties* – hang from the thorns to symbolise a wish made.

Hawthorn blossom was the original wedding confetti. Curiously enough, it also used to be taboo to bring hawthorn blossom into a house, as the blossom smelled of death – and therefore, death would follow. In fact, the blossom does contain *trimethylamine* – a chemical found in decaying tissue.

It used to be believed that attaching a branch to a cow barn will assist them in staying healthy and producing large quantities of milk.

In Medieval Europe, hawthorn was associated with *Wicca* and witchcraft. Witches are said to be able to transform themselves into a hawthorn tree.

It is associated with *Beltane*, the Gaelic May Day festival, a celebration of spring honouring *Belenus* the sun god. Young women wishing to remain beautiful would bathe in the dew of the hawthorn tree at dawn on Beltane.

The fair maid, who on the first of May,
Goes to the fields at break of day,
And bathes in the dew from the Hawthorne tree,
Will ever strong and handsome be.
Unknown

Hazel

One of the most popular woods for divining water and underground minerals, although willow and peach twigs are favoured by some. The practice originated around the 15th century and is still practised today.

Some Sorcerers do boast they have a rod,
Gather'd with vows and sacrifice,
And born about will strangely nod
To hidden treasure where it lies,
Mankind is sure that rod divine,
For to the wealthiest ever they incline.
An Epigram by Samuel Sheppard

A forked hazel stick was also used until the 17th century to divine the guilt of persons in cases of murder and theft.

In the Celtic world, hazelnuts gave the consumer

wisdom, inspiration and heightened spiritual awareness. *Fionn Mac Cumhaill*, a hunter-warrior of Irish legend, was said to have gained wisdom by eating 'the Salmon of Knowledge'. The salmon had gained this title by eating nine hazelnuts that had fallen into the Well of Wisdom.

Heather

Charms made from heather are worn or carried as protection against danger and violent crimes, and the flowers represent good fortune.

Burning it with fern outdoors produces an herbal smoke believed to attract rain.

A gift of heather is said to represent admiration.

Holly

In *Ogham* (the early Medieval alphabet of Ireland), the holly is known as *tinne* meaning *fire*. From it we get the word *tinder*, as holly will burn when freshly felled.

Intertwined with ivy, holly was traditionally made into a crown worn by the bride and groom at weddings.

It is thought that the practice of decorating one's homes with boughs of holly started with the Pagan druids and was carried on with the coming of Christianity in order to conciliate their Pagan neighbours. The Christians called the holly the 'holy-tree'. The Roman judicious practice of allowing indigenous religions and beliefs to continue under their occupation of Britain extended to them using sprigs of holly at Yuletide to accompany gifts.

Gather nine holly leaves in complete silence on a Friday after midnight, wrap them in a white cloth using nine knots to bind the cloth, place under your pillow and your dreams will come true.

Bunches of holly were used to clean chimneys. They were tied with rope leaving both ends long. The bunch was then pushed into the top of the chimney at roof level together with one long end of the rope which dangled down and was pulled to force the bunch downwards. It was them hauled back up from the roof.

This was a more humane method of cleaning a chimney compared to some other alternatives, these being either to send a small boy up to clean it, or throw a chicken or goose down it from the top – the frantic flapping of wings serving to dislodge the soot.

Ivy

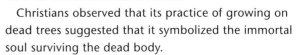

Whilst the clinging Ivy often symbolizes true love and faithfulness in relationships, it can also represent debauchery, carousing and the enjoyment of forbidden pleasures, due to its ability to thrive in the shade and darkness.

Christians observed that its practice of growing on dead trees suggested that it symbolized the immortal soul surviving the dead body.

Ivy, entwined with holly, is traditionally made into crowns for the bride and groom at weddings. These crowns were also worn by ancient poets and the ancient Greeks also presented these crowns to conquering heroes at the games.

Lime (also known as Linden)

Lime is a Slavic sacred tree and national emblem of the Slovak Republic, Slovenia and the Czech Republic.

The word lime is derived from its Saxon name *lind*, meaning both smooth and shield. Warriors' shields were often made of lime due to its ability to absorb a blow.

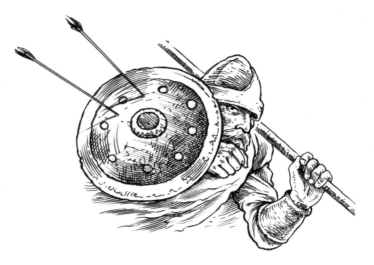

In Germany the lime was a symbolic and hallowed tree. Local communities assembled to celebrate and dance under the tree. Judicial meetings were also held under it.

Under the Lime tree
On the open fields
Where we had our bed,
You still can see
Lovely both
Broken flowers and grass.
On the edge of the woods in a vale,
Tandaradei
Sweetly sang the nightingale.
A mediaeval love poem by Walter von der Vogelweide

While softly rings
The evening's cool wind
Above me the holy Lime
Shakes its branch.
One Wish Alone Have I **by Mihai Eminescu**

Misteltoe

Mistletoe is the druid's most sacred tree. It is also believed by Romans and Germans to be the key to the supernatural.

Amongst whose awful shades the druids strayed,
To cut the hallow'd mistletoe, and hold high converse with their Gods.
Pliny the Elder, Roman author, philosopher and commander.

Hung above a cradle, Mistletoe was thought to protect the child from being stolen by bad faeries and to protect against werewolves.

Many people know the Yuletide tradition of kissing under mistletoe, but few are aware that after each kiss, a berry should be removed. When there are none left, the kissing privilege ends.

Oak

The *druids* took their name from the Celtic name for oak, which is often written as *dru*, but also *daur* or *duir*, or even *derw*, in its Welsh form. Combined with *wid*, the word for knowledge, druid roughly translates as 'oak-knower'.

In Celtic mythology the oak is known as the 'tree of doors' believed to be a gateway between worlds, or a place where portals were erected. Celtic offenders were tried by judges under a suitable oak tree – the accused being made to stand in a circle drawn by the chief druid's wand.

The Saxons also held their meetings under an oak tree. The work oak is similar to the Saxon *aack* or *ak* from which 'acorn' is derived.

As the oak attracts lightening, it is associated with the gods *Zeus, Jupiter, Tho*r and *Perkunas*.

The mighty oak is a symbol of strength and endurance. It has been chosen as the national tree by 13 countries.

Scots pine

The only truly native pine tree in Britain, it is thought that the practice of decorating a tree at Christmas time could date back in the times of the Pagan druids, who would decorate the Scots pine with tallow candles and home-made stars to emulate their ritual fires lit at the winter solstice, to invite the sun back. Others say that the practice of tree decoration originated in Germany.

The pine tree was associated with the Greek goddess *Pitthea*, and the wine god *Dionysis*. The pine cone was an ancient Greek fertility amulet. The Romans used Scots pine cones to flavour their wine. Greece, of course, is famous for its *retsina* wine, which is made using pine resin.

Pine forests are held in such reverence by Mongolian *Shamans*, they enter the forest in silence, in reverence to the gods and spirits living within.

Rowan (Mountain Ash)

Although it is sometimes referred to as the mountain ash, rowan is not a member of the ash family, but a member of the rose family.

Druids' staffs and wands were made from rowan branches, while the twigs were used for water divination and rowan was the preferred wood for rune sets. The

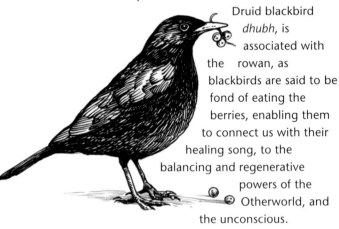

Druid blackbird *dhubh*, is associated with the rowan, as blackbirds are said to be fond of eating the berries, enabling them to connect us with their healing song, to the balancing and regenerative powers of the Otherworld, and the unconscious.

The druids so favoured this tree that they are found in large numbers planted near sacred stone circles.

It was, and still is, planted in Scotland where there is a superstition that it conveys health and wealth to a household.

It is often thought to offer protection against malevolent beings. Fires of rowan wood in Scotland were lit to protect cattle against evil faeries. Milk-maids and dairymen drove cattle with a rod of rowan. Sheep and lambs were driven through a large rowan hoop as protection from enchantment by evil. It was believed that bewitched horses could be controlled by a rowan whip.

Their spells were vain; the boys return'd
To the Queen in sorrowful mood,
Crying, 'that Witches have no power
Where there is Rowan-tree wood!
Unknown

Sycamore (Acer)

The name *acer* has Roman origins, being derived from *aeer, aeris/sharp* or hard, because of its use in

making spears and other sharp pointed instruments.

The Scots' first choice to hang people from, due to the accommodating splay of its lower boughs, hence its nickname *dool*, or sorrow tree.

Vine

Associated with *Jupiter* and the Moon, the God *Bacchus* and Goddesses *Venus* and *Minerva*.

Wine was, and still is, associated with most rituals and events. Wine, and therefore the vine from which it comes, is revered.

Eating grapes and raisins was said to increase fertility. Grape leaves, dried and carried around, were thought to repel evil spirits.

Walnut

An unsociable tree, it can secrete a poison called *juglone* from its roots, capable of killing a nearby tree which is competing for light and moisture.

The Greeks called it *Caryon* from *Kara* (a head) – its powerful odour allegedly causing headaches. Its shade was thought to be harmful to humans and vegetables, but its nuts were always revered as both a tasty and nutritious food, and an antidote to the bite of a mad dog.

Willow

Prevalent in English folklore, willow trees are often believed to be quite sinister, capable of uprooting themselves and stalking travellers.

They were once used to confess to, or share a secret with, as it was believed the

secret would remain trapped in the tree. The willow will also grant wishes if asked in the correct way. A rejected lover could wear willow as a charm to win back love.

To determine if you are to be married in the new year:

Throw your shoe high up,
Into the branches of a Willow tree,
If the branches catch and hold the shoe,
You soon will married be.

Often associated with death, willow coffins have become extremely popular. Victorian paintings of funerals often features willow trees. Willow wood is also thought to be good for wands, water divining rods, flutes and magical harps.

Yew

The yew is Britain's longest living tree, with some specimens more than 1,000 years old. Revered by both Pagan and Christian alike, the yew was often associated with birth, death and re-birth. A sprig of yew used to be placed into shrouds as a sign that death was acknowledged as a transitory process, passing through into another life.

Recently, its mystic regenerative ability has resulted in its needles being used as a basis for certain cancer treatments.

Yews have been planted in almost every churchyard in England, although there has been much speculation about the reasons for this. One theory is that because of their toxic foliage, they were planted to prevent livestock from rutting up the graveyards, and to provide protection for the churches during gales. The fronds and branches have often been used as a substitute for Palms on Palm Sunday.

The yew has important significance in the history of the Celts. *Catuvoolcus*, chief of the *Eburones,* poisoned himself with yew rather than submit to Rome.

In Spain, an Asturian tradition on All Saints Day was to bring a branch of yew to the tombs of those who had recently died so they would find a guide in their return to the land of shadows.

Yew was the premier wood used to make longbows. Ironically, although the British were by far the most prolific users of the longbow for hundreds of years, British yew was inferior to that available in the rest of Europe, and as a result, Britain almost decimated supplies of it with their need.

The Grave
Well do I know thee by the trusty Yew,
Cheerless, unsociable plant, that loves to dwell,
'Midst skulls and coffins, epitaphs and worms;
Where light heeled ghosts, and visionary shades,
Beneath the wan cold moon (as fame reports),
Embody'd thick perform their mystic rounds
No other merriment, dull tree is thine.

By 18th century Scottish poet Robert Blair

CHAPTER 27

Celtic tree astrology

Tree of Knowledge

Celtic priests, or druids (whose name derives from the old Celtic words for oak – *dru*, and wisdom – *wid*), based their religion mainly upon their perception of the energies and wisdom of the spirits, or *Dryads*, dwelling within the ancient trees, symbolically representative of the cycle of life, death and renewal.

They believed that the entire universe was in the form of a tree, known as the 'Tree of Life', or 'World Tree', and thought to derive from *Yggdrasil*, the mythological Norse ash tree. Yggdrasil's cosmic pillar held up the universe; its roots deep into the earth's core, branches reaching far into the sky and embracing the heavens. Throughout the world,

past and present, each country and religion has their own interpretation and image of this 'cosmic' tree – just look up tree of life on Wikipedia and be amazed.

The druids designated a sacred tree to each moon phase in their calendar year, in accordance with its magical properties, and an Ogham (tree alphabet) name for each tree. The Celtic month is based upon the cycles of the moon, with the year divided into 13 lunar months, each one being 28 days long, plus 1 extra day. The extra day is 23rd December and is not ruled by any tree, being the traditional day of the proverbial 'year and a day' derived from the earliest courts of law.

Month	Tree	Celtic Ogham Name	Associated Planet
January 21- February 17	Rowan	*Luis*	Uranus
February 18 - March 17	Ash	*Nion*	Neptune
March 18 - April 14	Alder	*Fearn*	Mars
April 15 - May 12	Willow	*Saille*	Moon
May 13 - June 9	Hawthorn	*Huath*	Vulcan
June 10 - July 7	Oak	*Duir*	Jupiter
July 8 - August 4	Holly	*Tinne*	Earth
August 5 - September 1	Hazel	*Coll*	Mercury
September 2 - September 29	*Vine*	*Muin*	*Venus*
September 30 - October 27	Ivy	*Gort*	Persephone
October 28 - November 24	Reed	*Ngetal*	Pluto
November 25 - December 22	Elder	*Ruis*	Saturn
December 23	The Secret of the Unhewn Stone		
December 24 - January 20	Birch	*Beith*	Sun

Celtic tree Ogham alphabet and symbolic meanings

The ancient Celtic Ogham alphabet dates back to at least the 4th century AD, with monumental engravings lasting from that time. Some scholars believe it was around in the 1st century AD, when it would have been most commonly used to write on sticks or trees. It consists of 20 simple characters, each associated with a sacred tree or shrub. Renowned for their intimacy with nature, the Celts also believed that each of their sacred trees projected symbolic meanings, and were thus used appropriately by druids in ceremonies and practices, as well as in everyday Celtic life.

Whilst the spelling of the Ogham name varies slightly with different interpretations, the lists on the right are a fair representation of the basic Ogham names.

Tree	Ogham Name	Ogham Symbol	Symbolic Meaning
Alder	*Fearn*		Endurance Passion Strength
Apple	*Queirt*		Beauty Generosity Love
Ash	*Nion*		Connection Surrender Wisdom
Birch	*Beithe*		Beginning Renewal Youth
Blackthorn	*Straiph*		Control Discipline Perspective
Elder	*Ruis*		Evolution Continuation Transition
Fir	*Ailm*		Achievement Clarity Energy
Gorse	*Ohn*		Exposure Resourcefulness Transmutation
Hawthorne	*Huath*		Consequence Contradiction Relationships
Hazel	*Coll*		Creativity Honesty Purity

Tree	Ogham Name	Ogham Symbol	Symbolic Meaning
Heather	*Ur*		Dreams Feelings Romance
Holly	*Tinne*		Action Assertion Objectivity
Ivy	*Gort*		Change Determination Patience
Oak	*Duir*		Nobility Stability Strength
Poplar/ Aspen	*Eadhadh*		Transformation Victory Vision
Reed	*Ngetal*		Growth Harmony Health
Rowan	*Luis*		Expression Connection Protection
Vine	*Muin*		Depth Introspection Relaxation
Willow	*Sail*		Imagination Intuition Vision
Yew	*Idhadh*		Illusion Passage Transference

Pines in mist

CHAPTER 28

The etymology of wood-related sayings

The ultimate wooden spoon, in Gullabo, Sweden

Some of the sayings that slip from our tongues today, even though they are often used out of their true context, have their origins in the wood trades. Others of course come from sources like the armed forces. Navy expressions like 'pressed', 'taken aback', 'skylarking' and 'hand over fist' are still regularly used in modern vocabulary, even though they all date back to the times of Lord Nelson's navy.

Here are a few of the lesser known ones about wood, or the wood-related trades.

Against the grain

OK, an obvious one, but any practitioner of wood working will know that it is infinitely harder to work against the grain than with it. The grain is the lighter and darker sections of the wood that runs like irregular stripes through the wood, and planing, cutting or sanding along these lines is the usual way to work. So it is that in life, going against the grain is a form of rebellion, or conscious choice to do things differently, even though it may not be the easiest option.

■ *Source – word of mouth*

Benchmark

The modern definition of this word refers to setting a standard, an example to be followed, a measurement to work to. Latter-day carpenters, and for that matter, modern-day carpenters, are stationed at a bench. For tasks that require marking or cutting a piece of wood either on a regular basis, or on a small production run, a mark, or marks, are either scored, chalked, taped or indicated by means of a fixed block of scrap-wood directly on the bench itself. A benchmark.

■ *Source – word of mouth*

By hook or by crook

Coal fires, as well as wood fires, need wood for kindling. Most of the fire-lighting wood used in towns is sawn and cleft from salvaged sawn timber, but in times gone by in the country, branch wood gathered out of doors still met the cottager's needs. In wooded districts of the North, this practice is known as 'sticking', and so long as only dead branch wood is picked up, no substantial harm is done to the forest thereby. In the New Forest there is an ancient privilege for the forest dwellers to gather wood 'by hook or by crook', for their own use, though not for sale. The term there implies that no cutting tool may be used, and therefore no tree may be damaged, although crooks may be used to dislodge any dead branch within reach.

■ Taken from *Woodland Crafts in Britain* H.L.Edlin (1949)

NB. On common land, it was also permissible to cut firewood from a pollarded tree. The resourceful commoner however, was not above increasing their supply by pollarding a previously maiden tree themselves and waiting until the new shoots grew, much to the disapproval of the local landowner.

Drunk as a Lord

A Lord was a name used by coopers to define a badly made wooden cask.

Things can go wrong in raising up a cask. If the cask is not raised up perfectly straight and upright the extent of the leaning will be much more noticeable after the cask is bent. Sobriety has not always been one of the cooper's virtues. A misshapen cask that leans to one side is called by coopers a Lord.

■ Taken from *The Cooper and his Trade* Kenneth Kilby (1971)

Knock on wood; touch wood

These actions or chants for good luck originated from the ancient practice of rapping on, or touching a tree trunk to summon protective spirits (dryads) from within it. Nowadays we automatically touch anything wooden immediately after saying something that we either hope to achieve, or something we want, or don't want to happen, in a wishful, failsafe reaction, without really knowing why we do it.

■ *Source – word of mouth*

Out for a duck

Coopers have a name for a cracked stave; they call it a 'duck'. The first time they try to heat bend it, the stave cracks. As in cricket, it's something you'd rather avoid. I don't know whence the word is derived, but it is used widely in the trade.

■ Taken from *The Cooper and his Trade* Kenneth Kilby (1971)

Re-makes

Often used in the film industry to describe the making of a new version of an old film, a common practice of a cooper was to take apart a large old cask and make a smaller one out of the parts. These were known as 're-makers'.

■ Taken from *The Cooper and his Trade* Kenneth Kilby (1971)

Scraping the bottom of the barrel

Many things were transported and stored in wooden casks, made by coopers. Coinage was one such commodity, and with paper money being only a recent practice, metal coins were the only hard currency. Clearly, when only a handful of coins were left in the coffers of the Lord of the manor, or King, funds were low, so they would be literally, scraping the bottom of the barrel.

■ Taken from *The Cooper and his Trade* Kenneth Kilby (1971)

Spitting image

From some unknown date before the Norman conquest in 1066, until the year 1826, certain accounts of the English Exchequer were made and preserved on sticks of cleft willow. These tallies, so named from the French verb tallier, to cut, were 'struck' in a singular fashion which required a light and readily cleft wood; so willow was chosen, though hazel and other kinds were sometimes used. When a sum of money, such as a tax payment, was paid into the Exchequer, a tally stick was taken, and on one side of it were cut notches of different sizes, in a simple code, to represent pounds, shillings and pence.

The marked stick was then split into two [lengthways] so that the man who paid could take away half as his receipt! The cut never ran from top to bottom of the stick, for the cutting tool was first entered from the side, close to one end, and then turned so as to follow the central pith for the main length of the tally. This left a broad butt on the retained portion, and insured that only the one genuine stick given as a receipt could be matched up against it.

Another check against the forging of these wooden receipts was that not only the notches, but the grain of the wood, must match on the two splitten images – an old adjective that survives in our phrase the 'spitten' image of his father or mother. It is a matter of history that when the tally system was at last abandoned in 1826, the fire lit to burn up the sticks got out of hand, and destroyed the Houses of Parliament!

■ Taken from *Woodland Crafts in Britain* H.L.Edlin (1949)

Top dog; underdog

Although it is commonly thought that these expressions are derived from the practice of bull- and bear-baiting with dogs – the top dog going for the throat, and the under-dog… well, you can guess the rest. However, a very plausible alternative derivation can be found in the traditional saw pit.

Professional sawyers worked in pairs, using a long two-handled saw. A log was suspended over a saw pit (a large, deep trench), with one man standing above the pit and the other below the timber, in the pit. The timber was held in place by metal rods with a sharp point on each end set at 90 degrees. These effective holding devices were known as dogs. One end of the dog was hammered into the log and the other hammered into the supporting pole placed tangentially over the saw pit. The man who took the position on the top of the saw pit, was the boss, or top man. His job was to mark out the log to be cut, and guide the long, two handled saw while balancing on the log. He could possibly have been called the top-dog. The poor pit man below, the under-dog would have the unfortunate and shoulder-aching job of being stuck at the bottom of the pit, very often standing on damp, muddy ground, pulling and pushing the saw whilst trying to dodge the inevitable showers of sawdust. They often wore wide-brimmed hats to keep the sawdust out of their eyes. Bearing in the mind the disparity of roles between the two sawyers, these expressions become very plausible.

■ *Source – word of mouth*

Twigged

In the past, fibrous and pliable Osier twigs were used to bind the end of Ash hoops used in cooperage. Twigging was the term used for this. 'He's twigged' may have derived from this practice.

■ *Source – word of mouth*

Wooden Spoon Award

Originating from the University of Cambridge, the wooden spoon was a booby prize, awarded to the student who had achieved the lowest exam result in their chosen subject. Presumably the opposite of 'born with a silver spoon in their mouth'. Inevitably, over the years, as the tradition became more fashionable, the wooden spoon became proportionally larger in line with its popularity, and so evolved in one case to become a five-foot wooden characteriser, well suited for photographic opportunities.

■ *Source – word of mouth*

CHAPTER 29

Woodland associations and organisations

The Ancient Technology Centre

Dorset • 01725 517618

www.ancienttechnologycentre.co.uk

An atmospheric hands-on learning centre, with an emphasis on experiencing how rural life used to be. There are open days and events, as well as opportunities to learn ancient crafts, including green woodworking, weaving, blacksmithing, charcoal burning and coppice crafts.

Arboricultural Association

Gloucestershire • 01242 522152 • www.trees.org.uk

An authority on arboricultural best practice and all things trees.

The Association of Pole Lathe Turners and Green Woodworkers

Local groups dotted all over the country

www.bodgers.org.uk

The association has over 500 members, publishes the quarterly magazine *The Bodger's Gazette* and organises the *Bodger's Ball* every May. Offers local services including pole lathe demonstrations.

Basketmakers' Association

Gloucestershire • www.basketassoc.org

Promoting the knowledge of basketry, chair seating and allied crafts, the association also keeps a large database of local basketmakers, weavers, and chairseaters and has a list of associated regional groups.

Bill Hogarth Memorial Apprenticeship Trust

Lancashire • www.coppiceapprentice.org.uk

Enabling apprenticeships in coppicing, and promoting the management of broadleaf woodlands.

BioRegional Charcoal Company

Surrey • 020 8404 2300

www.bioregionalhomegrown.co.uk

A network of regional charcoal producers, promoting charcoal produced from sustainable forests.

British Horse Loggers

Herefordshire • www.britishhorseloggers.org

An association promoting the benefits of horse logging, with contacts for independent full and part-time contractors who work horses in forestry locations.

British Reed Growers Association

Norfolk • 01603 629871 • www.brga.org.uk

Representing reed growers all over the UK, lobbying on behalf of members and co-ordinating research.

British Trust for Conservation Volunteers

Yorkshire • 01302 388883 • www.btcv.org.uk

International volunteering network that is dedicated to supporting conservation projects.

Centre for Alternative Technology
Powys • 01654 705950 • www.cat.org.uk
Fantastic rural eco centre and park demonstrating everything about sustainable living. They have growing expertise in sustainable woodland management and run a number of woodland courses.

Confederation of Forest Industries
Edinburgh • 0131 240 1410 • www.confor.org.uk
A membership organisation for forest owners and those who work in forests or with forest-related products, Confor supports sustainable forestry and low-carbon businesses through lobbying, promoting the market for forest products and helping members to develop their skills.

Coppice Association North West
Cumbria • 07990 952473
www.coppicenorthwest.org.uk
Promoting coppicing in our woodlands, as well as conserving woodlands and supporting those in coppice woodland management.

English Hedgerow Trust
www.hedgerows.co.uk
Established to redress the destruction of British hedgerows, they can provide technical expertise and sometimes labour and materials for suitable projects to re-establish hedgerows.

Fauna & Flora International
www.fauna-flora.org
Acts to conserve threatened species and ecosystems world-wide, including a number of tree species.

Forestry Commission
Bristol and Edinburgh • 0300 067 4321 (England) and 0300 067 6156 (Scotland) • www.forestry.gov.uk
Government organisation responsible for the management, protection and expansion of Britain's forests and woodlands.

Forest Stewardship Council (FSC)
www.fsc-uk.org
Certification initiative guaranteeing that timber comes from well-managed, sustainable woodlands.

Future Trees Trust
Gloucestershire • 01453 884264 • www.futuretrees.org
This charity provides a way for tree scientists to collaborate on their research, with the aim of improving broadleaved trees in Britain and developing the economic, social and environmental benefits of broadleaved woodlands.

Hedgelink
Yorkshire • 0845 6003078 • www.hedgelink.org.uk
An organisation helping farmers, land owners and the public to work together to understand and maintain British hedgerows, and providing information on hedgerows and their conservation and management.

The Herb Society
Cheshire • 0845 4918699 • www.herbsociety.org.uk
A educational charity, dedicated to the understanding, use and appreciation of herbs and their many uses and benefits.

The Heritage Crafts Association
Yorkshire • 01904 541411 • www.heritagecrafts.org.uk
An advocacy body, working with the government and other organisations to support individuals, groups and societies of traditional crafts people, with links to resources and advice on funding.

Institute of Chartered Foresters
Edinburgh • 0131 2401425 • www.charteredforesters.org
The professional body for those working in forestry and arboriculture in the UK, it aims to maintain standards in the profession, and keeps a nationwide directory of chartered members.

The National Council of Master Thatchers Associations
www.ncmta.co.uk
This council brings together the various county-based Master Thatcher Associations and has contacts for them on its website.

National Hedgelaying Society
www.hedgelaying.org.uk
This membership organisation aims to maintain the skills of hedgerow management, providing training, running events and helping people to find local hedgelayers.

National Institute of Medical Herbalists
Devon • 01392 426022 • www.nimh.org.uk
The national organisation representing herbal practitioners and providing information on herbal medicine, details of training courses and a directory of qualified practitioners.

National Society of Master Thatchers
Leicestershire • 01530 222954 • www.nsmtltd.co.uk
Helping to protect professional standards, this society provides contacts for its members around the country.

The National Trust
0844 800 1895 / 0344 800 1895
www.nationaltrust.org.uk
One of the largest owners of British countryside, coastline, forests and farmland, as well as stately homes. Its work includes the conservation of some of the UK's ancient woodlands.

Natural England
Worcestershire • 0300 060 3900
www.naturalengland.org
A government body for the conservation and enhancement of the natural environment.

Permaculture Association
Yorkshire • 0845 458 1805 • www.permaculture.org.uk
A national charity, educating people to understand and use permaculture design practices to improve individual lives, society and our environment.

Royal Forestry Society
Oxfordshire • 01295 678588 • www.rfs.org.uk
Educational charity dedicated to promoting the wise management of trees and woods.

The Silvanus Trust
Cornwall • 01752 846400 • www.silvanustrust.org.uk
This trust is working to regenerate woodlands in the south west for the benefit of local communities, businesses and the environment.

The Small Woods Association
Shropshire • 01952 432769 • smallwoods.org.uk
The national association for those involved in managing small woodlands, this organisation champions sustainable woodlands and teaches woodland skills. It also runs a website (www.coppice-products.co.uk), helping to support those trying to make a living from traditional woodland crafts.

Sustainability Centre
Hampshire • 01730 823166
www.sustainability-centre.org
An educational centre promoting all kinds of sustainability practices, from bee keeping to biomass boilers. The programme includes a course on *Making a Living from the Woodlands*.

Thatching Advisory Services
Devon • 08455 20 40 60
www.thatchingadvisoryservices.co.uk
A supplier of thatching products, but with helpful information and contacts for independent thatchers across the UK.

The Tree Council
London • 020 7407 9992 • www.treecouncil.org.uk
The Tree Council is the charity promoting trees and their benefits in both urban and rural environments.

The Tree Register of the British Isles
Bedfordshire • 01234 768884 • www.treeregister.org
Registered charity containing details of more than 150,000 of Britain and Ireland's most notable trees.

Wood Education Programme Trust
Cumbria • 01539 822140 • www.woodeducation.org.uk
A small charity providing people in Cumbria with educational access to woodlands.

Woodland Heritage
Surrey • 01428 652159 • www.woodlandheritage.org
Registered charity uniting wood producers with wood users, and helping to develop woodland management skills.

The Woodland Trust
Lincolnshire • 01476 581111 • www.woodlandtrust.org.uk
Registered charity caring for and protecting over 1,000 woodlands in the UK, covering 20,000 hectares. Also custodians of the superb website **www.british-trees.com**, which provides free, comprehensive information on the type, characteristics, history and mythology of 70 British trees.

CHAPTER 30

Acronyms of the woodland industry

AAC	Annual Allowable Cut (*see Glossary*)		**DBH**	Diameter at Breast Height
ADAS	Agricultural Development & Advisory Service		**DEFRA**	Department for the Environment, Food and Rural Affairs
AONB	Area of Outstanding Natural Beauty		**EA**	Environment Agency
ASNW	Ancient Semi-Natural Woodland		**EC**	European Commission
BAP	Biodiversity Action Plan (*see Glossary*)		**EMC**	Equilibrium Moisture Content (*see Glossary*)
BDS	British Deer Society		**EMS**	Environment Management System
BIHIP	British and Irish Hardwood Improvement Programme		**ESA**	Environmentally Sensitive Area
BTCV	British Trust for Conservation Volunteers		**EU**	European Union
CAI	Current Annual Increment		**FAO**	Food and Agriculture Organisation
CAP	Common Agricultural Policy		**FC**	Forestry Commission
CBD	Convention on Biological Diversity		**FCA**	Forestry Contracting Association
CCF	Continuous Cover Forestry (*see Glossary*)		**FDP**	Forest Design Plan (*see Glossary*)
CCW	Countryside Council for Wales		**FEI**	Forest Education Initiative
CLA	Country Land and Business Association		**FMU**	Forest Management Unit
CONFOR	Confederation of Forest Industries (UK)		**FOE**	Friends of the Earth
CPRE	Council for the Protection of Rural England		**FRCC**	Forestry Research Co-ordination Committee
CRC	Commission for Rural Communities		**FSC**	Forest Stewardship Council
CROW	Countryside and Rights of Way Act		**FWAG**	Farming and Wildlife Advisory Group
CSS	Countryside Stewardship Scheme			

FWPS	Farm Woodland Premium Scheme
FY	Forest Year (*see Glossary*)0
GIS	Geographic Information System
ha	Hectare
HAP	Habitat Action Plan
HSE	Health and Safety Executive
ICF	Institute of Chartered Foresters
IFS	Indicative Forestry Strategy
ISO	International Organisation for Standardisation
ITE	Institute of Terrestrial Ecology
ITTA	International Tropical Trade Agreement
ITTO	International Tropical Timber Organisation
IUFRO	International Union of Forestry Research Organisations
JNCC	Joint Nature Conservation Committee
LANTRA	Sector Skills Council for the Environmental and Land-based Sector
MAB	Man and the Biosphere Programme (of UNESCO)
MAI	Mean Annual Increment (*see Glossary*)
NDR	Net Discounted Revenue
NE	Natural England
NERC	Natural Environment Research Council
NFC	National Forest Company
NFU	National Farmers Union
NIFS	Northern Ireland Forestry Service
NNR	National Nature Reserve
NTFP	Non-timber Forest Products

NVC	National Vegetation Classification
NRW	Natural Resources Wales
OSNW	Other Semi-Natural Woodland
PAWS	Plantations on Ancient Woodlands Sites
PEFC	Programme for Endorsement of Forest Certification
RDA	Rural Development Agency
RFS	Royal Forestry Society
RICS	Royal Institution of Chartered Surveyors
RPNW	Recently Planted Native Woodland
RSFS	Royal Scottish Forestry Society
RSPB	Royal Society for the Protection of Birds
SAC	Special Area of Conservation
SAP	Species Action Plan
SFM	Sustainable Forest Management
SPA	Special Protection Area
SRC	Short Rotation Coppice
SSSI	Site of Specific Scientific Interest
SWA	Small Woodland Association
TPO	Tree Preservation Order
TRADA	Timber Research and Development Organisation
TROBI	Tree Register of the British Isles
UKWAS	UK Woodland Assurance Scheme
WGS	Woodland Grant Scheme
WWF	World Wide Fund for Nature
YC	Yield Class

CHAPTER 31

Compendium of terms for tools, woodlands and crafts

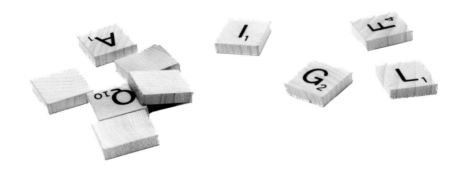

The words connected with trees, woodland management, tools, timber processing, green woodworking, turning, coopery, timber framing, wheel making, chair making, hedge laying, hurdle making, basket weaving, rake making, seat weaving and thatching can seem strange and alien to those new to woodland craft.

There is also much variation in the names given to tools, processes in woodland management, parts of a tree or parts and products made from a tree throughout the counties of the British Isles, so this glossary, although substantial, is by no means definitive. In fact, there is vast disparity throughout Britain, as the following quote from H.L.Edlin's jewel of a book, *Woodland Crafts in Britain*, published in 1949, explains so eloquently.

"In most parts of Britain thatching materials are secured to the roofs of thatched houses or stacks by narrow pegs of wood, usually hazel. One common name for these is spars, but they have many others: *spics, speekes, spikes, speaks, spits, splints, sparrows, sparrods, sprees, tangs, spelks, gads (cf.goad), privets, brotches, brooches, broaches, pricks, withynecks, ledgers* and *roovers* have all been recorded. Celtic names are *scolp, scallop* and *sgilb* in Wales, *sgolb* in Ireland and western Scotland and *scob, scobe, scoub* or *ecrobe* in eastern Scotland and Northumberland; these last eight variants illustrate how any word may change when it is seldom written down, even though it be current coin in the mouths of many countrymen."

Think of this glossary therefore, as a brave cross-section of our gloriously rich language and colloquial heritage, where nothing is right, wrong or definitive – and never bland.

A

Absolute humidity – A reading of the actual moisture content in the air measured in grammes (of water) per cubic metre.

Acre – A unit of land of 43,560 square feet, which is approximately 208 feet x 208 feet square (2.471 acres = 1 hectare, or 10,000 square metres).

Adze – Type of axe with a forged metal blade set at right angles to the wooden handle. Used to rough out a convex area into solid wood (chair seats), or in traditional timber framing for trimming oak beams, (where a flat cutting blade is preferred). Available with a short or long handle, and the choice of either a flat cutting head or a concave gouge, there are quite a few versions used by carpenters, coopers, wheelwrights and framers.

Adze, chequered – A general purpose tool looking like a hammer with a blunt end on one side of the head and a 'V' shape on the opposite face. Used by coopers as a hammer, a lever and a nail-pulling tool.

Adze, rounding – Extremely sharp and flat headed, used by coopers to cut the slope on the chime of a cask.

Adze, trimming – A general purpose cooper's adze for tidying up protruding pieces of hoop.

Adze, trussing – A heavy blunt version used by coopers to hammer home truss hoops when bending a cask.

Afforestation – Establishing trees on clear land.

Agro-forestry – Establishing tees on land also used for farming livestock or crops.

Air-dried – Wood that has been stored outside to dry slowly and has reached equilibrium moisture content (e.m.c.) with the environment, typically 25% in the winter and down to 15% in a good summer. Superior quality over kiln dried wood. Allow one year air-drying per inch diameter/thickness.

Ancient woodland – Woodland that has known to have been in existence since at least the 17th century (400 years).

Angiosperms – Taxonomic name for broadleaf, hardwood trees with covered seeds.

Annual Allowance Cut (AAC) – The volume of timber allowed to be cut in a sustainable way, from a designated area of woodland.

Apical dominance – When a dominant bud in a plant grows the most vigorously, usually indicating that it will result in a single, straight stemmed tree.

Area of Outstanding Natural Beauty – A designated area of high landscape and scenic quality designated by Natural England, or Countryside Council for Wales.

Arboreal – Associated with trees. Generic term to describe

Apple blossom

life living in or on trees, structures resembling trees, and actions directly involving trees.

Arboretum – A place where trees or shrubs are cultivated for their educational, aesthetic or scientific interest.

Arboriculture – The practice of cultivation, management and maintenance of individual trees.

Arborist – A practitioner of arboriculture.

Arris – Cutting edge of a tool where two ground bevels meet, or where two edges of a wooden board meet.

Ascending grain – Direction of wood fibre. Cutting with the grain results in a smooth cut, in contrast to cutting 'against the grain', which catches and tears instead of cutting cleanly. Often compared to stroking a short haired dog – rubbing your hand down the coat head to tail results in a smooth action. Rubbing your hand on the coat upwards tail to head catches and raises the fur, and also upsets the dog.

Aspect – The compass direction to which a slope of land faces.

Assarting – Old common term for clearing areas of forest for agricultural use.

Auger bit – Speciality boring tool used traditionally in a hand brace to bore round, accurate, flat bottomed holes.

Auricle – Small formation on the base of a leaf resembling an ear.

Awl – Thin, sharp pointed shaft set in a wooden handle, used to make an indent in wood where a hole will be drilled.

B

Backing – Shaping the outside of a wooden cask stave into a convex shape.

Backing knife – Curved drawknife used in coopery to cut

the back, outer face of a cask stave.

Back sawn – A log sawn in such a way as to produce the maximum number of cuts at 90 degrees to the growth rings.

Backsteady – Upright support for the middle of long, thin spindles when being turned on a lathe, to prevent them flexing in the middle.

Bagging hook – A curved blade similarly shaped to a sickle attached to a long pole, used to cut down overgrown undergrowth.

Ball rooted – Term for a young sapling with its roots still enclosed in a ball of earth, ready for planting out.

Banjo – Name given to the part of a lathe which slides along the bed and supports the T bar/tool rest. Also known as a saddle.

Bare rooted – Nursery plants lifted and supplied with roots bare of soil, for planting out.

Barking – Describes the process of peeling the bark from an oak tree, for use in leather tanning.

Barking iron – Tool used to remove the bark from oak trees by peeling. Curved metal blade shaped similar to a spoon with a long stem and wooden handle. Also called a *spud*.

Basal area – Cross-section area of a tree trunk 4.5 feet/1.3m above ground level. Used as an indicator of a stand density, expressed in square metres per hectare.

Basle – Bevel cut into a wooden cask lid or head, around the circumference.

Bast – The commonly known name in the UK for the inner layer of tree bark where carbohydrates flow through the cells to feed the tree. Soft and supple, and leather-like when wet. Used very effectively to weave post and rung chair seats. The most superior bast being hickory in the USA or wych elm in the UK. Cedar, lime, ash and oak can also be used. Known more commonly in the USA as phloem.

Baulk – A log roughly worked to a square section with an axe or adze.

Bavins – Bundles of sticks and twigs (cordwood and brash)

'Barking' – removing tree bark with a barking iron

Beech 'mast'

tied tightly together using a wythe. Traditionally used for a very intense blaze in hearths, bakers' ovens and brewers' maltings. Also used as a base for corn and hay stacks and to line the bottom of ditches instead of pipes, since water percolates freely through them. Also known as *faggots*.

Bead – A rounded, raised form running around a spindle in turning.

Beading – In cane seat weaving, the process of covering the holes in the frame with a wider cane, after the seating is complete.

Beading tool – A small, square-sectioned chisel used in turning to form a bead.

Bearing timbers – The bottom load-bearing supports under a stack of sawn timber set up to air-dry.

Beating up – Planting replacement tree stock in new woodland planting areas to replace losses. Also known as gapping up.

Beattle/Beetle – (pronounced *bittle*). Large, long-handled shop-made wooden mallet with iron rings on either end of the head. Used in conjunction with splitting wedges when opening up felled tree trunks. Tree root clusters are the ideal material.

Bed – Horizontal part of a lathe on which the headstock and tailstock run.

Bender (1) – Temporary woodland shelter made from bent hazel branches with a canvas covering.

Bender (2) – A concave piece of wood with a heavy roller set adjacent to it used to form cleft hazel rods into barrel hoops.

Bench dog – A square or round peg, driven into a corresponding hole in the top of a work bench. Used to hold work pieces.

'Browsing' deer

Benchman – Name given to a craftsman responsible for all the sawn parts of a chair such as the seat and back of a Windsor chair.

Bending strap – A steel strap placed along the length of a piece of timber, used to assist steam bending larger diameter billets and tight curves into compression, whilst absorbing tension which could otherwise break the piece. Used in conjunction with a wooden stop at each end.

Besom – Traditional broom comprising a bundle of fine birch twigs secured by a withe around a cleft wooden handle.

Besom horse – Very similar in construction to that of a traditional British shaving horse, except that the billet platform is replaced by a bracket at the front nose and a 'V' shaped fork, or forked stick behind it, directly underneath the pivoting clamp. Gives a firm grip on round poles.

Best formed tree – Describing a tree with the straightest stem and small diameter branches.

Bevel – The angle that is left after grinding a face on a cutting tool.

Bick iron/Beek iron – Tall metal upright post on which sits a small 't' shaped anvil with an indentation at each end, used in cooperage to assist beating rivets into a hoop.

Billet – Small section of cleft wood.

Bill – Wedge-shaped steel blades fitted at 90 degrees through a club-like handle, used by millwrights to dress mill stones.

Billhook – Traditional broad bladed cutting/riving tool shaped with a downwards hook on the front similar to a parrot's beak, with a wooden handle and a sharp edge on the underside. Used for coppicing, hedge laying, splitting withies for hurdles and removing the small twigs from slightly larger boughs (*snedding*). There are many regional patterns, each with its own unique application.

Binders (1) – Thin, whippy stems of hazel rods which are weaved into the top stakes of a newly laid hedge to form an attractive continuous finish. Also known as *ethers* or *heatherings*.

Binders (2) – Decorative hazel rods held down by broaches, used to secure thatch to a roof frame. Also known as sways.

Biodiversity – Describing the variety of plant and animal life in either a given area, or the entire planet.

Biodiversity Action Plan (BAP) – A plan containing proposals and targets for conserving and enhancing biodiversity.

Biomass – The waste product of the forest after felling, consisting of unusable branches, twigs and bark, chipped and used for fuel.

Bittel – See *beetle*

Birdseye – Attractive distorted cluster figuring on the surface of wood, resembling a bird's eye. Found in maple and sycamore.

Bird's mouth (1) – Initial wedge cut made in a tree facing the direction in which it will fall, prior to making the final felling cut from the other side of the tree directly behind. Also known as a face cut, dip, kerf, or sink.

Bird's mouth (2) – An uneven 'V' cut into the end grain of a piece of square section sawn timber enabling it to rest snugly on a perpendicular timber. Commonly used in timber framing – particularly roofing structures.

Black heart – A dark brown discolouration in the heartwood of a tree, particularly in ash. Does not always signify rot.

Blank – Term given to the form of a piece of wood which has been roughly prepared and shaped prior to the next stage of working. Most commonly referred to in turning.

Blaze – Mark left on a tree after slicing off a small area of bark.

Blazing – Removing bark from a tree or pole along its length after felling to enable it to season properly. Sometimes performed on poles with a special tool called a dolly.

Bleeding – The practice of extracting sap or resin from a tree by boring a small hole in the trunk and inserting a twig, from which the liquid will run into a container underneath.

Blind tenon – A tenon that does not go right through the mortise hole.

Block hook – A metal spike with a curved, flat head at the other end. The spike is driven into a wooden block near the top and is used to assist a cooper in gripping a cask stave while working on it.

Bob – Timber bob. A device consisting of a pair of wheels attached to a shaft placed underneath the butt of a felled tree to assist extraction. Also known as a timber janker.

Bodger – Name associated with a skilled woodland worker who specialised in riving, shaping and turning chair parts in a woodland camp during the summer season, to be sold later to factories that made chairs from those parts after they had seasoned.

Bog Oak – Oak which has been trapped under the surface of a bog for thousands of years and turned black as a result of its chemical marinating. The timber is also rendered unusually hard. Highly prized for certain types of furniture and decorative artefacts.

Bole – Trunk of a standard tree from ground to first branch.

'Bolts' of freshly-cut rush

Bolling – Trunk of a pollard tree from ground to first branch.

Bolt (1) – A sizeable piece of log formed by riving.

Bolt (2) – Rush seat weaving. Name given to a standard bundle of weaving rush, or willow, containing various thicknesses and lengths, usually weighing about 2-3kg (5-6 lbs).

Bonds – Bindings of cleft ash, bramble, chestnut, hazel or oak, used to tightly hold besom broom heads together. Also known as *laps*.

Bond poker – A tool unique to besom broom making. Its purpose is to allow the free end of the bond to be securely tucked away under itself. Also called a *lap poker*.

Booges – Metal hoops fitted nearest the middle/pitch of a wooden cask.

Bool – Oval-shaped ash or hazel hoop around which cleft laths of oak were woven to make a spelk/spale/swill basket. This hoop is also sometimes known as a *bow*.

Boreal period – A period between 9,000-6,200BC, when hazel was the dominant tree species.

Botany – The study of plants, fungi or algae.

Box hearted – A squared length of tree bole, with the pith still remaining in the centre.

Botch – See *Spar*.

Bottoming – Term used to describe the process of carving or weaving a chair seat.

Bound moisture/water – Moisture bound/trapped within the cell walls of wood. Loss of bound water results in dimensional shrinkage and loss of weight but will not occur until the free water/moisture has been extracted from the wood first. Bound moisture starts to be lost after the cells collapse at under 30% moisture content.

Bow – Ash or hazel hoop used to make a spelk/spale/swill basket. This hoop is also sometimes known as a *bool*.

Bowl gouge – A turning tool with a heavy cross-section and a deep flute ground to a 40-60 degree angle, for turning bowls.

Box – A removable wooden gripping handle on the tail end of a two-man pit saw, attached by means of a kerf and wedge.

Boy – A device for clamping a bundle of birch twigs in the making of a besom broom, or a bundle of faggots.

Brace – A slanting piece of timber used extensively in general construction, commonly affixed at 45 degrees to two other pieces of timber to give rigidity.

Brace/bit brace – Traditional hand-held boring tool that consists of a pommel, crank and chuck. Usually used with auger or spoon bits.

Bract – The leaf-like structure arising from the base of a flower.

Brake (1) – Riving brake. An arrangement of posts driven into the ground and nailed horizontally, that allows wood

An old beech tree

in the round to be held conveniently so that pressure can be applied during riving (the process of splitting wood down the grain).

Brake (2) – Two springy metal rods bent and set upright together in a wooden frame. Used to strip bark from willow rods.

Brand – Unconverted pieces of partially burnt wood left over from a charcoal burn. These were used to start the next kiln burn.

Brash – Also known as brushwood or brousewood. Term given to the small twigs left behind after a tree has been felled and snedded.

Brash mats – Small diameter branches of brash spread on the ground on extraction routes where vehicles are travelling, to help reduce soil damage.

Brashy – Derogatory term for inferior grained, or old and dying wood.

Breast bib – Block of wood with a hollow in it held in front of the chest by straps or from a string around the neck. Used in conjunction with a traditional brace and bit to drill holes in wood; the borer uses the chest to apply pressure on the brace while drilling. A slightly larger, flat version can be used to protect the abdomen and lower ribs from injury caused when a wooden billet, held in a shave-horse, catches on the drawknife blade on the pull stroke, slides through the clamp and rams into the body.

Breast height – Historically 4 ft 3 in (1.3m) up from the ground. This is the height at which a tree's diameter is measured.

Broadleaf – A tree that has flat, broad leaves (usually a hardwood) rather than having needles(softwood/conifer).

Broach – Thin, cleft rods of hazel, pointed at both ends and twisted, used to hold down the under-thatch on roofs. Also known as a botch, spar, spec, spick.

Broadleaf tree – General description of a deciduous, hardwood, non-narrow leaf, or excessively resinous tree.

Broom hook – A billhook with an extra, oblong, fin-shaped blade opposite, giving the tool a kind of double edge. Used in exactly the same way as a bill hook with the extra blade used for trimming off the ends of besom brooms.

Brown ends – Term for charcoal that has not completely carbonised, which will be separated and put back into the next burn.

Brown willow – Green willow which has been steamed and dried (see also *buff* and *white willow*).

Browse – Twigs, shoots and leaves eaten by woodland mammals.

Browsing – The act of eating low shoots and leaves by woodland mammals.

Browse line – The height at which the largest woodland mammal cannot reach to browse woodland foliage.

Brushwood (1) – See *brash*

Brushwood (2) – Wood of a certain type suitable for making brush heads and backs. Typically alder, beech and broom.

Brushwood (3) – Collective term for a thicket consisting of small trees and shrubs.

Buck – To crosscut a felled tree trunk into shorter lengths.

Buck saw – Large wooden frame saw used mainly in woodland applications to crosscut round wood held in a wooden holding device called a saw buck.

Buckingham Woodstation – Job-specific holding device. Adjustable metal cage designed to securely hold a quantity of long lengths of round wood for the purpose of cutting them into firewood using a chainsaw.

Buff willow – Green willow which has been boiled, kept in the water for 24 hours and dried. The natural tannin in the bark stains the rods a rich golden colour (see also *brown* and *white willow*).

Buffering – Additional planting around woodlands of a tree line intended to protect the woodland from extreme weather and agricultural activities.

Buffing – An attractive reddish brown colour achieved by 'buffing' or boiling the willows, causing the colour from the bark to penetrate the stems.

Bungee – Another name for a flexible shock cord. Useful on a pole lathe.

Bumping – Startling or disturbing a deer from cover in a woodland.

Bung flogger – Wooden long-handled mallet used to beat either side of a barrel bung to loosen it.

Burden – A number of gathered and graded bundles of straw roofing thatch ready for carrying up the ladder on a pronged fork called a *jack*.

Burly – Timber featuring irregular grain, compacted wood tissue and/or burrs/burls.

Burr (1) – A minute metal flap (wire edge) formed on the opposite side of a cutting tool edge during sharpening and honing. Usually honed off on most blade edges but retained on cabinet scrapers.

Burr (2) – A wart-like swelling beneath the bark of a tree as a result of a tight compaction of small dormant buds or twigs, known as epicormic growth. Much prized by bowl turners.

Burl – See *burr*

Burnish – Polishing by friction. Rubbing a piece of work with dry wood shavings to produce a smooth finish and lustre. These shavings are also sometimes known as 'Bodger's sandpaper'. This finish is only suitable in preparation for waxing.

Burnisher – A length of super hard steel, usually set into a wooden handle. Used to drag along the side of a cabinet scraper to form a burr.

Burrow – An area of cut or sold coppice. Also known as a cant, coupe or fell.

Butt (1) – The lower, usually wider portion of a stem, pole or tree.

Butt (2) – The thick, lower end of a length of rush.

Buttresses – Feet-like swellings on the base of a tree curving down and out, denoting the beginning of the roots. Also known as *claws, toes, spurs* or *stams*.

Buzz – Three-cornered chisel used to clean out the corners of a square or oblong mortise.

C

Cabinet scraper – Thin sheets of flexible metal on which a burr is raised on the end with a burnisher. Used to scrape seasoned wood at an angle to produce fine shavings and a good subsequent finish.

Cage – Referring to a post and rung chair frame.

Coils of wych elm 'bast'

Cambium – The inner layer of cells between the inner bark (bast) and sapwood of a tree, where carbohydrates convert into wood cells on the inner side of the cambium.

Caning – Weaving a chair seat with thin strips of rattan vines.

Canker – A fungoid disease in trees.

Canopy – Top layers of tree foliage forming the roof of a forest or woodland.

Canopy level – Highest foliage level in a woodland, receiving the most light from the sun.

Cant – An area of coppice cut or sold in a season. Also known as a *coupe, fell* or *burrow.*

Cant hook – Long wooden handle attached to a curved metal arm used to manipulate large logs on the ground. See also *peavey* and *ring dog.*

Caliper – Metal measuring device or compass, used for transferring measurements from one part to another.

Carbon dioxide (CO2) – A gas made up of carbon and oxygen, created by animals (including man), but particularly livestock, through respiration and exhaust, and by burning carbon-based fuels such as oil and petrol. CO2 is absorbed by plants during photosynthesis.

Carbon fixing – Occurs during photosynthesis when a tree 'locks in' carbon dioxide. It will only be released with the demise of the tree, either by dying and rotting, or when the wood is burnt. One hectare of forest can 'fix' two tons of carbon dioxide each year.

Carbon footprint – A measurement of how much carbon dioxide an individual or organisation produces over a period of time, usually measured in tonnes per annum.

Carbon sequestration – The process by which green plants absorb/remove carbon dioxide from the atmosphere and store it as carbon biomass within their trunks, branches, foliage and roots.

Carbon trading – An idea dreamed up around the Kyoto Protocol suggesting that if one member country exceeds its agreed capacity of greenhouse gas and another member country has a surplus of agreed capacity, the former can pay the latter for the right to use the latter's surplus capacity.

Carcassing – Softwood timber used for the structural content of house building.

Carr – Describes an area of woodland situated in wet or boggy ground, usually containing alder or willow.

Cast – Twists and buckles in sawn timber planks which have distorted due to uneven grain or seasoning; or wood which was under stress while growing. Also known as *warp*.

Caulked handle – Tool handle with the end opposite the head formed to a blunt beak-like shape. Helps prevent handle slipping out of the hand when in use. Popular design for axe, billhook and machete handles.

Cawel – Woven hazel farm basket mostly found in Wales. Sometimes called a *lippe*.

Cellulose – An abundant organic chemical derived from the cell walls in green plants. Has many applications, but mainly used in the production of paper-based products.

Centres – The two parts in immediate contact with and holding the work piece (between centres) on a lathe.

Chairstick – A length of narrow flat timber usually the height of a chair back on which is marked all positions for mortise holes, tapers, and all other relevant dimensions and instructions. Also known as a *story stick*.

Check – **(shake)**. The term used to describe splits in wood incurred in the process of drying. Most noticeable on end grain. Checking is more likely in wood dried too quickly, or in reaction wood.

Cheek – The convex area of an axe head around the eye.

Chime (1) – A bevel cut around the inside edge of a wooden barrel with a small-adze.

Chime (2) – Metal hoop fitted to the ends of a wooden cask.

Chince – A chisel with a flattened edge used to push flag/river rush into the inner groove of a howel prior to fitting the wooden head/cask lid.

Chive – Specialist wide cutting blade, set into a wooden stock with a semi-circular fence, used to cut the howel on the inside of a wooden barrel. A *jigger* was also used as an alternative tool.

Chlorophyll – Name derived from the Greek *chloros* (green). Green pigment found in algae and plants, critical to photosynthesis, which gives leaves their colour in spring and summer.

Chuck – Holding device for the work piece on a lathe.

Clacks – Traditional leather-covered leaded valves in wooden water pumps.

Clapse – A colloquial name for a wooden latch on a cow stall.

Claws – Feet-like swellings on the base of a tree curving down and out, denoting the beginning of the roots. Also known as *buttresses, toes, spurs* or *stams*.

Clearance angle – The angle between the lower face of a blade and the wood being cut.

Clear fell – The removal of all trees in a given area larger than 0.25 hectares (approx .6 acre).

'Clear' felling

Clear lumber – Felled timber free from knots, twists and shakes.

Cleave (1) – To split wood down and along its grain following the natural direction of its fibres.

Cleave (2) / Cliff – Palm-sized oval wooden-bodied tool with three to four fins of wood or metal on one end, pushed through a pre-scored end of a willow rod and pushed down the entire length to produce skeins used for weaving and basketry.

Cleft – The result of cleaving.

Climate change – Long term weather and temperature changes commonly linked to a rise in the emissions of greenhouse gasses into the atmosphere.

Clinch – Where a nail is hammered through a lap joint and turned/hammered over at the protruding point at 90 degrees back to the face of the wood.

Clinker-built – A construction of overlapping boards. A common boat building method (also used in trug making).

Clinometer/inclinometer – A sophisticated instrument very much like a compass with a hydroscope used in conjunction with basic trigonometry, to measure the length and incline angle of a tree in order to calculate its height.

Closed forest – A forest with over 80% tree canopy cover.

Coed – The Welsh word for wood.

Colonisation – The natural regeneration of trees on new previously un-wooded areas.

Collets – Metal gripping parts in a chuck.

Compression – In steam bending this is the compression of the structure of wood along its length on the concave underside of the bend. A bending strap and stops help to control this process.

Compression wood – Distorted softwood formed in leaning trunks on slopes and on large overhanging branches of trees. Compression wood dries unpredictably, often twisting and cracking. Contains many tension and compression forces in the trunk and boughs, so care must be taken when felling this type of tree. Known as *reaction wood*.

Commander – Very large and heavy two handled mallets, usually made from the butt of a small tree with a stout handle fitted at 90 degrees. Looking like the old fairground hammers, they were used by timber framers to 'persuade' the newly joined heavy timber framework of a building to 'fit together'.

Common(s) – Land for use in part as communal.

Community woodlands – Areas where there is free access for local communities to engage in maintenance, educational and recreational activities.

Compartmentation – Fencing off a newly felled area to prevent livestock eating the re-generated shoots.

Conifer – General description of a non-deciduous softwood tree which has needles as opposed to broad leaves, and bears cones.

Conky – Term used to identify wood suffering from fungus decay. Conk wood.

Container grown – Young trees and shrubs grown in a container in order to encourage the root system to form a compact ball within the container soil to protect its roots when planting out.

Continuous Cover Forestry (CCF) – Managed system of high forest ensuring a continuous canopy cover.

Conversion – Turning felled logs into useable products, like sawn boards and construction timber.

Cooper's axe – Long thin-bladed axe with a wooden handle offset from the head. Used to dress/shape a wooden cask stave.

Cooper's shave – See *Inshave*.

Coping saw – Deep-framed U-shaped cutting device, holding a blade similar to that of a band saw. Used extensively before band saws, these versatile devices are used to cut wooden stock and can cut curves.

Coppice, coppicing – Underwood trees cut close to ground level every few years and left to re-generate into poles.

Coppice cycle – The number of years left in between cutting for each designated area of coppice.

Coppice-with-standards – A two-storey woodland management system where, amongst the coppice (underwood), a proportion of trees are left to grow on as larger trees called standards.

Copse – Name for a previously coppiced area of woodland now containing standing trees.

Corbels – Timber lintels projecting through a wall to support weight.

Cord – Standard woodland stack of firewood in the round, measuring 4ft x 4ft x 8ft (128 cubic feet), stood on a raised log-stacking rack and weighing approximately 1 tonne when seasoned.

Cord wood – Small branches of wood suitable for firewood.

Corrack – A special rake used in charcoal burning.

Corridors – Essential creation of new woodland habitats linking fragmented patches of woodland to encourage the harmonisation of habitat.

Couching – (Cane seat-weaving). The method of using a narrow cane to hold down the beading cane.

Coupe – Describing either an area designated to be felled at a particular time, or a total amount of felling in a year.

Cover – Vegetative shelter for wildlife against predators and bad weather.

Crank – A threaded length of metal fitted through the poppet of a pole lathe to support the work piece being turned.

Creel – Woven hazel basket used in Ireland for carrying fish and peat.

Crest rail – Upper horizontal panel on the back of a chair seat. Usually curved.

Crib – A livestock feeder consisting of a long frame of bent rods of hazel or willow. Its purpose is to hold hay off the ground in the cage to prevent the hay being trodden into the mud.

Crook – A natural or contrived longitudinal bend or elbow in timber. Very desirable in boatbuilding and timber framing.

Crook knife – A one-handed knife similar to, but longer

Coppiced lime tree

than, a spoon bowl carving knife. Held in one hand and pulled to cut while the other hand holds the work piece. Originated from North American Indians who used them to carve canoe parts.

Crop Tree – Those trees in a stand designated to form the final crop. Usually the best quality and highest value specimens.

Crosscut – Saw cut at 90 degrees to the wood's grain.

Cross-cut – A saw cut perpendicular to the grain.

Cross grain – An irregular grain in timber, neither running lengthways or in only one direction, caused by interlocking fibres or uneven annual rings.

Crotch – Area immediately below the fork of a tree where the branch grows from the trunk, or where the trunk divides into two. Sawing or riving along the grain reveals beautiful fan-like figuring.

Crown – The live branches, twigs and foliage of a tree.

Crown closure – The calculated percentage of a given area covered by tree crowns.

Crown trees – Smaller trees sprouting from the cambium layer of a recently cut tree, forming a circle of new growth.

Cruck – A bent or forked-shape tree branch. Inspiration for cruck-framed timber buildings.

Cruise – The undertaking of a forest inventory to obtain information about the forest. Usually part of a forest management plan.

Cruz/Croze – Specialist long, narrow, adjustable cutting blade set into a wooden stock with a semi-circular fence, used by a cooper to cut a deep groove within the howel of a wooden cask to accommodate the head/cask lid.

Cultivars – Cultivated, domestic varieties of trees, grown and maintained in gardens and parks.

Cup chuck – A lathe chuck containing a deep recess into which a spigot on the work piece can be driven.

Cupping – The result of a curved distortion, best seen when looking at the end grain of a board. Caused during the process of curing. Quartersawn boards eliminate this problem.

Cup-shake – A shake in wood caused by growing conditions the tree was subjected to, resulting in lack of cohesion between successive annual rings.

Curing – Another name for seasoning – the slow, natural drying of timber.

Current Annual Increment (CAI) – A measurement in cubic metres per hectare representing the annual or medium term incremental growth within a stand of trees.

D

Dader – Specialist hammer-like hand tool for enlarging and shaping a drilled mortise in a hurdle. Also sometimes called

a *trybill, twivil* or *twybil*.

Danish oil – A wood sealer/finish made from polymerised linseed oil.

Dappled shade – Method of woodland management designed to retain 30-50% canopy cover while the wood is replanted.

Daubing – Cutting away the feet, or buttresses, spurs, or toes, on the base of a tree, prior to felling. Also referred to as facing, rounding up, or setting up.

Dead centre – A cone centre used on a lathe which does not revolve with the work it is holding.

Dead hedge – Long piled rows of brushwood left lying on the woodland floor for working up into a hedge to create a biodiversity resource.

Deadwood – Dead trees either left standing or felled and left on-site to create a biodiversity resource.

Deciduous – Definition of a broadleaf tree which sheds its leaves in autumn, the end of the growing season. Name derived from the Latin meaning 'falling down'.

Decomposers – Generally fungi and certain bacteria, that break down the dead tissues of plants into nutrients available for other live species to use.

Decoy tree – A lure tree intentionally deadened or felled and left to attract bark boring beetles in order to protect nearby growing stands of trees. Also known as a *trap tree.*

Deforestation – The complete removal of trees from a designated area.

Descending grain – Direction of wood fibres running down into a cut producing a snagging rough surface.

De-stumping – A post-felling practice of removing stumps to prevent the spreading of butt rot fungus to nearby newly planted trees.

Dendritic – Broadleaf tree form characterised by multiple

Author carving a cherry eating spoon

Chisels

branching from the main stem.

Dendrochronology – The practice of studying of tree rings to determine its age and the history of the environment during the life of the tree.

Den tree – A tree containing holes and cavities suitable for birds and small mammals to nest in.

Dew point – The temperature at which water vapour condenses from the air.

Diameter at Breast Height (DBH) – The diameter of a tree calculated after having measured its circumference at 4ft 3" /1.3 mtr from ground level.

Differential shrinkage – The different rates of wood shrinkage parallel with the rays, compared with shrinkage tangential to the growth rings.

Diffuse porous – A hardwood species where pores are approximately the same size and are distributed evenly across each growth ring. Examples are maple, birch and beech.

Dillaxe – An alternative name for a *froe*, or *frommard*, used in the south east.

Dip – Initial wedge cut made in a tree facing the direction

in which it will fall, prior to making the final felling cut from the other side of the tree directly behind. Also known as a *face cut, kerf, birdsmouth* or *sink*.

Dog – Securing device used in forestry. Long metal rod usually square or round in section with right angle bends at either end filed to a point. Points are driven into a felled log and an anchoring spot. Much used to secure logs held over saw pits.

Dog-leg gouge – One handed gouge with the blade almost at ninety degrees to the handle with a convex spoon blade at the end. Used to carve out the inside of bowls and cups.

Doles – The two side gripping handles on a scythe handle, usually made of Beech. Also known as *snees*.

Dolly – A specially made one handed tool/shave, designed to remove strips of bark from poles along the length in a process known as *blazing*.

Downright shave – Heavy wooden-bodied spokeshave with a concave blade. Used by a cooper with a pushing action to finish the outside of a wooden barrel.

Drawboring – Advanced jointing method used particularly in timber framed building where a mortise and tenon is secured with a seasoned dowel driven through a hole, pre-drilled into the mortise and tenon, but slightly offset in one of the pieces to enable the joint to draw together very tightly when the dowel is driven in.

Drawbore pin – Tool used to assist in drawboring.

Drawknife/Drawshave – A green woodworker's cutting tool with a straight or slightly curved blade and a bevel on one side, commonly 8 to 12 inches (20 – 30 cm) long, with perpendicular handles at each end. Invariably used to shape cleft wood billets clamped in a traditional shaving horse.

Drawn up – The result of selective cutting of hazel rods, as opposed to coppicing the whole stool indiscriminately.

Drawn – Trees grown close together which are unable to develop wide crowns.

Dressing – Initial shaping of a wooden cask stave with a cooper's axe.

Dressing out – Trimming the off-side brash from coppiced rods with a billhook.

Drifts – Piles/layers of rods from cut-over coppice systematically laid in rows all in the same direction, prior to sorting and bundling. Brash drifts remain on the forest floor to encourage wildlife habitation.

Druxy – Colloquial term for wood cut from an old or dying tree which has lost its strength and flexibility. Also referred to as *frow*.

Dry cooperage – Wooden casks not required to be watertight, made from fir and pine to hold a variety of commodities – apples, tobacco, coins, etc. (See also *tight dry, wet* and *white cooperage*).

Duck – Coopers name for a split wooden cask stave which, if not properly made, would crack when it came to bending and assembling. Possible origin of 'out for a duck'

Dumb head – Continental style of shaving horse using a block of wood to clamp the work piece.

Dutch elm disease – A fungal tree disease carried by beetles first introduced in the 1930s which devastated the UK elm population in the 1960s.

Dutch hand – Levering device operated by foot, used when bending cask staves together, consisting of a wooden plank into which stout rope is threaded through holes and noosed around the perimeter of the cask.

E

Earlywood – Early thin-walled cells laid down in stems and branches in the early part of growth, evident in the growth rings. Lighter than the later summer/latewood. Also known as *springwood*.

Ecology – Study of how plants and animals interact with each other and their surroundings.

Ecosystem – All plants and animals in a particular area and how they relate with one another.

Equilibrium Moisture Content – (e.m.c.) Moisture content (m.c.) within the cells walls in a piece of wood, or pieces of jointed wood containing different moisture content after full adjustment to the ambient humidity at the time.

Emparked – Detained within the boundaries of an enclosed area of land.

Encased knot – The dead residue of a branch embedded within the resulting growth of the trunk which encompasses it.

Encoppice – To enclose an area of young coppice after cutting to prevent browsing of young shoots.

Endemic – A species, plant or animal only to be found in one particular country or area.

End grain – A wood surface consisting of exposed cross-grain.

End rounder – Cutting tool which produces a radius on the end of wooden poles. Suitable for use in chair making.

Epicormic – Shoots sprouting from the outer layers of wood.

Epicormic branching – Branches growing out of the main stem of a hardwood tree from dormant buds compacted under the bark, usually in response to damage or in areas of increased light.

Epicormic growth – A wart-like swelling beneath the bark of a tree as a result of a tight compaction of small dormant buds of twigs. Much prized by bowl turners.

Epidermis – Outer covering of young shoots.

Estovers – Old common term for the wood gathered by tenants for fuel and various general use.

Ethers – Thin, whippy stems of hazel rods which are woven into the top stakes of a newly laid hedge to form an attractive continuous finish. Also known as *binders*.

Evergreen – Description of a coniferous, softwood tree which retains its leaves/needles during the winter.

Excurrent – Conifer tree form characterised by a straight, dominant main stem with subordinate lateral branching.

Extraction – Removal from site of felled timber, to a roadside location.

Extraction route – Woodland track, or ride agreed or created for the purposes of transporting felled timber to a roadside location with the least possible disturbance to the woodland ecosystem.

Extractives – Deposits left in wood after the transition from sapwood to heartwood.

Eye – The oval hole in an axe handle in which the handle is fitted.

F

Face cut – Initial wedge cut made in a tree facing the direction in which it will fall, prior to making the final felling cut from the other side of the tree directly behind. Also known as a *sink, dip, kerf* or *birdsmouth*.

Facing – Cutting away the feet, or buttresses, spurs, toes on the base of a tree prior to felling. Also referred to as *daubing, rounding up,* or *setting up*.

Faceplate – Circular plate held on the head stock of a lathe to which the work piece is attached by screws.

Face turning – Turning a work piece where the wood grain runs perpendicular to the axis of the lathe.

Faggots – A bundle of sticks and twigs (cordwood and brash) tied tightly together using a wythe. Traditionally used for a very intense blaze in hearths, baker's ovens and brewer's maltings. Also used as a base for corn and hay stacks and to line the bottom of ditches instead of pipes, since water percolates freely through them. Also known as *bavins* in some areas.

Faired down – The result of shaving a thin cleft of ash, oak or birch leaving it wider in the middle and narrower at each end, which is used to make trugs.

Fall of timber – An area of trees either felled and awaiting extraction, or marked out for felling.

Fascines – Tied bundles of small diameter brash with many uses, such as strengthening earth structures and preventing soil erosion, effective in minimising flash flooding along river banks, laying over wet and boggy terrain as a pathway and as dead hedges.

Feathered tree – Nursery grown young tree with plenty of branches near ground level.

Fell – An area of cut or sold coppice woodland. Also known as a *coupe, cant* or *burrow.*

Felling – The act of cutting down a standing tree.

Felling cut – The final cut made on the back of the tree behind the face, or wedge cut.

Felloes – (Pronounced *fellies*). Curved blocks of ash, beech or elm joined together to form the outer rim of a wooden cart/waggon wheel.

Ferret – Hooked carving tool used on a pole lathe. A specially designed chisel used to extract fibre from the bottom of a mortise.

Ferrule – Protective brass or rubber tip on the bottom end of a wooden walking stick.

Fibre – Fine tubular structures of wood which determine the grain direction.

Fibre saturation point – The condition when wood cells are fully saturated with bound water but the cell cavities are empty of free water. The moisture content would have reduced to approximately 30% after which shrinkage/drying commences.

Fiddleback – Attractive wavy, ripple effect figuring on the surface of some maple and sycamore when quarter sawn. Traditionally used for the backs of violins, hence the name.

Fids (1) – Pointed metal centres attached to the headstock and tailstock of a pole lathe.

Fid (2) – Slender, cone shaped half sectioned wood or metal cylinder, used for rope splicing and very useful for finishing the last weaves of a rush chair seat.

Field layer – Layer of small, non-woody herbaceous plants growing usually no more than one metre from the ground.

Figure – The pattern visible on the surface of wood caused by a combination of the features of grain, growth rings, rays, tissue structure, colour, knots, burrs, growing conditions and damage, and the orientation of the surface when cutting.

Fillet – A narrow strip of wood.

Final crop spacing – The density of growing trees prior to felling them for commercial timber.

Fipple – A round dowel with a flattened top along its length ('windway'/oscillating valve) inserted into the mouthpiece of a rustic whistle, enabling the airflow to creates the 'whistle'.

Firmer – A chisel bevelled on both sides.

Fishtail – A chisel or gouge with a splayed cutting end resembling a triangle.

A French drawknife and two spokeshaves

Fissile – The property of wood that allows it to be riven/cleft, depending on the straightness of the grain (softwoods) or the arrangement of the fibres and rays (hardwood).

Fitching – One of many types of weave used in the construction of willow baskets.

Flag – Cooper's tern for river rush.

Flare – Name given the part of an axe head that flares out towards the shoulder.

Flatsawn – Pieces with annual rings intersecting the surface at less than 45 degrees.

Flitch – The half of a tree which has been sawn lengthways.

Flitch sawn – A section of timber sawn lengthways in a series of parallel slices (see *through and through*) retaining the original waney bark edges of the log. This produces not only back sawn and quarter sawn boards, but also some of them will be a combination of both.

Flittern – A young oak tree.

Flush – The first vigorous burst of leafing buds on trees in spring.

Fluted parting tool – A cutting tool in wood tuning with a wedge shaped section and a flute on the wider of the two edges.

Fingernail – Term coined to describe the shaped, ground end of a spindle gouge used in turning.

Fold bar – Metal rod resembling a large, fat nail with a forged eye two thirds of the way down and a point at the end. A tool to aid installation of sheep hurdles in fields. Two-fold use – firstly to drive two holes in the ground with the aid of a beetle, and secondly to fit the eye over each of the two hurdle heads in turn to avoid splitting the end grain when driving them into the pre-made hole in the ground with the beetle.

Forest – A biological community dominated by trees and other woody plants. Used by kings to keep deer on.

Forest Design Plan (FDP) – Long term (over 20 years) outline design including detailed proposals of felling, regeneration and environmental management in the first few years.

Forest wetland – An area dominated by woody vegetation taller than 20 feet where soil is at least periodically saturated, or covered by water.

Forest Year (FY) – The 12 months from October 1 to September 30.

Forestry – The art, science and craft of tending woodlands to derive benefit to humans.

Formative pruning – Removing the branches/stems of young broadleaf trees usually 3 to 10 years after planting to ensure that it grows in a single stem with light branching.

Forstner bit – A speciality wood cutting bit that rides on semi-circular spurs. Makes a clean, flat bottom hole.

Forwarder – A forestry machine used to carry out cut timber for stacking prior to collection.

Foxing – A yellow/brown/orange staining caused by fungal infection.

Fragmentation – The gradual loss of whole or parts of woodlands to agriculture, roads or building development, resulting in unlinked patches of surviving woodland, isolating wildlife populations and reducing biodiversity.

Framer – Name given to a craftsman who would assemble the component parts of a chair and carry out any finishing details.

Frame saw – Traditional saw comprising of a blade held in a wooden 'H' frame consisting of a pair of mortised cheeks held apart at 90 degrees by a stretcher and tensioned by a hemp cord twisted like a windlass with a wooden toggle. Typically the blade length varied from 8 to 16 inches (20 - 40cm).

Framed pit saw – Long frame saw consisting of a long blade fixed lengthways in the middle of an oblong wooden frame. Used by two men to saw boards from logs over a saw pit.

Framing pins – Timber framing. A long, round tapered pin with a 'T' handle used in place of an oak peg during construction and replaced with an oak peg on final assembly.

Fraying – Damage to the bark of trees when deer rub their antlers against them to either mark their boundaries or remove surplus velvet from them.

Free water/moisture – Moisture within cell cavities of wood, not in the cell walls. Loss of free water does not result in appreciable shrinkage. Most free water is removed when wood dries down to under 30% moisture content, after which the cell walls start to collapse and the bound water/moisture starts to be lost in the wood.

Froe – A riving (splitting) tool with a straight blade usually 8 to 12 inches long (20 - 30cm) and a sturdy perpendicular handle. Usually struck on the top edge of the blade with a beetle, or similar wooden club. Very effective for splitting shingles. Also known as a *Frommard.*

Frommard – French word for a *Froe.*

Frog – The angled section of a spokeshave body that supports the blade.

Frost hollow – A dip of low lying land harbouring cold air and frost even into late spring and early summer, not helpful in ensuring healthy young tree shoots.

Frow – Colloquial term used to describe brittle timber which would have been cut from an old, dying or dead tree. Also sometimes referred to as *druxy.*

Full Stocking – Trees grown in sufficient volume to form closed canopy woodland.

Fuming – The process of darkening oak without effecting the grain, by enclosing the timber, or a finished piece in an airtight chamber containing ammonia. Half a pint (.25 litre) of ammonia in a shallow container will produce an olive green shade in 12 hours in a chamber of 200 cubic feet (5.6 cubic metres).

G

Galleries – Shallow tunnel networks excavated by beetle larvae under the bark of a tree. Removing the bark reveals these intricate labyrinths, and an artistic eye may view them as quite beautiful.

Gapping up – Planting trees and shrubs to replace dead ones to maintain stock level. Also known as *beating up.*

Ghost – A dead tree, or other woody structure whose presence remains as a hedge, landmark, or parish boundary.

Girdling – Removing the bark and cambium layer from a tree trunk completely around its circumference.

Forest willow

Girt/Girth – A quarter of the circumference of a tree. To measure the cubic capacity of a standing or felled tree, a string was passed around the circumference, aided by a metal sword/needle in the case of a fallen log, and doubled, then doubled again. This, minus an allowance for the thickness of the bark, was measured and formed the basis for determining the cubic capacity of the log. Once calculated, the log would be marked/scribed using a race.

Glade – A clearing within a woodland, often grassy and grazed by mammals.

Glassing – Focussing on a distant object through binoculars or a spotting scope, usually when observing wildlife, or culling deer.

Global warming – A term used for the greenhouse effect as a result of increased emissions of greenhouse gasses.

Glut – Tapered wood or metal splitting wedge.

Gouge – Turning tool with a 'U' shaped cross section cutting edge.

Grain – The longitudinal wood cells of a tree. Described as straight, interlocking, diagonal and wavy grain.

Grannies – Term given to ancient scots pine trees.

Green – A small common.

Green belt – Areas of open land retained around towns and cities upon which there are strict planning restrictions upon development.

Green tonne – Expression sometimes used to describe the weight measurement of freshly felled green timber still containing free water.

Greenhouse effect – The effect produced as greenhouse gasses allow solar radiation to pass through the earth's atmosphere, but prevent most of the infa-red radiation from the surface and lower atmosphere from escaping into outer space.

Greenhouse Gasses (GHG) – Gases, including water vapour, carbon dioxide, methane, nitrous oxide, halogenated fluorocarbons, ozone, perfluorinated carbons and hydroflourocarbons, which accumulate in the earth's atmosphere and trap heat.

Green wood – Any unseasoned wood with a moisture content above the fibre saturation point (approx. 30%). Below this, the bound water within the cell walls will start to disappear and the seasoning/shrinkage will commence.

Green woodworking – A recently adopted phrase describing an ancient approach to woodworking that takes advantage of the structural qualities of freshly felled timber. These include the use of rived (split) parts with little grain run out, easy cutting with hand tools, and superior bending characteristics. After it has been worked, the green wood is dried to various appropriate moisture contents before wet/dry assembly which involves very tight fitting mortise and tenon joinery and takes into account the orientation of growth rings to ensure maximum adaptability to fluctuating moisture levels and no dependence on glue.

Grit – A term adopted to describe the grade of particles in sandpaper and sharpening stones to determine the aggressiveness of the cut.

Grove – A small wood.

Ground layer – The woodland floor up to 10cm from the ground containing mosses, herbs and seedlings from shrub and canopy layers.

Group selection – Management intervention where small groups of trees are felled and allowed to re-generate in order to introduce a diversity of tree age, or to cultivate valuable individual trees.

Growth rings – A layer of new wood cells added to a tree trunk or stem around its girth during the growing season. Prominent once a log/tree has been crosscut. New wood produced in the latter part of the year (Sept/Oct to March/April) after the sap has stopped rising is darker than that produced when the sap is rising (April/May to August/Sept).

Grub/grubbing) out – Clear-felling an area of trees and extracting their roots.

Grumplings – Low stone walls at the base of timber frames buildings.

Gun – Name used in coopery for a fired wooden cask.

Gymnosperms – Taxonomic name for conifers/softwoods with naked seeds.

H

Habitat – The ecosystem in which a plant or animal lives and depends on for cover, breeding sites, food and water.

Habitat pile – A heap of brash left on the forest ground after felling to enrich biodiversity.

Haft – The handle of an axe or hammer.

Half pointed – The bevelled top of a post which assists in avoiding splitting when driving in the ground, and helps rainwater to run off.

Hand pin – Side handle on a scythe. Also called a *dole* or *snee*.

Hanger – A wood growing on the side of a hill.

A German treadle lathe

Hardwood – Collective term for the group of deciduous trees which loose their leaves annually (*gymnosperms*). Not all hardwoods are hard. Their hardness varies between species. Balsa and basswood are hardwoods that are quite soft.

Harr – The upright on a field gate onto which the hinges are fixed.

Head – Wooden cask lid.

Headstock – Assembly sited on the left side of the bed on an electric or pole lathe. Supplies the drive for the work piece on an electric lathe.

Heart shake – A shake emanating from the heartwood.

Heartwood – The inner, expanding dead cell core of a tree trunk which supports the tree.

Heathering – In hedge laying, a finishing weave consisting of three or four horizontal layers of very small diameter, pliable material like hazel or hawthorn ends, or even bramble, intertwined between the tops of the upright stakes.

Hectare – An area of land 100 x 100 metres (10,000 square metres) and equal to 2.471 acres.

Heel (1) – The corner at which a chisel bevel meets the back of the blade.

Heel (2) – Upright at the hinged end of a field gate

Height – Work used in Coopery to denote the proportional radius of a wooden cask stave in its middle/belly/pitch once assembled.

Helve – A tool, or implement handle, usually associated with axes.

Hewing – Shaping, squaring or levelling a log with an axe or adze.

High forest – A dedicated, single stemmed tree woodland managed without underwood coppice.

Forest 'high seat'

High seat (*pictured left*) – Wooden or metal structure discretely placed within a forest, with a seat at the top, accessed by ladder, used to view and/or cull deer.

Hollow auger – Tool used to form cylindrical tenons used for stools and solid bottom chairs.

Hollow grind – A minute concave form ground on the bevel of a chisel mirroring the radius of the grinding stone used.

Hollowing out – Shaping the inner face of a wooden cask stave to remove some of its stoutness.

Hollowing knife – Drawknife with a concave blade used to cut the inner face of a barrel stave.

Hollow shoulder tool – Used to cut round tenons with a concave shoulder.

Honeycombing – Checks / irregular splits in the interior of a piece of wood, caused by rapid drying.

Hone, honing – The second step in sharpening, between shaping (grinding) and polishing. Usually performed by hand on a stone.

Hookgate – (Sizing tool). A hook shaped attachment to a square parting tool enabling the work piece to be sized to a pre-set dimension on a lathe.

Hooper – Name given to a craftsman who produced hazel hoops for wooden barrels.

Hoppus measure – A theoretical allowance measurement made for wastage when converting timber in the round, to a square log. There are 27.8 hoppus feet to a cubic metre. A hoppus foot is roughly 20% less than a cubic foot.

Horticulture – The art and science of cultivating and the creation of gardens.

Howel – A concave groove cut around the inner circumference of a wooden cask near the top at each end.

Hung timber – Felled tree caught up in the canopy of other standing trees preventing it from falling to the ground. Must be dealt with immediately rather than leave it to fall down without warning at any time after. Known as a *widow maker*, due to the danger to forest workers.

Hurdle – A moveable barrier to control farm stock, usually sheep. Two types – gate or wattle hurdles. Gate hurdles are very light gates comprising upright posts, cross-bars and braces best made from cleft sweet chestnut, ash or willow. Wattle hurdles are best made from cleft and whole hazel rods weaved around a series of uprights called sails.

Hydrophilic – Wood with a strong tendency to absorb and bind water.

Hydrophobic – Wood with a strong tendency to repel water.

Hydroscopic – Wood with the ability to absorb and/or lose moisture/bound water within the wood cells from the atmosphere with changes in humidity, resulting in dimensional changes in the wood.

Hypsometer – Simple sighting device used to calculate the height of a standing tree.

I

Inboard turning – Face turning performed on the bed of a lathe on the right hand of the headstock.

Incannel – The surface of a gouge sharpened on the concave surface.

Included angle – The sum of the two faces of a cutting edge.

Increment – The amount of measurable new wood put on by a tree in a year.

Increment Borer – An auger-like tool with a hollow bit designed to extract a sample core from a living standing tree to determine age and growth history, without having to cut it down.

Index plate – A plate which locks the drive shaft on an electric lathe into a series of pre-set positions.

Indicative Forestry Strategy (IFS) – Local Planning Authority strategy highlighting the strategic impacts of afforestation according to sensitivity in different areas.

Industrial roundwood – Felled, unconverted/processed trunks and branches for commercial, non-fuel use.

Inshave – A type of deeply dished drawknife, usually with two handles, but sometimes with only one. Used to sculpt the saddled section of Windsor chair seats, or convex scoopings from solid bowls. Probably had its origins originally in the cooper's trade for shaping the inside of wooden barrels.

Inside shave – A small rounded wooden plane with a wooden handle either side used to smooth the inside of a wooden cask.

Interlocking grain – A grain which has multiple directions within alternating layers. Difficult to work or split.

Introduced Species – A non-native species intentionally or unintentionally introduced into an area by humans.

Iron – An 'iron' refers to the blade of tools such as a plane or spokeshave.

J

Jack – A pronged fork used to carry a burden of about eight bundles of straw roofing thatch up a ladder.

Jambs – The side timbers in doors and windows.

Janker – Timber janker. A device consisting of a pair of wheels attached to a shaft placed underneath the butt of a felled tree to assist extraction. Also known as a *timber bob*.

Jarvis – Hollow-bladed plane used to round off wooden wheel spokes.

Jigger – Long knife with a hollow concave blade used to cut the howel around the inner circumference of a wooden cask. A chive was also used as an alternative tool.

Jointing – Carving a bevel down each side of a wooden cask stave using a jointer.

Jointing plane/jointer – Floor mounted long wooden block plane, raised at one end with the blade facing upwards. Used in coopering to cut a bevel edge on a wooden cask stave.

Juvenile wood – The core of the first few growth rings around the pith.

K

Kerf – The width of slot formed by a saw cut.

Kerf cut – Initial wedge cut made in a tree facing the direction in which it will fall, prior to making the final felling cut from the other side of the tree directly behind. Also known as a *face cut, dip, birdsmouth* or *sink*.

Kiln dried – Wood dried by heat below the moisture content attainable by air-drying. Approx 6 to 12% m.c.

Kind – Describing high quality coppice poles that are easily rived, and are straight and smooth.

Knocker-up – Bent piece of metal tubing used to lever up the head of a cask into position by means of access through the bung hole.

Knot – A portion of a missing branch encased within the subsequent growth of the trunk. A dead knot is usually dark in colour and has a tendency to fall out. A live, or tight knot is usually a similar colour to the surrounding wood, which knits it into place permanently.

Kyoto Protocol – A legally binding agreement between 159 countries (including Great Britain) who met in Kyoto, Japan in 1997 to agree reduction targets for six greenhouse gasses.

L

Lammas growth – Meaning 'loaf mass' after a Christianized Pagan festival. A second flush of leaves put out by oak trees in May and June if the first spring leaf crop has been decimated by caterpillars.

Landing (1) – A cleared area within a working timber harvest where felled logs are piled, processed and loaded for transportation.

Landing (2) – A cleared, flat circular ground area within a woodland acting as a base for charcoal burning by the traditional stack method.

Lap board – A sloping table on which a basket in the making is placed, with the weaver sitting under with legs outstretched.

Laps – Bindings of cleft ash, bramble, chestnut, hazel or oak used to tightly hold besom broom heads together. Also known as *bonds*.

Lap poker – A tool unique to besom (broom) making, its purpose to allow the free end of the bond to be securely tucked away under itself. Also called a *bond poker*.

Lateral roots – Roots that run out from a tree horizontally just below the surface.

Latewood – Thick walled cells laid down in mid-growing season in stems and branches evident in the growth rings. Darker in colour that the spring/earlywood. This is also known as *summerwood*.

Lat-axe – Another word for a froe, but sometimes a smaller, thinner version used for splitting lathes and shingles.

Laths – Long thin strips of cleft timber employed traditionally in building work. Weaved similar to wattle hurdles and nailed to walls and ceilings they form a base for traditional plaster. Also used to make swill or spelk baskets. Best cleft from oak, sweet chestnut or, sometimes willow.

Laths after lime plaster has been removed

Ash ladderback rocking chair with rush seat made by the author

Ladderback – Term used to describe a post and rung chair with between two to five horizontal thin slats usually steam bent for extra comfort and mortised into the back posts, to resemble a ladder. Shaker chairs were mostly ladderback.

Lanes – Courses of straw roofing thatch in 30" (76cm) widths.

Lath – Flat cleft riven from straight grained oak, chestnut or hazel into flexible components approx 1.5 x 0.25 x 48 inches (approx. 4 x 1 x 120 cm) long, nailed to, or woven into frames (wattle) to be installed as interior sub-structural walls and covered with plaster (daub) consisting (traditionally) of soil, clay, sand, animal dung and straw.

Lath Axe – Specialised sharp knife hit with a mallet to split riven oak into finer spelks used for weaving baskets.

Layering – To peg down a living tree stem into the ground, to encourage rooting for another tree. Sometimes occurs

naturally in some tree species.

Leader – The main top shoot of a tree.

Leggat – Wooden paddles for dressing reed and wheat reed thatching.

Let in – A term used in wattle hurdle making to describe when a new cleft rod of hazel is pushed between and weaved in and out of the upright 'sails'.

Lignin – Simply put, it is the pitch, sap, or semi-liquid (a polymer containing nitrogen), that remains in wood after it has seasoned. Lignin is the 'glue' that binds the wood fibres together. When it is heated, the lignin softens slightly making bends possible, hardening again when cooled.

Liner – (Cane seat weaving). A piece of fairly thick centre cane or Palembang cane used to line the inside of the seat frame, for the purpose of knotting the close cane over it.

Line-out – Marking down the length of a log using a chalk line, prior to sawing lengthways down that line.

Linish – A final sharpening/polishing process on a blade involving it being rubbed on a surface such as a leather strop containing a fine abrasive paste.

Linseed oil – A wood sealer/finish made from the seeds of flax plants.

Lippe – See *cawel*.

Listing – Chopping an angle and taper on the sides of a wooden cask stave using a cooper's axe.

Live centre – A centre in the tailstock of a lathe which revolves with the work piece.

Log house drawknife – Large drawknife with approx 12 inch (30cm) blade curved from the centre towards the user, with a slight concave shape. Used to quickly remove bark, shape and smooth logs for constructing log houses etc.

Log scribe – Marking out tool used in timber framing.

Longitudinal shrinkage – Shrinkage of wood cells along its length, from end to end. Typically less than 0.1%.

Lop and top – Chopping waste branches from poles and timber trees and leaving them on the forest floor to encourage biodiversity.

Lord – Word used by coopers to describe a misshapen wooden cask that leans to one side. Possible origin of the saying 'drunk as a lord'.

Lumber – American term for converted wood.

Lynchet – The difference in ground level after ploughing.

M

Maiden – A single stemmed tree, grown from seed, not from coppicing.

Mandrel – A means of holding a work piece for turning by means of a rod of wood or metal.

Mare (1) – A framework barrow made for and used by charcoal burners for carrying wood.

Mare (2) – A shaving horse differing slightly in design to the traditional English one, in that the clamping pivot resembles the American 'dumb head' design. The mare design was favoured by English 'swillers' who made spelk/swill baskets.

Mast – The irregular production of the fruit of oak & beech.

Masting – When a tree produces seeds on an irregular cycle subject to local conditions.

Mast year – A year when fruit crops are heavy.

Maul (1) – Alternative name for a wooden club.

Maul (2) – A log splitter. Long handled axe with wide head shaped for splitting timber.

Medulla – The pith of a tree.

Medular rays – Pockets of wood cells which run radially from the pith to the cambium layer, most prominent in oak. Very attractive figuring.

Mean Annual Increment (MAI) – The average rate of volume increment measured on a stand since planting, to the present, measured in cubic metres per hectare.

Meetings – The average cubic content calculated for a 'parcel' of standing trees. If, for instance, a number of standing trees measured about ten cubic feet each, they would be referred to as 'ten foot meetings'.

Mellowing – Willow and rush work. After soaking in water, bolts of willow or rush are wrapped tightly in a blanket for several hours, or overnight to become soft and pliable – 'mellow' – before use.

Mensuration – The measurement of individual or stands of trees.

Merknife – Timber framing. A two-handled drawknife/gouge used for cleaning up the hollow in the underside of a log.

Micro bevel – A narrow sub-bevel ground behind, and a few degrees greater than, the normal bevel angle on a blade.

Mill bill – A metal cold chisel held in a club-like wooden handle used in a similar way to an adze. This is the tool for dressing mill stones.

Minimum intervention – Hands-off management of a woodland involving only the bare minimum input to ensure protection of habitat and species.

Mire – Permanently waterlogged shallow area of low-lying ground.

Mixed woodland – Woodland comprising broadleaf and coniferous trees.

Moisture content – (m.c.) Represents the percentage of moisture in a piece of wood that is not completely dry.

Moisture meter – Hand-held electrical device with a small battery and circuitry which sends a small voltage through two integral metal spikes which are inserted into the wood. The resistance between the metal spikes is calculated and displayed on the meter as a percentage moisture content in the wood.

Monoculture – A stand of only one species of tree.

Morse taper – The taper of the end of a lathe/drill chuck enabling it to be installed or removed.

Mortise – A round or rectangular cavity into which a similar sized tenon is fitted.

Mortise chisel – A special chisel used to cut mortises by hand.

Mother tree – A mature tree left to produce seed to encourage natural regeneration.

Mottle – Term describing a figuring in wood caused by adverse weather and growing conditions resulting in attractive interwoven, swirling, twisting grain that, when caught by the light, gives the impression of depth and movement. Much used in cabinet making.

Motty Peg – The central wooden log used to start and support the stack of wood in a traditional charcoal earth burn, which is removed prior to lighting.

Mould – A small tree trunk split in half lengthways and drilled with holes on the convex side where sails are inserted in the process of making a hurdle.

N

Native species – Tree species which colonized prehistoric Britain naturally (without human assistance) after the recession of the last ice age and before the English Channel was formed.

National Vegetation Classification (NVC) – A comprehensive record of vegetation in the UK.

Naturalised species – Trees introduced by humans after the formation of the English Channel. Good examples are sweet chestnut (introduced by the Romans, a native of Italy and southern Europe) and sycamore (introduced in Tudor times, a native of central Europe).

Natural Resources Wales (NRW) – The agency responsible for forest management in Wales.

Neb/Nib – A large pair of wheels on a concave axle with shafts. Used to manipulate and carry a felled tree butt. The device is rolled lengthways down the butt, a wheel on either side, to the middle and the shafts raised in the air. A chain is secured to the butt and the shafts lowered, raising the butt for moving. Also known as a *timber bob*.

Needle/Sword – A slender metal rod with a small hook forged at the point on one end. Pushed under a felled tree, it enabled a string to be looped on the hook which was then pulled back under the tree. The continuous length of string remaining determined the girth of the tree (less a calculation for the bark and sapwood) and was used at the purchasing stage for the buyer/seller to determine the price of the tree.

Net Discount Revenue (NDR) – An analysis of the cost and revenue over a complete rotation period to assess the profitability of various management methodologies.

Nagura – Paste forming stone used in conjunction with polishing grade Japanese water stones.

Natural edge – The tip of a turned bowl or goblet which still retains some of the outside layers of the tree, including bark.

Natural regeneration – Perpetuation of woodland without human assistance.

Non-intervention – Or minimum intervention by humans in the natural regeneration of a woodland, either by planting, felling, coppicing or path creation.

Non-Timber Forest Products (NTFP) – Fruits, medicinal plants, resins, mushrooms, wildlife and other non-wooden assets obtained from forests.

Nug axe – Used by hurdle makers to trim off and finish a panel. Looking similar to a small fro, wooden handle with narrow metal blade with bevel at the tip.

Nurse crop – Sacrificial fast growing trees (usually conifers) grown alongside slower growing species to both protect and encourage them to grow straight and tall. Once the slower growing trees are established, the nurse crop is felled.

O

Open forest – Forest with between 10-30% canopy cover.

Other Semi–Natural Woodland (OSNW) – Woodland established since 1,600 AD comprising of mainly native species that has regenerated naturally.

Outcannel – The surface of a gouge sharpened on the convex surface.

Overbark – The volume measurement of a standing or felled tree inclusive of its bark.

Overstood (coppice) – Coppice that has been uncut and neglected for many years rendering it out of rotation for useful coppice products.

Overstory – Trees comprising the upper canopy of a woodland.

Oxygen – The colourless, odourless essential element of life produced by trees, making up 20% of the earth's atmosphere.

P

Pale – Fence of wood clefts nailed to horizontal rails.

Palembang – A brown cane used for the liner in chair seats named after a port in Java near where it grows. Much harder than centre cane, it is also used to make very strong baskets.

Three Scots pine

Paling – Fence of wood clefts up to six feet high (traditionally chestnut) wired together and rolled up for easy transportation.

Pannage – Old common term for allowing pigs to forage in a forest.

Pare – To make small, methodical reduction cuts.

Paring chisel – Bevel edge chisel with a slim blade used for light carving. Not intended to be struck with a mallet.

Park – Enclosed area of land commonly used for keeping deer.

Parting tool – For parting off in turning which involves cutting off waste from the finished work piece or dividing it into sections.

Patina – Richness and depth of colour evident in wood as it matures and darkens over decades.

Pea sticks – coppiced poles of small diameter used to support the growth of peas.

Peavy – A log moving tool similar to a cant hook, or ring dog with a spike at the end, instead of a hook.

Pecky – Work used to describe timber showing patches of decay.

Peeling knife – (Timber framing). Large curved drawknife used to remove bark from logs prior to building.

Perambulation – Legal document defining a piece of land by describing its boundaries.

pH – A measure of acidity and alkalinity on a scale from 0 to 14. pH7 is neutral, less than 7 is acid and greater than 7 is alkaline.

Phloem – Inner bark of a tree. Word more commonly used in the USA to describe the area through which the carbohydrates flow that feed the tree. Soft and supple/leather-like when wet. Used very effectively to weave post and rung chair seats. The most superior phloem being hickory in the USA or wych elm in the UK. Cedar, lime, ash and oak can also be used. Known more commonly in the UK as *bast*.

Photosynthesis – A process used by plants to convert light from the sun, carbon dioxide from the air and water into carbohydrates which are essential food for the tree. Ironically, the waste product from this process is oxygen, which keeps us alive.

Picking over – (Basketry). Trimming off projecting ends of a willow weave so they lie neatly in with the weaving.

Pigs – Collective name sometimes given to earwigs and wood lice found beneath the outer bark of seasoned logs.

Piles – Cleft oak fence stakes. (Also called *spiles* and *stobs*).

Pimp – Another word for a bunch of tied faggots used for fire lighting.

Pin chuck – A lathe chuck with a metal or wooden pin jammed into a hole drilled in the work piece.

Pin knot – Very small knot up to a quarter of an inch diameter.

Pinetum – Botanical collection of conifer trees, including, but not exclusively pines.

Pioneers – The first plants and trees to colonise bare ground.

Pith – Narrow, hollow channel found in the middle of a tree trunk, branch or twig.

Pitch – Number of teeth per inch (t.p.i.) on a saw blade.

Pith – Narrow, sometimes hollow, channel found in the middle of a tree trunk, branch or twig residue from the first year's growth.

Pit roll – A principle straight grained log, laid across a saw pit, having been shaved lengthwise to a hexagonal cross-section with cross mortises on each end to take a lever. Its function is to assist moving the log to be sawn, lengthways, backwards or forwards along the top of the pit.

Pit saw – Two-man operated long tapered saw used in conjunction with a saw pit to produce boards from logs. Also see *framed pit saw*.

Pitstead – An area in the woodland cut and cleared for producing charcoal.

Plane iron – The metal cutting blade on a hand plane.

Plain – Open area within a wooded forest.

Pleach – To interweave branches and twigs in hedge laying. Also called *plashing*.

Pleacher – A cut stem of living wood ready to, or already woven into a hedge.

Pleaching – In hedge laying, notching and layering the stems of an old hedge to induce new growth.

Pole – A coppice stool shoot of more than 2"/50mm in diameter.

Pole lathe – An ancient device made from wood with the same function as a modern day lathe, except that the work piece revolves between centres by means of a cord wrapped around it with one end of the cord attached to a springy pole overhead and the other end to a foot treadle. A semi-rotary action where the cut is made when the piece rotates towards the operator and the tool withdrawn at the end of the stroke when the piece rotates away.

Pole stage – A stand's growth stage when the canopy has closed and above head height, and the timber (small diameter thinnings under the normal size for milling into sawn timber) is cut.

Pole wagon – Like a normal horse-drawn wagon but just a skeleton version consisting of a round trunk of wood attached to which are four wheels and front shafts. Large felled trees are then secured for transport.

Polymer – A large molecule consisting of many sub-units with unique properties of toughness and viscoelasticity. Lignin in all trees is a polymer.

Poll – The area of an axe head directly above the eye.

Pollarding – The practice of coppicing a tree 8 feet (2.5 m) or more above the ground so the tree can re-generate saplings safely beyond the reach of cattle or deer. This also encourages burrs.

Pompeyed – A wooden cask having been charred inside during the firing process, allowing beer to mature more effectively

Post-and-rung-chair – Chair style consisting of vertical posts and horizontal rungs with vertical or horizontal back rests and a woven seat.

Pressier borer – Device for extracting a round core from a tree trunk at chest height without felling the tree in order to determine its age by counting the annual growth ring in the sample.

Pricking up – In basketry, when willow stakes are bent sharply upwards over the point of a knife so that they kink and do not crack.

Prickers – Timber framing. Metal rods of various diameters with a small spike on one end offset $3/16$"/5mm closer to the shoulder from the centre. Used to mark tenons through pre-drilled mortise holes. The tenon is then removed and a hole drilled (off-centre) where the mark indicates. When the joint is re-assembled and the wooden peg is driven through, the offset holes will cause the joint to fit very tightly together.

Primary woodland – A woodland that has been in place since trees re-colonised the British Isles after the last ice age.

Prog – A thick, forked pole used to manipulate trees during felling, especially if they have become hung.

Promote – To select a coppice pole on a stool and allow it to grow on to produce timber.

Propagate – To grow a new plant from its parent plant.

Provenance – Defining the region where a tree or seed originates.

Pulp – Product from which paper is made originating as waste and small wood in the round which is processed. The main timber used is aspen, fir, hemlock and spruce.

Pummel – A section of a turned spindle which is left in square section. Often a feature in chair and table legs.

Punky – Describing wood containing decay, or a soft, unuseable heartwood.

Puppet – Part of a lathe that houses either of the two lathe centres.

Purlins – Strengthening beams affixed horizontally to roof rafters.

Purpreture – Old common term for fencing off part of a forest for livestock grazing, or to build upon.

Putchers – Hazel salmon traps consisting of a woven, tapered open cone placed directly in the tidal salmon run.

Q

Quarters – Metal hoops fitted below the chime hoops on a wooden cask.

Quartersawn – A log is cut longitudinally into quarters. Boards are then sawn usually at 45 degrees to provide the maximum number of cuts radial to the centre of the log. Creates more waste than other sawing methods, but resulting in very stable boards less prone to warping, shrinking and splitting.

Queens – Term given to ancient beech trees.

Traditional 'pimp' – 25 individual bundles of fire kindling – Moreton Wood Coppice Products

R

Race – A knife, often adapted to a folding type with the point turned back in the shape of a hook and sharpened at the bend. Used for scoring marks in newly felled timber on-site and delivered and sorted timber to-site, symbolizing identification and usage/length etc. The marks are sometimes referred to as scribings.

Rack – Lines of trees cut out at first thinning to allow access for inspection or extraction.

Radial – A hypothetical plane that radiates from the pith outwards towards the bark of a tree. Perpendicular to tangential.

Radial shrinkage – Shrinkage of wood in the direction from the centre of the tree (pith) to its outside edge. Varies between species but between 4 and 6%, and up to 8% in some species.

Rack – A purpose build track in the forest for timber extraction.

Racking – Force applied to a chair when rocking it back while sitting on it.

Raft shackle – A short, stout chain with spikes affixed either end used by lumber men to attach floating logs together to form temporary rafts for timber transportation.

Raised grain – Effect in wood caused by dampness. An otherwise smooth surface can 'raise' up and ripple as the cells absorb water and swell.

Raising up – Putting wooden cask staves together within a rising up hoop prior to bending and assembly.

Raising up hoop – Ash hoop used to assist in the assembly of the wooden staves in a cask.

Randing – one of many types of weave used in the construction of willow baskets.

Rake (1) – The angle of saw blade teeth.

Rake (2) – Term used to describe the back lean angle of a chair.

Rasp – Type of course metal file used in woodcarving.

Rays – A cluster of wood cells that are arranged radially to the growth rings, emanating from the centre of the wood. Very prominent and attractive in oak.

Reamer – A cone-shaped hollow cutting tool used to taper the inside of round mortises. Similar shaped tenons fit into these holes.

Reaction wood – Distorted hardwood formed in leaning trunks on slopes and on large overhanging branches of trees. Reaction wood dries unpredictably, often twisting and cracking. Contains many tension and compression

Teaching the use of a pole lathe – Moreton Wood

forces in the trunk and boughs, so care must be taken when felling this type of tree. Known as 'compressed wood' in softwoods/conifers.

Recently Planted Native Woodland (RPNW) – Woodland of native trees and shrubs planted on open ground.

Reforestation – Re-establishing forests on land previously containing forests.

Regeneration – Woodland management to replace old or diseased trees by planting or encouraging natural regeneration.

Relative humidity – The general term for water/moisture vapour within the atmosphere at a certain temperature.

Residual stand – Tree remaining uncut following felling operations.

Re-space – Cutting out selected young trees before the thinning stage to allow the others to grow on.

Retention – A stand of trees allowed to grow beyond its optimum commercial felling age for either conservation or aesthetic reasons.

Retort – Metal cylindrical container, usually double lined and insulated specially designed for efficient charcoal burning.

Ridding – Very rough trimming of rods, in the initial cut stage leaving a few inches of twig instead of trimming them off against the stem. Useful if the rod is to be part or fully seasoned before use, as it avoids sere spots of dead wood which loos unsightly and dull the edge of a work tool.

Riddle – Device used to sieve out the dust and ashes from newly made charcoal.

Ride – A rough woodland access and thoroughfare, particularly useful for extraction of coppicing. Also see *rack*.

Rinding – Removing bark from poles. Usually peeled off in the summer months when the sap is rising, making the bark easier to remove.

Riffler – Slender metal file used in wood carving to file out small, contoured areas. Resembles a paddle shape, often double ended.

Ring-barked (1) – Squirrel damage on trees where the bark is gnawed around the entire circumference of a bough causing it to die from lack of supply of essential nutrition under the bark surface.

Ring-barked (2) – The deliberate removal of all the bark around the trunk of a tree to either stimulate reactionary seed production, or to leave standing deadwood to assist biodiversity.

Ring dog – Traditional tool for manipulating felled logs consisting of a metal ring and spike on a wooden lever. Similar design to a cant hook, or peavey.

Ring porous hardwood – A hardwood species that develops a ring of relatively large pores/vessels during early annual growth and much smaller pores/vessels later in the season. This results in very distinctive annual growth rings. Examples include oak, ash, hickory and elm.

Ring shake – A shake appearing between the annual rings.

Rip – A saw cut made parallel to and down the grain.

Rive – Splitting wood down the grain following the natural fibres and contours.

Riving break – A rough configuration of upright and angled timber to assist in the riving poles.

Road – Wide, unsurfaced woodland road ditched on at least one side, making it suitable for access all year round, as opposed to rides, or racks, which are semi-permanent, or seasonal.

Rods – Poles under 2"/50mm diameter taken from coppiced trees.

Rooted set – A single 8 foot (2.5m) rod of cricket bat willow 2 to 3 years old ready to be transplanted and grown specifically to make cricket bats.

Rootstock – The root onto which a scion is grafted.

Rotary plane – see *rounding plane.*

Rotation – Period between successive cuttings of coppice poles.

Roughing gouge – A large, square-nosed gouge with a 35 to 40 degree bevel, used by turners to convert riven and square stock and into a cylinder section.

Ring barking

Rounding plane – Cutting tool resembling a large pencil sharpener producing even cylindrical lengths of wood to pre-determined diameters. Used to cut round tenons for chair making.

Rounding up – Cutting away the feet, or buttresses, spurs, toes on the base of a tree prior to felling. Also referred to as *facing, daubing* or *setting up*.

Roundwood – Term used to describe logs and boughs which have not been sawn or cleft.

Rubber – Name sometimes used for a sharpening stone.

Runner (1) – Cleft or round hazel rod woven horizontally in and out of upright sails to form a wattle hurdle.

Runner (2) – Cleft Ash hoop used in coopery to assist the bending and assembly of wooden cask staves.

Runout – When a split runs from the centre of a pole to the outside, spoiling the cleft.

Rush – A natural, grass-like fibre used to weave post-and-rung chair seats.

S

Saddle – Name given to the part of a lathe which slides along the bed and supports the T bar/tool rest. Also known as a *banjo*.

Saddle tree – Name for the internal structure of a horse saddle, traditionally made from laminated beech or birch, around which the leather saddle is constructed.

Saddling – Carving the contours in the upper side of a solid chair seat.

Sail(s) – Upright rounds of hazel between which cleft hazel is woven to make a wattle hurdle.

Samson – Wheelwright's device consisting of a wooden bar through which a long hooked metal bar is pivoted near the end. Used to pull two spokes together enabling the spoke tenons to fit into the felloe mortises. Also known as a *spoke dog*.

Sapwood/Xylem – The outer growth rings between the heartwood and the cambium layer, which are a physiologically active part of a living tree. Sapwood is usually lighter than heartwood, and lacks decay resistance.

Savin coal – Charcoal made from juniper wood, suitable for making quality gunpowder.

Saw buck – Free standing wooden construction of two pairs of 'x' jointed timber held spaced apart at hip height by a horizontal bar. Used to rest round wood on whilst cross cutting with a buck saw.

Sawlogs – Round timber of the size and quality suitable for conversion in a saw mill.

Sawtooth bit – Type of Forstner bit which is more useful when drilling flat bottom holes in end or cross grain.

Saw pit – Oblong trench dug in the ground approximately 10 x 4 x 6 feet (3 x 1.25 x 2m) deep, over which a log would be suspended by resting on lengths of hewn timber.

Sawyer – Trade name given to the operator of a long, two handled saw. Sawyers would work in pairs to saw logs suspended over a deep pit.

Scab – A noticeable bulge in the trunk of a tree where it was once damaged and covered by protective growth.

Scarification – Removal of unwanted vegetation on the forest floor to stimulate natural regeneration.

Scarf – To join the ends of pieces of wood by bevelling so they overlap without increase in thickness.

Scion – Cuttings for grafting onto a rootstock.

Scorp – A type of deeply dished drawknife, (almost round) usually with one handle. Used to sculpt the saddled section of Windsor chair seats, or convex scooping from solid bowls, or for hollowing spoons.

Scotch eye auger – Long, metal hole boring tool, forged with a ring at one end to accommodate a removable wooden rod/handle fitted at right angle to the tool. Used for manually boring in wood at slow speed.

Scotch – Metal bracket placed behind the wooden wheel of a horse-drawn vehicle to prevent the cart/wagon rolling backwards on a slope. The process was known as *trigging* in some areas.

Scrapers – Thin sheets of flexible metal on which a burr is raised on the end with a burnisher. Used in turning to achieve a fine internal finish inside bowls and goblets. Similar shapes to cabinet scrapers.

Scratch awl – Marking out knife. Used in place of a pencil when a precise mark is needed prior to cutting.

Screw chuck – Lathe chuck with a single screw fixed in the centre to which the work piece is attached.

Scribings – Identification and measure marks scored on a tree with a hooked knife called a race.

Scroll chuck – Lathe chuck with the teeth on the underside of the four jaws engaging in a raised spiral/scroll on the back plate. Movement of the back plate causes the jaws to move in unison.

Scrub – Young woodlands.

Scrub wood – A small tree with stunted growth.

Seagrass – Chair seating. A course grass or sedge which grows mainly in the far East. A cheaper and slightly rougher alternative to rush.

Sealing – First step in the process of putting a finish on a piece of work. A sealer is applied to the bare wood which fills the grain and acts as a barrier against dirt and more importantly, moisture. This is the base for future finishing coats of wax, oil or paint.

Seasoning – The process of drying wood by lowering the moisture content, usually in open air, before processing.

Secondary woodland – Woodland created in an area since 1600 AD which was originally farmland or moorland.

Seed tree – A mature tree left uncut to provide seed for regeneration of a harvested stand.

Seed year – A year when seed is widely produced in abundance during a good summer.

Sere – Dry, discoloured dead wood, often showing where twigs have been snedded from a branch or pole. Dulls the edge of working tools.

Sessile – Without a stalk, i.e. sessile oak, which bears acorns without a stem.

Set (1) – The side offset of alternate teeth on a saw blade which forms the kerf (the width of the cut), which is slightly wider than the thickness of the blade to provide clearance as it passes through the work piece.

Set (2) – The final shape of a bent wooden cask stave after assembly.

Setting up – Cutting away the feet, or buttresses, spurs, toes on the base of a tree prior to felling. Also referred to as *facing, daubing* or *rounding up.*

Shade bearer – A tree able to grow in low light conditions under a partial or full canopy.

Shake (1) – Long, hand riven shingle.

Shake (2) – Term used to describe a split in wood.

Shaker tape – Woven webbing used by the American Shakers for chair seating. Originally woollen, later chairs used cotton tape. Nowadays comes in a multitude of colours in $5/8$ of an inch or 1 inch width.

Shaving horse – Ancient wood holding device consisting of a low, long narrow bench on feet and a pivotal arrangement designed to hold billets, using foot pressure whilst leaving two hands free to work the wood.

Shell augur bit – A drill used in turning on a lathe for long holes needed in items such as table lamps.

Shelter belt – Strips of trees planted to provide shelter from wind.

Shingle – Wooden roofing tile. Typically oak or cedar, cleft radially along the grain, hence they do not warp.

Shock(ing) – To lay newly sawn planks upright on-end against a frame resembling a goal post for a few weeks, prior to lying flat to dry between wooden spacers (stickers).

Shool – A long handled shovel used in charcoal making.

Shores – The two outer/end rods of a wattle hurdle which are pointed and driven into the ground.

Shot – Bevel angle on the edge of a wooden cask stave

Shoulder – Part of an axe head directly above the bevel.

Shaving horse in author's woodland workshop

Shredding – A management technique practised where the side branches and top are removed fro a living stem every two or three years for fodder and firewood.

Shrie – To remove the thorns from a bramble stem, often before using the fibrous stem to make a strong twine.

Shrub – A multi-stemmed, woody plant that comprises the understory of a forest.

Shrub layer – The understory of woody plants growing below the tree canopy.

Silva – Latin word for forest.

Silvan/Sylvan – Generic term applied to all things associated with woodlands and forests.

Silviculture – The practice of assisting and controlling the growth, quality, health and wellbeing of forests.

Silvology – The study of forests and woodlands.

Sink – Initial wedge cut made in a tree facing the direction in which it will fall, prior to making the final felling cut from the other side of the tree directly behind. Also known as a face cut, dip, kerf, or birdsmouth.

Snedding – removing the branches from a felled log

Singling – Converting a coppice stool to a single stemmed tree.

Site of Specific Scientific Interest (SSSI) – Designated example of the best UK wildlife and geological sites which are conservation areas.

Sizing tool – (Hook gate) A hook shaped attachment to a square parting tool enabling the work piece to be sized to a pre-set dimension on a lathe.

Skeins – Flat, cleaved strips of willow used for weaving and basketry, obtained by applying the use of a cleave/cliff.

Skew chisel – A turner's chisel with an angled cutting edge for fine cuts and tapers.

Skewing cut – Using a drawknife, spokeshave, chisel or plane at an angle, as opposed to perpendicular to the cutting edge.

Skidder – A tractor used to extract felled timber by dragging it.

Slab off – When a coppice pole tears away from the main stool.

Slabwood – The first and last cutting pass in a sawmill when sawing a log into planks. The result is an irregular plank with one oval face usually retaining some bark.

Slasher – A long handled tool with a billhook-like end used for crude, rapid ground brush clearance.

Slath – These are the upright sticks tied together by the first few rows of weave on a traditional basket.

Slay – Piles of brushwood laid in windrows awaiting conversion into faggots/bavins.

Slewing – One of many types of weave used in the construction of willow baskets.

Slicing cut – Shifting a tool's edge from one side to another during a cut. This has the same effect as 'skewing'.

Slick – Large, long handled, heavy duty chisel used in timber framing.

Slight – Word for a thin wooden bucket stave.

Slip/slipstone – A convex or concave shaped stone used to sharpen non-flat tools such as gouges.

Sloyd – Swedish term for 'craft', or 'handcraft' and the make of Swedish carving knives.

Slope – Angle of a chair seat from front to back

Slype – (Basketry) A slanting cut made at the end of a willow rod.

Snag – A standing dead tree.

Snaith/Snead – Scythe handle. Name derived from the Anglo–Saxon word sneadan (to cut).

Sned, snedding – To cut away the side branches from the standing bole of a tree or pole.

Snee – Side handle on a scythe. Also called a dole, or hand pin.

Snub ring – Metal spike attached to a metal ring hammered into the end grain of a stray floating log and attached by rope to a boat for towing.

Snigging – Extraction of felled timber sometimes with horses. Also known as tushing.

Softwood – Collective term for the group of non-deciduous trees including all conifers, which do not lose their leaves annually. Some soft woods can be quite hard, like certain species of pine, which are harder than some hardwoods.

Spade bit – Budget, fairly crude, aggressive but effective drilling bit used to drill larger flat bottomed holes.

Spalting – An irregular, dark linier pattern made in wood showing the first stages of fungus, caused by storing wood in damp conditions. If the wood is dried to below 20 degrees m.c. the fungi will cease multiplying. Most commonly affecting beech. Now considered by some as a desirable attribute in a finished artefact.

Spale – See *Spelk.*

Spar – A cleft hazel stick bent and twisted into a large hairpin shape with pointed ends, used to secure thatch in place. Also known as a botch, broach spar, or spec.

Spar gads – Hazel rods in the round approx 1 inch/25cm average diameter by 27 to 30 inch/ 70 to 76 cm long from which spars are cleft and bend.

Spar hook – One of many types of billhook. This one is used to assist the making of thatcher's spars.

Spec – See *Spar.*

Spelk (1) – The word spelk is derived from Old Norse *Spelker*, meaning a shaving or splinter of wood. Thin cleft strips (laths) of oak, 1 - 2 inches wide and approximately one $1/8$ inch thick (20 - 50mm x 3mm) were woven into a spel basket (also known as a *spale* or *swill*).

Spelk (2) – The original name for the large oval basket made from spelks. The basket resembling a miniature coracle. Very strong and versatile, used to carry anything from foodstuffs and coal, to a baby.

Spick – See *Spar.*

Spiles – Cleft oak fence stakes. (also called *piles* and *stobs*).

Spilling – A technique of planting and weaving living willow fences along river banks and streams to deflect potential flood water and resist soil erosion.

Spindle – A slender, cylindrical chair part.

Spindle gouge – Lathe tool for shaping beads and coves on spindles. Is ground to a finger nail shape with a cutting edge of 30 to 40 degrees.

Spinney – A small wood, or thicket.

Splat – A flat, thin board, usually shaped and mortised vertically into the centre area of the backs of English Windsor chairs.

Splay – The visual angle of chair legs protruding in any direction from the seat of a chair, measured in degrees from horizontal.

Splice – (Seat weaving). Method of joining seagrass and pre-twisted rush.

Spoke dog – Wheelwright's device consisting of a wooden bar, through which a long hooked metal bar is pivoted near the end. Used to pull two spokes together enabling the spoke tenons to fit into the felloe mortises. Also known as a *samson.*

Spokeshave – A finishing cutting tool with two handles housing a small blade mounted in the centre.

Spoon knife – Wooden handled knife with tightly curved (almost round in cases) blade with an edge on one or either side. Carves the hollow in a spoon.

Spoonbit – A wood boring bit with a rounded nose at the front. Sometimes called a *'chairmaker's bit'.*

Spray – Finely branched 'twiggy' wood from the top of a coppice pole; used for besoms, pea sticks etc.

Spring – The new regrowth of a coppice.

Springwood – Early thin-walled cells laid down in stems and branches in the early part of growth, evident in the growth rings. Lighter than the later summer/latewood. Also known as *earlywood.*

Spud (1) – A flat oblong board with a spade-like handle used by a thatcher to drive home pegs into the thatch.

Spud (2) – Tool used to remove the bark from oak trees by peeling. Curved metal blade shaped similar to a spoon with a long stem and wooden handle. Also called a *barking iron.*

Spurs – Feet-like swellings on the base of a tree curving down and out, denoting the beginning of the roots. Also known as *buttresses, claws, stamms* or *toes.*

Spurtle – A traditional Scottish wooden porridge stirrer. Cylindrical stick approximately 12"/300mm long by $1/2$"/13mm diameter. Can be quite ornate, or just tapered and plain. Also excellent for scrambled eggs, custard etc.

Staghead – Dead crown of a veteran tree.

Stail – Name for cleft wooden handle for a rake or besom broom. Very often made with a stail engine.

Stail engine – Wooden rotary cutter placed over a cleft and rotated down its entire length to form a round stail, or snaith, a handle for a rake or besom broom.

Stams – Feet-like swellings on the base of a tree curving down and out, denoting the beginning of the roots. Also known as *buttresses, claws, spurs* or *toes.*

Stand – A collection of growing trees of a similar type or species.

Standing volume – Calculation of the volume of trees in a stand before felling, normally expressed in cubic metres overbark.

Standard – Term for a single stemmed tree planted and allowed to grow straight to eventually be used for quality timber. Not coppiced.

'Snigging' or 'tushing' – extracting timber by horse – Moreton Wood.

Star shake – A group of splits visible on a cross cut log, running away from the pith, resembling a star.

Stave – Steam-bent curved wooden barrel components.

Steam bending – Placing wood in a chamber full of steam to temporarily heat and soften the wood's lignin, (pitch, sap, glue-like semi-liquid), before bending it over a form to the desired shape.

Steer – An arrangement of wooden boards stacked vertically for the purpose of drying.

Stem density – The number of larger trees in an area expressed as stems/hectare.

Stewardship – The act of taking responsibility for caring for land in the long term, regardless of short term financial gain, ensuring that it is left in as good, if not better condition as when first acquired.

Stick – An unspecified term for chair parts that are roughly cylindrical. Post-and-rung chairs are sometimes called 'stick' chairs. Also refers to bow and comb supports on Windsors when they are shaved instead of turned.

Stickers – Thin scraps wood strips inserted between stacks of green sawn timber to allow good air circulation through the stack enabling even air-drying. Normally $^3/_4$ inch to 1 inch (approx 2.5mm) square and as long as the width of the board, the most common woods used are fir, spruce or poplar, as they will not taint the boards. Using stickers made from unsuitable wood results in yard stain.

Stobs – Cleft oak fence stakes. (also called *piles* and *spiles*).

Stool (1) – The bottom living stump of a coppiced tree from which new stems grow.

Stool (2) – Traditional solid top three or four legged low seat.

Stooling – The burying of a stool to ensure re-growing stems produce roots which can be cut and planted as new trees the following winter.

Stoop/Stoup plane – Rounded wooden bodied plane used to smooth the inside of a cask.

Stop – Wooden end pieces/handles designed to attach either end of a metal bending strap used in the process of steam bending billets of wood into curves. Used in conjunction with the bending strap, these end pieces 'stop' the billet breaking under tension in the bending process.

Store – To leave coppice out of rotation either to save for future uses, or to grow into small trees.

Stored coppice – A slightly overstood coppice that is still capable of being brought back into rotation.

Story – A level of forest canopy, often consisting of various collective heights.

Storystick – A length of narrow flat timber, usually the height of a chair back, on which is marked all positions for mortise holes, tapers, and all other relevant dimensions and instructions. Also known as a chair stick.

Skeins – (Basketry). Thin strips of willow split off from either white or buff rods using a small cleave.

Stocking – The density of trees or stools in a woodland, usually the number per acre.

Stock knife – Large piece of steel approximately 30"/750mm in length bent slightly towards its middle. The lower half is fashioned into a stout blade and terminates in a hooked projection, while the upper half forms a curved handle with a wooden hand-grip fixed at right angles to its end. By means of the hook, the knife is fastened to a steel ring driven into a low wooden bench and, with this ring acting as a pivot point, the knife is used with a levering action to make powerful downward cuts while the other hand holds the work. Mostly used to rough out beech clog blanks and ash tent pegs.

Stool, stole – The base of a coppiced tree from which new shoots emerge.

Store – To leave young trees in coppice uncut to provide future standards.

Strake(s) – Flat lengths of metal nailed directly into the felloes around the circumference of a wooden wheel. Eventually replaced by heat-shrunk metal tyres.

Strop – A piece of leather and a process by which a fine

abrasive paste is placed on the leather and a blade rubbed over it as a final finish to sharpening.

Structural diversity – The degrees of spatial distribution both horizontally and vertically evident in woodlands.

Stumpage – The calculated value being the difference between the market values of felled timber and the cost of felling, transporting and processing it for market.

Sucker(ing) – Shoots growing from the roots of an older tree. Elm and aspen form clones of genetically identical trees by this method.

Summerwood – Thick walled cells laid down in mid-growing season in stems and branches evident in the growth rings. Darker in colour that the spring/earlywood. This is also known as latewood.

Sun scorch – Damage caused to tree bark by sudden exposure to the sun, usually when another tree shading it has been felled.

Sun shoots – Fresh stems that grow from the base of over-stood hazel coppice.

Sustainability – The ability of the natural environment to supply goods and services to man for the indefinite future, without being overexploited.

Sustainable Forest Management (SFM) – The concept of best practice in forest management to encourage sustainability and diversity.

Swales (1) – Contour ditches intended to collect water and absorb it into the soil.

Swales (2) – Brushes made of a bundle of birch twigs resembling a miniature besom broom without the handle, used in ironworks to brush off the residue from red hot steel.

Sway – Name of a decorative hazel stick held down and secured horizontally by broaches midway up a layer of thatch. Also known as *binders*.

Sweep – The term used to describe the curvature of a gouge, ranging from nearly straight to a gentle curve.

Swill Basket – See *Spelk*.

Swiller – Name given to a person who made spelk/swill baskets.

Swiller's mare – Foot-operated vice on which you sit, very similar to a shaving horse, made and used specifically to shave a spelk – a cleft, thin strip of timber (lath) used to weave a swill, or spelk basket.

Swingle-tree – A wooden type of yoke used to control two horses working side by side.

Sword/Needle – A slender metal rod with a small hook forged at the point on one end. Pushed under a felled tree, it enabled a string to be looped on the hook which was then pulled back under the tree. The continuous length of

Burnishing with spokeshave shavings

string remaining determined the girth of the tree (less a calculation for the bark and sapwood) and was used at the purchasing stage for the buyer/seller to determine the price of the tree.

Sylvan, Silvan – Generic term applied to all things associated with woodlands and forests.

Symbiotic – A mutually beneficial relationship between two organisms.

T

Tail – Another name given to the handle of a besom broom.

Tail stock – The moveable assembly to the right of the head stock which runs along the bed of a lathe.

Tang – A tapered projection on one end of a tool/knife/file/drawknife which can be tightly fitted into a handle.

Tangential – Perpendicular to radial.

Tangential shrinkage – Shrinkage around the annual growth rings. Varies between species, but averages from 7 to 8% and up to 12% in some species.

Tannin – A toxic secondary metabolite exuded by trees; notably Oaks, to discourage insects and mammals from eating bark and leaves. Bark was harvested from felled oaks and used extensively for softening and preserving leather.

Tapering plane – A tenon former with the blade set at an angle for making conical tenons. A matching reamer must be used to make the tapered mortise.

Tapped tree – A live, standing tree which has been bled for its sap, or resin.

Tare – The net weight of a vehicle without its fuel or load.

Tap root – Original and main root of a tree, put down from the germinating seed.

Taw – A type of lath (thin strip of cleft wood) varying from $^1/_2$ to 2 inches wide and approximately $^1/_{16}$ of an inch thick (12 – 50mm x approx. 1.5mm) used in the making of swill or spelk baskets.

Taxonomy – The science of classifying living things into different groups, classes, families, species, genus.

Tear-out – Broken or torn wood fibres generated typically as a cutting tool exits a cut at the end. Usually occurs during crosscutting cuts as the blade exits, or if a hand plane is not lifted off the cut before it reaches the end.

Tenon – A rectangular or cylindrical projection made to fit into a matching mortise. Used in mortise and tenon construction for many chair joints. Cylindrical tenons can be made on a lathe, or by hand, or by using specialist 'former' or 'rounding' tools.

Tension – In steam bending this is the tension of the structure of wood along its length on the convex outside of

Stock knives used for clog making

the bend. A bending strap and stops help to control this process; otherwise there is a possibility of the fibres breaking on bends with a tight radius.

Tension (assembled in) – In the case of post and rung chairs, where the compound angles of the drilled round mortises are deliberately drilled with a slight misalignment, so when the frame is assembled, it is slightly under tension, and in the case of Windsor chairs, where the middle stretcher is cut slightly long, so when assembled, pushes the rungs outward under tension.

Tension rod – (*Cane seat weaving*). A round or flat rod which will reach from side to side of the seat, over which the warp is put on to the seat, thus allowing 'play' for the weaving.

Thread – To clean a rod of knots smoothly with a billhook.

Throat – The slot on the sole of a plane or spokeshave where the blade protrudes, and through which shavings are ejected.

Through and through – Term for the conversion of logs into boards by sawing in parallel cuts along the full depth of the log. This produces not only back sawn and quarter sawn

the butt for moving. Also known as a *neb* or *nib*.

Tine – Old English word for thorn. Cleft wooden rake teeth usually made from ash or oak.

Tine cutter – Cylindrical metal tube, with a tapered grind on the outside of one end which was secured vertically on a bench and a cleft piece of slightly oversized wood hammered through it to form a round tine for rake heads.

Tithe – A small part, or tenth of the produce from the land originally paid to the Church.

Toes – Feet-like swellings on the base of a tree curving down and out, denoting the beginning of the roots. Also known as *buttresses* or *claws, spurs* or *stams*.

Tool rest – 'T' shaped part of a lathe which fits into the banjo and supports the cutting tool.

Topman – Senior sawyer in charge who stood on the top of a saw pit and held the top handle tiller of a long two handled saw, while his assistant pitman stood in the bottom of the pit controlling the other end of the saw.

Topping plane – Wooden semi-circular plane used in coopery to level the top ends of cask staves.

Trace(s) – The two side straps, ropes or chains by which a horse draws a plough, pulls logs etc.

Touchwood – soft fungal decayed wood easily combustible, so a favourite for tinder.

Trapezoid – (In chair making). Name given to a structure when the width of the front rail of a chair seat exceeds the width of the back rail, thus resulting in a structure that is not square.

Trap tree – A *decoy tree* intentionally deadened or felled and left to attract bark boring beetles in order to protect nearby growing stands of trees.

Traveller/Tyre runner – Thin circular disc of metal 6" to 7" diameter with a wooden handle kerfed at one end to accommodate the disc and pinned in the disc's centre. Used mostly by wheelwrights to determine the inner and outer circumferences of a wooden wheel or metal tyre by running the traveller around the entire inner or outer circumference.

Travisher – (chairmaker's shave, bottomer's shave) A spokeshave with a convex curve on the blade; used for finishing saddling on Windsor seats, or inside of carved bowls. Body usually made from wood.

Tree – A perennial plant with a self-supporting single trunk growing to 6m/20feet or more, with branches.

Tree monkey – Non-derogatory name (used in a similar way as Bodger) occasionally applied to a tree surgeon or their assistant who climb trees with the aid of ropes etc. in order to trim and fell them.

boards, but also some of them will be a combination of both.

Throw – To fell a tree in a pre-determined direction.

Thumbstick – A wooden walking stick with a natural 'V' shape at the top to accommodate the thumb. Probably the most comfortable, useful and versatile stick to own. Best examples made from hazel or blackthorn.

Ticketer – A round piece of metal, usually with a handle used to rub firmly along the end of a cabinet scraper, to form a burr edge.

Tight – (*Dry cooperage*). Wooden casks required to be watertight, made from fir, spruce and white elm to hold a variety of commodities – Herrings in brine, butter, syrup, soap, gunpowder etc. See also *dry, wet* and *white*.

Tiller – Wooden handle attached at 90 degrees to a metal rod fixed to the top end of a two-man pit saw.

Timber bob – A large pair of wheels on a concave axle with shafts. Used to manipulate and carry a felled tree butt. The device is rolled lengthways down the butt, a wheel on either side, to the middle and the shafts raised in the air. A chain is secured to the butt and the shafts lowered, raising

Treenails

Tree Preservation Order (TPO) – A legislative order regulating the care and removal of trees, particularly prevalent in urban areas.

Treen – Collective name of Saxon origin given to domestic household goods produced by local green wood craftsmen – bowls, platters, ladles, spoons, clothes pegs, etc.

Trenails (tree-nails) – Collective name for riven, wooden pins/nails/dowels slightly tapered at one end, and well-seasoned. Sometimes called *trunnels*. Ranging in all diameters and lengths, use for green wood joinery (particularly in timber framing), boatbuilding and in the case of furniture, as an additional decorative and functional enhancement. The wood used must be extremely hard and durable, so oak was traditionally preferred in Britain, but acacia and locust trenails, were also imported from America in large quantities.

Trigging – Procedure of placing a metal bracket (scotch) behind the wooden wheel of a horse-drawn vehicle to prevent the cart/wagon rolling backwards on a slope.

True out of wind – expression used for a flat, level surface.

Trug – Hand-made oval wooden container made from overlapping cleft strips of ash, oak or birch, nailed to a steam-bend hazel frame with a carrying handle. The word is derived from the Anglo-Saxon word trog meaning boat. Traditional boats were 'clinker-build' using overlapping boards. Trug construction adopts a similar method.

Trug Runner – See *Dog-leg gouge.*

Trunnel – see *Trenails.*

Trying sticks – Two small wooden square-sectioned sticks placed at opposite ends of a piece of planed timber and sighted by eye to determine if there is any level discrepancy, or wind in the plank. If the plank was perfectly flat it was known as 'true out of wind'.

Tumulus – Mound built on top of a burial site.

Tung oil – Oil used for wood finishing, extracted from Tung nuts.

Turning saw – Traditional saw comprising of a blade held in a wooden 'H' frame consisting of a pair of mortised cheeks held apart at 90 degrees by a stretcher and tensioned by a hemp cord twisted like a windlass with a wooden toggle. Typically the blade would be thin, About $^1/_8$ inch (3mm), allowing the cutting of curves (Windsor chair seats) with blade lengths averaging about 12 inches (30 cm).

Tushing – Extraction of felled timber sometimes with horses. Also known as *snigging.*

Twillie – A reinforced rectangular hole made from twisted cleft hazel weaved into a hurdle to enable carrying by means of a stick passed through and lifted onto the shoulder.

Twists – Longitudinal warping caused by uneven grain, stresses in the growing timber, or uneven seasoning.

Twybil – Specialist double-headed hammer-like hand tool with one end sharpened like an adze, used for enlarging and shaping a drilled mortise in a hurdle. Also sometimes called a *trybill, twivil, twiver, clader, timyhawk, mortice knife* or *dadder.*

Twca cam – Welsh long handled crook knife used to finish carving the hollow of a spoon.

Tyre – Continuous flat strip of metal heat-shrunk around the circumference of a wooden wheel. Previous to this, flat lengths of metal called strakes were nailed directly into the felloes around the wheel.

Tyring – The process of heat fitting a metal tyre on a wooden wheel.

U

Under-bark – The final measurement of a log after the thickness of the bark has been deducted.

Underbrush – Large forest plants that do not grow into trees.

Undercutting (1) – The process of cutting the roots of a young tree in a nursery at a depth of 3 - 4 inches (8 -10 cm) below the surface to stimulate root growth.

Undercutting (2) – Cutting away from an edge on finished wooden components forming a bevel to create the illusion of thinness.

Underplanting – Planting a new crop under the canopy of an existing one which will eventually grow up to replace the original.

Understory – Layer of shrubs beneath the main canopy of a forest.

Underwood – Coppiced trees growing under standard timber trees.

Upsetting – (Basketry). A shaping and strengthening stage in willow weaving.

V

Vascular system – Term for early elongated cells in the stem of young shoots which later grow under the bark, known as the cambium layer.

Vascular cells – Under-bark tissue. These cells transport fluid and nutrients internally. They are the main components of *vascular system*. Known as *xylem, bast* or *phloem*.

Veiner – A small, deep vee-shaped carving gouge often used to define detail.

Veneer log – A high quality, high value product grown and managed in such a way as to produce a straight, knot and branch free, large diameter tree suitable for slicing and peeling for veneer production.

Veteran tree – A tree with great age, size or physical condition considered of value to landscape, wildlife or human wellbeing.

Virgin – Forest untouched by felling.

W

Wald – Old English word for a wild, or wooded place. Also weald, or wold.

Waling – one of many types of weave used in the construction of willow baskets.

Wane(y) – Sawed timber with its natural bark edge intact. Produced by flitch (through-and-through) sawing.

Warp (1) – In weaving a chair seat, the initial strands wrapped around the front and rear rungs.

Warp (2) – Twists and buckles in sawn timber planks which have distorted due to uneven grain, seasoning, or wood which was under stress while growing. Also known as cast.

Wass/Wace – Long fibres produced by pulling cleft willow through fine, comb-like blades. This fibre was then either woven into bags and hats, or used for packaging material.

Wasting – The rapid removal of wood by hand using an axe, adze, knife or rasp, prior to finer shaping.

Waterhouse pile – A log pile specifically created for the well-being of invertebrates.

Water table – An underground level in which the pores of soil are saturated with water.

Wattle – Name for a weave of cleft, coppice hazel producing a hurdle – a lightweight temporary fence used for penning sheep.

Wayfinders – Trees were often planted along drove roads (paths to market). Their purpose was to act as boundary markers, and 'way finders', making it less likely to stray off the road in bad weather conditions such as heavy rain and mist.

Wayleave – Strips of land either side of power lines where tall trees are not permitted to grow and interfere with the power line.

Weald – Old English word for a wild, or wooded place. Also wald, or wold.

Wedge (1) – A square sectional tapered device resembling a wedge of cheese, made in either metal or, traditionally, wood. Used to prize open logs by inserting the tapered end into a pre-made split and hammering.

Wedge (2) – Small version of the splitting wedge used for hammering into a pre-made saw kerf in a tenon to secure firmly in a mortice.

Wedge cut – Initial face cut made in a tree prior to the final felling cut.

Weft – In weaving a chair seat, the strands that are woven across the weft (from side rung to side rung) forming a pattern.

Wet cooperage – Wooden casks required to be very watertight and long-lasting, made from oak to hold beer, wine and spirits etc. (See also dry, tight dry and white cooperage).

Wetlands – Ponds, swamps, marshes and bags saturated by surface or groundwater sufficient to support wetland vegetation exclusively adapted to saturated soils.

Whimbel – Thatching tool similar in appearance to a hand brace, used to twist straw into rope for sewing thatch to the rafters.

Whip – A young, two- to four-year-old transplanted nursery grown tree.

White cooperage – Wooden casks and hollow ware required for general domestic and commercial use, depending on application, made from ash, beech, chestnut, elm, fir, oak, pine or sycamore, for use as buckets, tubs and general hollow ware etc. (See also *dry, tight dry,* and *wet cooperage*).

White willow – Green willow harvested in autumn and kept in running water until spring. (Also see *brown* and *buff willow*).

Whorl – Describes the yearly radial growth of branches around the trunk circumference on a conifer. Counting these annual whorls will indicate the age of the tree.

Widow maker – Felled tree caught up in the canopy of other standing trees preventing it from falling to the ground. Must be dealt with immediately rather than leave it to fall down without warning at any time after. Also known as *hung timber.*

Wildwood – Prehistoric forest, untouched by man.

Wind (1) – To twist a small rod to form a withe, or a twist in a hurdle.

Wind (2) – A natural spiral twist in a length of wood.

Wind-firm – Trees that remain stable in strong winds often situated on the outskirts of fields and woodlands.

Winding sticks – Pair of straight lengths of stable timber used as an aid to help flatten boards planed by hand. When placed perpendicularly at either end of a board, the user sights across the tops to discern if there are any remaining high points on the planed surface of the board.

Windrow (1) – Long piled rows of brushwood left lying on the woodland floor for working up into a dead hedge.

Windrow (2) – Cut wood, stacked and left to dry in the woodlands to be used for charcoal burning.

Windsnap – A tree which has had its trunk or branch(es) snapped due to strong winds, but has remained rooted.

Windthrow/Windblow – Tree, or a stand of trees partially or wholly uprooted by strong winds.

Withe, Withy – Thin rods of hazel, willow, elm or birch twisted and used to tie faggots, bundles of coppice – product etc., or for tying the twigs to the handles on besom brooms.

Wold – Old English word for a wild, or wooded place. Also *wald*, or *weald.*

Wolf tree – A large, quick grown poorly formed tree with low timber value.

Woodbank – Ancient man-made boundary bank surrounding or subdividing a woodland to mark old parish boundaries.

Woodman's grip – Simple but effective device consisting of two poles tied apart roughly three quarters of the way down. The top of the poles are griped in each hand and the bottom ends placed either side of a bundle of coppice rods raised slightly off the ground, leaving the string resting on the top of the pile. The poles are then opened out at the top causing the lower assembly to tighten around the pile, which is then secured with twine. This gripping device works well for all manner of bundles, including brushwood bavins, birch besom heads and hazel pea sticks.

Wood pasture – Open-grown and pollarded trees in a grazed woodland.

Wood tar – Byproduct of charcoal burning. A solidified liquor, re-heated to a brushing consistency and used by shipwrights for waterproofing. Pine tar was considered the best and was found in evidence on the Mary Rose.

Work up – To trim and sort coppiced rods or poles.

Wymbyll – A very large auger bit similar in shape to a scotch eye auger – a long, metal, hole-boring tool, forged with a ring at one end to accommodate a removable wooden rod/handle fitted at right angle to the tool. The wymbyll is, however, on the end of a very long extension rod and was used for the purposes of boring a hole lengthways through the centre of an elm tree trunk to make a water pipe. The long extension rod was supported in the middle by a wooden support.

X

Xylem/Sapwood – The outer growth rings between the heartwood and the cambium layer, which are a physiologically active part of a living tree. Sapwood is usually lighter in weight and colour than heartwood, and lacks decay resistance.

Ash hurdle and willow screen

Y

Yards stain – Stain on air-dried boards developed during seasoning. Often caused by using the wrong wood for the stickers, which are spaced between the boards.

Yard stick – A graduated wooden rod three feet (one yard) long.

Yelming – The process of grading and gathering straw roofing thatch into manageable bundles.

Yield Class (YC) – A measure describing a species growth potential on a site.

Yoke elm – Disused name for hornbeam.

Yurt – A domed wooden framed transportable shelter with a canvas covering, similar to a *bender* but much more substantial. A popular, longer-term woodland shelter.

Z

Zales – Wattle hurdle uprights.

Walnut leaves and unripened fruit

CHAPTER 32

Recommended resources

There are many useful and inspiring books on the market these days. The selection below comprises books I own and have actually read. There are certainly many more great ones that I have yet to read. I have added a selection of organisations, websites and periodicals I have found useful. I am indebted to some of the authors listed below for some sourcing of information included in this publication.

Chapter 1

Chamovitz, Daniel – *What a Plant Knows* (2012) One World Publications.
Absorbing and eye-opening book which investigates and affirms the sensory capabilities of plants and their interaction with nature.

Pakenham, Thomas – *Remarkable Trees of the World* (2002) Orion Publishing
The stunning result of the author's five-year odyssey travelling the world in search of the most remarkable trees on the planet.

Tudge, Colin – *The Secret Life of Trees* (2005) Penguin Books
Superb, critically acclaimed book about trees and their inextricable link with us through time, as well as how their future wellbeing is so vital to us. Written in a style to engage right through to the last chapter, every politician in the world should be forced to read this.

Chapter 2

Hill, Jack – *The Complete Practical Book of Country Crafts* (1979) David & Charles
A really comprehensive book full of old photos and good illustrations describing all these useful crafts, crammed full of authentic, useful information. This is such a good book, that in my opinion, it stands next to John Seymour's *The Forgotten Arts and Crafts*. They should both have a place in your library.

Seymour, John – *The Forgotten Arts and Crafts* (combined with *Forgotten Household Crafts* in one volume) (1984) Dorling Kindersley
This should be a standard in all schools. A comprehensive book on these subjects. An inspirational volume covering all the trades, with poignant and philosophical introduction by the author.

Tabor, Raymond – *Traditional Woodland Crafts* (1994) Batsford
Very good introduction to this subject.

Manners, J.E. – *Country Crafts Today* (1974) David & Charles Ltd
Another comprehensive, well researched account of rural crafts covering a good variety of them and their relevance to life in the 1970s.

Edlin H.L. – *Forestry and Woodland Life* (1947) Batsford
Out of print but available second-hand, a book of the background, natural history, life and management of our forests. (I was delighted to discover that the copy I obtained was signed by Edlin in 1956).

Law, Ben – *The Woodland Way, a permaculture approach to sustainable woodland management* (2001) Permanent publications
Absorbing and informative book at a ground roots level.

Chapters 3, 4, and 5

Hagenender, Fred – *Yew* (2007) The History Press
A truly unique and remarkable achievement containing the

most comprehensive study of a single species of tree (yew) covering just about everything you would need to know, in a beautifully presented volume.

Hart, Cyril & Raymond, Charles – *British Trees in Colour* **(1973) Book Club Associates**
Extremely good reference book with excellent illustrations of 63 of the most likely trees to be found in this country.

Johns, Rev. C.A. – *The Forest Trees of Britain* **(1892) Society for Promoting Christian Science**
A truly enjoyable book. It is well worth investing in a classic, beautifully bound, embossed edition if you can find one (perhaps on eBay). Extremely thorough and enlightening information on each of our native trees and shrubs including origins, characteristics, extensive European history, and folklore; beautifully eloquent and generously endowed with picturesque engravings throughout. The experience of reading and handling beautiful books like these will never be surpassed by the e-reader.

Mitchell, Alan – *Collins Field Guide, Trees Britain and Europe* **(1974) Harper Collins**
Very comprehensive, once you get used to it.

Rackham, Oliver – *Trees and Woodlands in the British Landscape* **(1976) Pheonix Press**
The definitive history of Britain's woodlands.

Chapter 6
Langsner, Drew – *Green Woodworking, a hands-on approach* **(1995) Lark Books**
Very good introduction to green woodworking from an American practitioner, including very useful information on the properties of wood.

Hoadley, Bruce R – *Understanding Wood, a craftsman's guide to wood technology* **(2000) The Taunton Press**
Best-selling publication telling you most things you need to know about understanding wood. A must for any serious woodworker.

Star, Chris – *Woodland Management, a practical guide* **(2005) The Crowood Press**
Very good book on the subject.

Fine Woodworking – *Wood and how to dry it* **(1986) The**

Taunton Press
41 articles on the subject selected by the editors of *Fine Woodworking*. These publications are good value for money and always interesting.

Chapter 7
Abbott, Mike – *Living Wood, from buying a woodland to making a chair* **(2002) Living Wood Books**
Extremely interesting and informative – this book taught me how to make traditional chairs. I bought it from Mike at a woodland show. He signed it for me and was very helpful when I subsequently emailed him to clarify a couple of things in it while I was making my first ladderback chair. It is now full of notes and well thumbed. Highly recommended. Thanks Mike.

Oaks, Rebecca & Mills, Edward – *Coppicing & Coppice Crafts* **(2010) The Crowood Press**
Delightful and comprehensive book on these two subjects, with excellent photographs throughout and useful advice.

Tabor, Raymond – *A Guide to Coppicing* **(2014) eco-logic books**
Excellent and cheap guide to coppice and coppicing.

Tabor, Raymond – *The Encyclopaedia of Green Woodworking* **(2000) eco-logic books**
Very useful and comprehensive book with particularly good sections on all the many products that can be made from coppice wood.

Chapters 9 and 10
Milner, Edward – *Trees of Britain & Ireland* **(2011) Natural History Museum**
Portrait of our native trees covering background, uses, folklore and place in our ecosystem, beautifully photographed.

Warren, Piers – *British Native Tree, their past and present uses* **(2006) Wildeye UK**
Personable little book consisting just 83 pages of interesting information on uses past and present of our most common trees, written by a tree surgeon.

Chapter 11
Jenkins J. Geraint – *Traditional Country Craftsmen* **(1965) Amberley Publishing**

Another extremely accurate summary of country crafts, paying particular attention to the specialist tools used for each type of craft. Over 200 illustrations with a wealth of old black and white photos.

Chapters 13 and 14

Hock, Ron – *The Ultimate Guide to Sharpening for Woodworkers* (2009) Ron Hock

As the title suggests, a great guide for the practitioner and 'techie' alike. Totally up-to-date information to inspire anybody who is serious about their tools and their craft.

Mercer, Henry C – *Ancient Carpenter's Tools* (1960) Dover Publications

Extremely good record of hand tools and implements used by lumbermen, joiners and cabinet makers, coopers and general carpenters from the 18th century onwards.

Chapter 15

On the crafts of the past

Jones, Andrew & George, Clive – *Stickmaking* (1999) Guild of Master Craftsman

Very comprehensive 'how to' book packed with information and high quality photographs and illustrations.

Kilby, Kenneth – *The Cooper and his Trade* (1971) Linden Publishing

Written by a cooper it is a detailed account of the life of the specialist craftsmen, the tools, techniques and social history of coopering.

Rose, Walter – *The Village Carpenter* (1937) Stobart Davies

Engaging and intimate little book by a third generation master carpenter reminiscing about the craftsmanship and the community spirit in Victorian times.

Sturt, George – *The Wheelwright's Shop* (1923) Cambridge University Press

Unique glimpse into 19th century craftsmen and craftsmanship, sensitively written by Sturt, who took over the running of a wheelwrights after the death of his father.

Massingham, H.J. – *The English Countryman* (1942) Batsford

Delightful study of the social, geographical and aesthetic

existence of English country life, and craftsman, prior to the industrial revolution. Now out of print but it is certainly worth tracking down a second-hand copy.

On green woodworking and furniture-making

Abbott, Mike – *Green Woodwork, working with wood the natural way* (1989) Guild of Master Craftsmen

Very good and widely read introduction to green woodworking from a true practitioner.

Abbott, Mike – *Going with the Grain, making chairs in the 21st century* (2011) Living Wood Books

A compilation of photos, notes and invaluable advice on making chairs by hand, collected over a three-year period, after decades of practice.

Brown, John – *Welsh Stick Chairs* (1990) John Brown. Stobart Davies Ltd

Widely read and enjoyable little book all about Welsh solid seat chairs, which, perhaps pre-date the 'English Windsor'. Written by a chairmaker, for chairmakers and chair devotees alike.

Gilborn, Craig – *Adirondack Furniture and the Rustic Tradition* (1987) Harry N. Abrams

The definitive book on American rustic furniture from its conception in Europe to its adoption over the Atlantic. Packed with text and photographs.

Hill, Jack – *Country Woodworking, how to make rustic furniture, utensils and decorations* (1995) Reed Consumer Books

Not only a 'how to make' book with a few projects, but also lavishly decorated throughout with beautiful photography depicting very atmospheric country style interiors.

Kylloe, Ralph – *Rustic Furniture Makers* (1995) Gibbs Smith

An inspirational American 'coffee table' type book with informative text, from the point of view of the makers and featuring their stunning work.

Langsner, Drew – *Green Woodworking, a hands-on approach.* Op.cit.

Langsner, Drew – *The Chairmaker's Workshop, handcraft Windsor and post and rung chair* (1997) Lark Books

Large, comprehensive and very informative volume on these subjects.

Mack, Daniel – *Making Rustic Furniture, the tradition, spirit and technique with dozens of project ideas* (1992) Lark Books
Reading this inspirational book was where it all started for me – it changed my life. Elevates sculptural rustic stick furniture to an altogether higher level and beyond. Not for the traditionalists. Thanks Dan.

Mack, Daniel – *The Art of Rustic Furniture, traditions, techniques, inspirations* (1996) Lark Books
More of the same. Brings out the artist in you.

Mursell, James – *Windsor Chairmaking* (2009) Crowood Press
Nicely informative book written by a practitioner specialising in the history and making of 18th century Windsor chairs by hand.

Ospina, Alison – *Green Wood Chairs* (2009) Stobart Davies
Inspiring book of sculptural stick furniture. Similar to those of Daniel Mack on the subject of American makers, but what makes this so pleasing is that its about Irish chair makers. Great chairs and beautiful photography too.

Chapter 16

To find out more about the Chiltern bodgers, seek out a fantastic old black and white film, available to view on YouTube, entitled *The Chiltern Bodgers.mp4*. Lasting nearly 10 minutes, and filmed by Eustace A. Alliott, when he was 88 years old, this nostalgic gem shows bodgers working in the Chiltern beechwoods, and also includes fascinating footage of some local cottage industry workers assembling Windsor-style chairs from component parts supplied by bodgers. For detailed information on how Windsor-style chairs were assembled in small factories, log onto Wycombe District Council's website **www.wycombe.gov.uk** and look under *Furniture making in High Wycombe*. You will find very comprehensive information on the subject.

You might also like to look at Stewart King's website **www.stuartking.co.uk**. Do a search for *bodgers* and you will be rewarded with two excellent articles:
The Chiltern Bodgers of Buckinghamshire
Samuel Rockall – Last of the Chair Bodgers

Chapter 17

A thorough history of the shave horse is available on **www.bloodandsawdust.com**. The website also includes an extremely good history of the lathe.

If you visit **www.stuartking.co.uk** and click on *History of the lathe* you will be rewarded with a comprehensive and fascinating record of lathes from the year dot to the present.

The Association of Pole Lathe Turners and Green Woodworkers, **www.bodgers.org.uk**, has more than 500 members and publishes a quarterly magazine called *The Bodgers Gazette*. It also holds the famous Bodgers Ball every May and provides many other services including demonstrations and insurance.

Hoadley, Bruce R – *Understanding Wood, a craftsman's guide to wood technology* Op. cit.

Tabor, Raymond – *Green Woodworking Pattern Book, over 300 traditional craft designs* (2005) Batsford
A labour of love by the author and well worth owning. Traditional patterns for everything from a wooden whistle to a pole lathe.

Chapter 21

Arnold, James – The Shell Book of Country Crafts *(1968)* John Baker (Publishers) Ltd
A woodland crafts classic, including an interesting section on charcoal burning.

***Charcoal Production – a handbook* (1999) eco-logic books**
Practical guide to charcoal production and technology – strong technical content.

Edlin H.L. – *Woodland Crafts in Britain* (1949) Batsford
Now out of print but still available second-hand, this is a classic, a real gem, and still one of the most comprehensive accounts of the traditional uses of trees and timber in the British countryside, including charcoal burning, crammed with much valuable and rare information.

Kelly, D.W. – *Charcoal and Charcoal Burning* (1986) Shire Publications
A very informative and comprehensive historic study.

Chapter 22
Rackham, Oliver – *Trees and Woodlands in the British Landscape.* **Op cit.**
Also covers the hedgerow.

Nozedar, Adele – *The Hedgerow Handbook* (2012) **Square Peg**
Nicely illustrated little book about hedgerows, their history, culinary, medical and mythical properties.

Chapman, Lesley – *The Living History of our Hedgerows* (2001) **Orchard Publications**
Small but extremely informative self-published book crammed with useful and interesting information about what comprises a British hedgerow.

Chapter 23
Conway, Peter – *Tree Medicine* (2001) **Judy Piatkus (publishers) Ltd**
Great publication with the first part introducing the phenomenal medicinal uses of our trees and the second part a comprehensive guide to the healing power of over 170 tree types.

Culpepper, Nicholas – *Complete Herbal* (1995) **Wordsworth**
Very famous classic 17th century publication on herbal medicine.

Grieve, M – *A Modern Herbal* **Dover Publications**
First published in 1931 and still an indispensable and encyclopaedic publication in two volumes covering the folklore, properties and application of herbs, trees and shrubs.

Chapters 26 and 27
Andrews, Julian – *The Sculpture of David Nash* (1999) **Lund Humphries**
The spirit of the woodlands, of the maker, of the medium, reviewing the entire range of artist, naturalist and green wood sculptor David Nash's wonderful and unique life-work. A hero of mine!

Blamires, Steve – *Celtic Tree Mysteries* (2005) **Llewellyn Worldwide**
Interesting book about trees and the Celtic magic associated with them.

Hageneder, Fred – *The Living Wisdom of Trees* (2005) **Duncan Baird**
Well illustrated and beautifully photographed. A book about the natural history, folklore, symbolism & healing properties of trees.

Hight, Julian – *Britain's Tree Story* (2011) **National Trust Books**
Well researched and beautifully illustrated record of Britain's oldest, largest and most famous trees through legend, literature and folklore.

Miles, Archie – *The Trees that made Britain* **BBC Books**
Detailed portraits of individual tree species revealing fascinating stories of how they have influenced the culture, myths and fabric of the nation.

Paterson, Jacqueline Memory – *Tree Wisdom* (1996) **Thorsons**
Very good book covering the legendary, healing and magical properties of our British trees together with many of the customs that relate to them.

Spence, Lewis – *Mysteries of Celtic Britain* (1998) **Paragon**
A peripheral book with reference to trees but nevertheless a very good book on Pagan practices, in particular the druids, who based their religion around trees. Cuts through a lot of the romantically manufactured dross sometimes churned out about the Celts.

Useful periodicals
Living Woods Magazine – **Freshwood Publishing**
For just about anyone involved in rural woodcrafts, trees and wildlife, woodfuel and eco-living. Fantastic bi-monthly magazine with a circulation of around 2,500. Available by subscription. Sign up now!

Permaculture Magazine – **Permanent Publications**
Quarterly issue full of very interesting, useful and thought provoking contributions from all over the world.

Cherry tree in blossom on the volcano Mount Koma, Northern Japan

A bit about the author

Born in London, Barry Mays lived the life of a successful, well-paid employee in the field of IT sales. That is until one day, in March 1998, shortly after his 45th birthday, he walked into his office and decided then and there to resign.

A couple of years later he had swapped his air-conditioned office, a regular salary and all the comforts and security of a life in the capital for a drafty, breeze-block chicken shed on the Cornish borders together with all the delights that only poverty and insecurity can bring. No more a slave to the crazy intensity of the hi-tech world, he embraced the spiritual, solitary existence of a green woodworker, teaching himself the creative, low-tech craft completely from scratch.

Fifteen years later, through his new found career, he had acquired a cornucopia of information and wisdom about his craft and he decided to write it all down so others could share his knowledge and enthusiasm. And thus, three years on, the Green Wood Companion was completed.

Barry still lives and works in the beautiful Tamar Valley. He has worked hard at his craft, seeking to perfect his skills. His natural wood chairs and furniture have become sought after objects in their own right.

He spends his spare time writing, walking in the woodlands with his dog, eating Sunday pub lunches with his sons, playing a cigar box guitar, and thinking about getting some chickens; not necessarily in that order.

He hopes you will enjoy his book and that you will find it inspiring, entertaining but above all useful.

PHOTO ACCREDITATIONS

Wikimedia Commons is an on-line, free media file repository making available public domain and freely licensed images, sound and video clips to everyone through the generous donation of time and personal skills, from volunteers worldwide. It has been a very useful source of many of the photos in this publication and I would like to extend a collective thank you to all those, mainly amateur photographers, who have helped present the visual content of this book. These files are licenced under Creative Commons Attribution – Share Alike 2.0, 2.5 and 3.0 (CC BY-SA 2.0, 2.5, 3.0)

PAGE NO	MEDIA	CAPTION	COPYRIGHT
Front cover	photo	Alder trees in the Beaulieu River, New Forest	Jim Champion
Dedication	photo	Old beech tree	RhinoMind
Intro 8	photo	Bluebells in sweet chestnut coppice. Flexham Park, West Sussex	Charlesdrakew
Intro 9	photo	Part of author's bookcase	Barry Mays
Intro 10	photo	The author using a shaving horse	Bernard Cole
11	illustration	Bill's oak, Tutwell	Sue Bryant
12	photo	Tree canopy in the Tamar Valley	Barry Mays
12	photo	Coiled lime bast in basket harvested and woven by Carol Horsington	Barry Mays
13	illustration	The layers of a tree	Barry Mays
14	photo	Exposed sycamore tree roots	Rosser 1954
14	Illustration	Tree profile	Barry Mays
15	photo	Cross section of a tree showing the growth rings	Arnoldius
15	photo	Strangler fig on a host tree	Vinayarji
16	photo	Elephant eating leaves	Charles J. Sharp
16	photo	Red squirrel	Volker
16	photo	Jay collecting acorns	Hans Jorg Hellwig
17	photo	The many colours of autumn	Hamon
17	photo	Pine trees	Rojypala
18	photo	Women planting	Yann
19	photo	Thatcher at work in Escheburg, Germany	Joachim Mullerchen
20	photo	Baskets and hat made by Carol Horsington, Cornish Willow	Barry Mays
20	photo	Ash Hurdle and Willow Screen	Moreton Wood Coppice Products
21	photo	Traditionally made besom broom by Mark Cottrell	Hen and Hammock
22	photo	Discovering the woodlands with Little Oaks Forest School, Cotehele	National Trust
23	photo	Ring kiln charcoal burning at Moreton Wood	Moreton Wood
23	photo	Traditional 'pimp' 25 individual bundles of fire kindling	Moreton Wood Coppice Products
24	photo	Traditional spoon carving	Christine Bra
24	photo	Author with 'Tipi' chair	Bernard Cole
25	photo	Ash ladderback rocking chair with rush seat made by the author	Barry Mays
26	photo	Scots pine forest	Bartosz Cuber
27	photo	Silver birch	Willow
28	photo	Guelder rose	Quartl
29	photo	Sweet Chestnut tree on the edge of a small wood	Jean-Pol Grandmont
31	illustration	The different branch structures of broadleaf and conifer trees	Barry Mays
31	photo	Norway spruce trees in Iceland	Axel Kristinsson
32	photo	Sunset clouds behind winter tree branches	Public Domain.com
33	photo	Alder trees in the Beaulieu river, New Forest	Jim Champion
33, 34	illustrations	Leaf illustrations	Barry Mays
34	photo	Avenue of English elm, Fitzroy gardens, Melbourne	Melburian
35	photo	Hornbeam tree in Barnet Gate Wood, London	Dudley Miles
35, 36, 37	illustration	Leaf illustrations	Barry Mays
36	photo	Rowan tree, also known as mountain ash	Mehmut Karatay
37	photo	Western red cedar. South Whidbey State Park, Washington, U.S.A.	JT Morgan
38	photo	Tree bark angel wings	Gayle Karen
41	photo	Weeping willow	Geaugagrri
42	photo	Coppiced lime trees in South Ayrshire	Rosser 1954
43	photo	Willow pollards in morning fog, in Dulmen, Germany	Dietmar Rabich
43	photo	Newly cut ash coppice stools	Barry Mays
43	photo	Coppiced ash stool re-growth after just six months – multiple stems reaching two metres high	Barry Mays
44	photo	Weaving a natural fence at Moreton Wood	Moreton Wood
47	photo	U.S. economics officer rough measuring age of a tree	US Airforce master Sgt. Brian Boisvert